Collection Development in the Digital Age

Collection Development in the Digital Age

Edited by
Maggie Fieldhouse and Audrey Marshall

facet publishing

Published by Facet Publishing,
www.facetpublishing.co.uk

Facet Publishing is wholly owned by CILIP:
the Chartered Institute of Library and
Information Professionals.

British Library Cataloguing in Publication Data
A catalogue record for this book is available
from the British Library.

ISBN 978-1-85604-746-3

First published 2012
Reprinted digitally thereafter

Reviewers: To save your readers time and
shipping expense, please include "distributed
in the U.S. by Neal-Schuman Publishers"
following publication information in your
review. Please see attached press release for
additional information.

Text printed on FSC accredited material.

Mixed Sources
Product group from well-managed
forests and other controlled sources
www.fsc.org Cert no. SA-COC-1565
© 1996 Forest Stewardship Council
FSC

Typeset from editors' files by Facet Publishing
in 10/13pt Garamond and Frutiger.
Printed and made in Great Britain by MPG
Books Group, UK.

Contents

Foreword

Liz Chapman

The Digital Age has brought us opportunities and challenges. Most library services face attacks from those who believe that we are no longer needed as 'everything is on the internet'. We face challenges from governments who in the light of economic uncertainty fail to see value in public libraries. We face challenges from students whose fee regimes imbue them with entitlement aggression about what a library can and should do for them.

Yet we know that our work in developing collections is important to preserve the past, support the present and plan for the future. Our fundamental responsibilities in collection development have not changed, but our methods have.

One hundred years ago in 1911 the British Library of Political Science (now the LSE Library) reported that in six months it had received and made available 29,287 books; a rate which the Librarian noted was twice that of the British Museum (now the British Library). In those times the Librarian would go out and search for materials. Sidney and Beatrice Webb came back from the USA laden with library materials, an agreement to an exchange of publications with Columbia University and a dislike of ice cream.

Building the collection was paramount, but despite vaulting ambitions no collection could ever cover everything. It was probably never possible, even in ancient Nineveh to bring together all recorded knowledge. We cannot hope to do this in the 21st century, but we do need to develop clear policies on what we will collect and maintain for future generations. Collections on library shelves or in remote physical storage must now be mirrored by storage and preservation of the digital. We must make policy in consultation with those we serve but also have an eye to the future. It may sometimes seem like a thankless task but future generations will thank us. Equally we must decide when we need to do the procuring and when we can pass basic work to others. Finally, and this horrifies some library users, we need to know how to weed out unwanted stock.

This book stands on the shoulders of previous texts, notably Jenkins and Morley's *Collection Management in Academic Libraries* (second edition 1999) and Clayton and Gorman's *Managing Information Resources in Libraries: collection management in theory and practice* (2001). At the end of the 20th century these authors pointed to the speed with which journals were becoming electronic and there was an idea that books might go the same way albeit more slowly. Now we are in the enviable position of being able to read a digital version of Samuel Pepys's *Diary* on a clear portable screen and immediately discover the meaning of arcane words or a photograph of a location from a touch of the screen. This implies a different kind of collection development but still requires an eye to future preservation.

Collection development (building) and collection management (maintaining) are merging as the digital pushes its way to the fore. It is not sensible or economical to develop duplicate collections which may not be used, or for which we might not have space, and at the same time we are pushing services outside our library walls – spinning out content and 'signposts' to offices and homes.

We use networks to spread our collections outwards – both within our institutions and beyond. We use networks to direct our users towards other useful services they may need and to build collections co-operatively with others. Networks help us to operate in an Open Access environment and to build collections in digital repositories. We have our own networks to support our work: professional networks, to share collections and those which intersect with publishers and suppliers. The continued vibrancy of the 30 year old Charleston Conference is one such version of a professional network. Yet despite the advances in technology and the concomitant increased accessibility of collections, our work still depends on people. We need people who can build and bring in collections in all formats. We need people who can explain what we have and how to use it. Finally of course we need people to use the collections we develop. It's all about the people.

In our better moments I hope that library staff would agree that we are privileged to work in an area which is constantly changing and which gives us the opportunity to develop our roles and to learn new ways of doing things. This book will help us to consolidate this learning and move on confidently in collection development.

Liz Chapman
Director of Library Services
London School of Economics and Political Science

Contributors

David Ball is Head of Academic Development Services at Bournemouth University. He is recognized as a leading practitioner and speaker, particularly in the field of library purchasing, having led innovative tenders for e-books, books and journals, and chairing national and regional library procurement organizations in higher education. Most recently he has led, on behalf of all the English universities, probably the most valuable and complex tender for books and e-books yet seen. He also has experience of procuring and implementing virtual learning environments (VLEs). He is a member of various bodies, such as the Board of SCONUL and the JISC Collections Electronic Information Resources Working Group. He has a strong publishing record and is a frequent speaker at conferences, particularly on e-books, VLEs and procurement.

David Brown has been involved in scholarly communication for nearly 40 years, which have included ten years with Elsevier in Amsterdam, Pergamon Press in Oxford and a number of years in the USA and the UK with various intermediaries (Faxon, Blackwells and Ingenta). He also recently spent six years at the British Library investigating scholarly communication developments. For many years he also ran his own consultancy, DJB Associates, which focused on scholarly publishing trends. David was joint editor of the monthly *Scholarly Communication Report* from its inception to conclusion, and has produced a large number of research articles on document delivery as well as two books published by Bowker/Saur entitled *Electronic Publishing and Libraries* (1996) and *The Impact of Electronic Publishing* (2009). David is currently an honorary research fellow and is also reading for a doctorate degree at University College London. He is also part of the CIBER research team.

Josh Brown is a programme manager for the Joint Information Systems Committee (JISC) in the UK, managing research and development projects in the areas of research information and scholarly communications. Before joining JISC, he was Project Officer for the SHERPA-LEAP digital repository consortium within the University of London, advising the 14 consortium members on a range of issues including research reporting, e-theses, non-textual content, overlay journals and Open Access. He also contributed to the Research Excellence Framework data collection pilot whilst working at the University of Sussex and worked on Sussex Research Online, the university's digital repository. His research interests include evolving digital repository practice, scholarly communications, copyright and open access.

Terry Bucknell is Electronic Resources Manager at the University of Liverpool where he manages an extensive collection of e-journals, databases and e-books, as well as the online services, including EBSCO Discovery Service and SFX, through which they are accessed. He gained a BSc in Physics from the University of Manchester before gaining his MA in Librarianship at the University of Sheffield. He was previously Engineering Librarian at the University of Leeds. Terry is a member of the COUNTER Executive Committee, a member of the editorial board of *The Serials Librarian*, and is a former member of the UKSG management committee. He was a member of the JISC E-Books Observatory Project Board, was Project Leader for the JISC-funded ticTOCs project and is a member of several publishers' Library Advisory Boards. He has published articles in *Serials* and *Learned Publishing* and has presented plenaries at the UKSG and ASA conferences.

Sheila Corrall is Professor of Librarianship and Information Management in the Information School at the University of Sheffield, where she is Graduate Research Tutor and Head of the Libraries and Information Society Research Group. She co-ordinates the Academic and Research Libraries module and lectures on information resources, collection management and the management of library, information and IT services. Before moving to Sheffield, she worked as a chief cataloguer, information specialist, library manager and strategic director in public, special, national and academic library and information services, most recently as Director of Academic Services at the University of Southampton. Her research interests focus on the application of strategic management concepts to library and information services and the development of professional roles and competencies. She served as the first President of the Chartered Institute of Library and Information Professionals (CILIP) and led the group that developed a definition of information literacy for the UK.

Bradley Daigle is Director of Digital Curation Services and Digital Strategist for Special Collections at the University of Virginia Library. He is also Principal Investigator on a grant funded by the Andrew W. Mellon Foundation entitled: Born Digital Materials: An Inter-Institutional Model for Stewardship. He has published on topics such as mass digitization, digital stewardship and sustaining digital scholarship. His research interests also include the history of the book, early modern natural history and James Boswell.

Diana Edmonds is Head of the Libraries Division of GLL, a charitable social enterprise which currently manages leisure services for more than 20 local authorities. She was formerly Assistant Director of Culture, Libraries and Learning in the London Borough of Haringey. Before moving to Haringey, Diana was Managing Director of Instant Library Ltd, a company which specialized in the outsourcing of a range of library and information services. She has published extensively, regularly gives papers at conferences and workshops and is particularly interested in the design of libraries and in the use of technology in libraries.

Jil Fairclough is Medical School Librarian at Brighton and Sussex Medical School (BSMS), Brighton, UK. She has worked in healthcare libraries for over ten years, including within the National Health Service (NHS) and more currently higher education. She manages library services as well as being the lead for e-learning at BSMS. In her life before libraries, she worked in advertising and has a particular interest in the exploitation and marketing of library services. She has written and spoken on marketing and usage of e-resources, particularly in partnership environments. She teaches information skills and evidence-based medicine on the undergraduate curriculum at BSMS.

Maggie Fieldhouse is a Lecturer at the Department of Information Studies at University College London, where she is module tutor for the Collection Management and Management modules on the MA Library and Information Studies Programme. Previously Deputy Librarian and Information Services Manager at the University of Sussex she has extensive experience in academic libraries and has also worked for a library management system supplier. She is actively involved in research, having interests in information literacy and information seeking behaviour and participated in the CIBER/JISC/BL Google Generation project, contributing to the final report and presenting the findings at LILAC, Umbrella and other conferences.

Jane Harvell is Head of Academic Services at the University of Sussex Library. She has over 20 years' experience working with researchers and research collections at the British Library, London School of Economics (LSE) and Sussex. She has written and spoken on alternative methods and models of providing core collections and support services during a time of limited resources in academic libraries and on the changing nature of scholarly communication. She is particularly interested in the potential for developing collaborative relationships between scholarly publishing and academic libraries. Jane is on the editorial board of *The Serials Librarian*, is a member of the Marketing Committee of UKSG and is on the SAGE Library Advisory Board.

David House studied German Language and Literature at the University of East Anglia and Librarianship at University College London. After a short spell in Norfolk County Library, he joined Brighton Polytechnic as a lecturer in library and information studies. Subsequently he moved into the polytechnic's library service, becoming its head in 1982. In 1988 he was appointed Assistant Director at the Polytechnic, with a particular responsibility for managing its transition from a local authority institution to a corporate body. From 1991 to 2010 he was Deputy Vice-Chancellor at the University of Brighton, with responsibility for corporate planning, information services, personnel and estates development. He has held office in the Library Association and CILIP, with a particular interest in education and accreditation and has been a member of the main board of JISC since 2001. He currently chairs the board of JISC Collections, which provides digital resources to the further and higher education communities in the UK.

Audrey Marshall is a Senior Lecturer in the School of Computing, Engineering and Mathematics at the University of Brighton, UK, where she is course leader for the MA in Information Studies. She teaches collection development and information service management. Before joining the university, she worked in a range of library and information sectors, including public libraries and health information services. Her research interests revolve around the uses of information and ICTs for health, focusing particularly on information literacy in a public health context. She has published articles in a range of library and information journals and publications.

Tracy Mitrano is Director of Information Technology Policy and Computer Policy and Law Programs at Cornell University. She also holds an academic appointment as an adjunct assistant professor in Information Science. She has a doctorate in American History from New York State University at Binghamton and a Juris Doctor degree from the Cornell University Law School. She currently writes a blog for the US online journal *Inside Higher Ed* entitled 'Law, Policy and IT?'

Martin Palmer is Principal Officer for Essex County Council's Library Service, where he has worked in a variety of roles since the mid-1970s. He led the Essex element of a LASER Foundation-funded scheme to test the feasibility of e-books in public libraries in 2004, and has been closely involved in the further development of e-services there ever since. Martin is also a member of the operational board of Book Industry Communication (BIC), and chairs BIC's E4Libraries Committee (promoting the use of standards in library technology) and the BIC/CILIP RFID in Libraries Group. He is also the Society of Chief Librarians' representative on the Public Lending Right Management Board, and is the author of a number of items on e-books and RFID, including Facet Publishing's 2009 publication *Making the Most of RFID in Libraries*.

Karrie Peterson is Assistant Director for Research and Instruction at the University of Pennsylvania Libraries, where she leads the development of library programs to support student learning of information and media literacies for the digital age. Her particular interests include advances in learning sciences and assessment of student learning, new technology-supported pedagogies, innovation in academic libraries, knowledge management for user-centred services, and organizational effectiveness.

Wendy Shaw is a Teaching Fellow in the Department of Information Studies (DIS) at Aberystwyth University. She is also a Fellow of the Higher Education Academy (FHEA). A short-term contract as a Development Officer for the department, on the 'NOF ICT Training for Public Librarians' project, led her to working in the department's Open Learning Unit (OLU) until 2008. She now has teaching responsibilities in the department in the areas of Collection Management and in School Libraries and Learning Resources, to full-time and distance learning students at undergraduate and postgraduate level. Research interests include sports and motivation, learning styles and lifelong learning.

Ruth Stubbings is Head of Academic Services at Loughborough University Library. She leads the Library Faculty Teams that support the information needs of the academic departments. She has worked in a variety of library and information sectors, including special, commercial and higher education. She is particularly interested in the development of student study skills, including information literacy; the exploitation and marketing of library services; and managing users' expectations. To this end she has been involved in several projects that ensure greater access to resources and the development of teaching material that helps develop students' academic literacy skills. She is Deputy Chair of the CILIP CSG Information Literacy Group, Chair of the editorial board of the Journal of Information Literacy, Webmaster of the Information Literacy website and a member of the SCONUL Working Group on Information Literacy.

Introduction

Audrey Marshall and Maggie Fieldhouse

The building and maintaining of collections has been at the heart of library and information work for a very long time. In the 7th century BC, the Great Library at Nineveh housed clay tablets which represented a treasure house of Assyrian ideas. In ancient Egypt, the legendary libraries of Thebes and Alexandria housed precious collections of religious, medical and literary material on papyri. With the advent of paper and then the printing press, individuals and organizations were able to build extensive book collections, often using them to demonstrate their knowledge, wealth and power. This activity culminated in the 19th century with an upsurge in the number of national libraries, very often in the form of grand buildings housing prestigious collections of material relating to national cultures and identities. Towards the end of the 20th century the situations began to change, with unprecedented developments in digital technology, which have contributed to a very different outlook for libraries and collections. These developments have accelerated into the 21st century, bringing with them fundamental changes in the nature of scholarly artefacts, library service provision and public expectation around access to information and reading for pleasure. These changes are having a profound influence on the ways in which library collections are developed and managed. Some professionals argue that collection development is no longer relevant or possible, that it's dead in the water, while others make a passionate case for adapting existing policies and practices. At the core of this book is a desire to confront the changes we are experiencing in a very explicit way and to question whether or not the rational strategic approaches to developing and managing collections, which have been at the heart of librarianship for years, are still relevant.

The goals of the book are:

1 To investigate the key developments in collection development and their impact on policy and practice.
2 To explore the role of information professionals in this changing environment and the new skills set they need.
3 To chart a path for the future.

Book organization
The book is divided into four parts, allowing you to approach the subject from different perspectives. It begins with a consideration of the concept of collection development

and how the thinking and practice around this has evolved over the years. It moves on to the heart of the matter, trends in the development of e-resources. The trends in electronic journals, e-books and open access material are set to change publishing, information retrieval and reading for pleasure forever and the pace of change is presenting new challenges to those responsible for keeping collections and services relevant. An exploration of new approaches to library supply follows logically from the section on e-resources and, given current economic constraints, considers the cost benefits of outsourcing. The book concludes with some thoughtful and practical attention to the key issue of making and keeping collections effective.

The book consists of a mix of chapters and case studies, where the chapters examine the issues in a general and discursive way, while the case studies focus more on illustrating the issues through practical examples and experience. Most of the chapters end with a 'coda' consisting of four or five bullet points or questions designed to make you think about the key issues raised in the chapter and to help you think through what you might want to do with this information.

The contributors represent a cross-section of stakeholders in collection development. They are a mix of academics, practitioners and 'insider' experts and while most of the contributors are UK based we also have contributions from US colleagues. A full list of contributors is included at the beginning of the book, with biographical information on each person. We thank them all for their help in developing this book.

Part 1   The concept and practice of collection development

Part one consists of two chapters, which establish the context for the book as a whole. Sheila Corrall explores the concept of collection development in the digital world, challenging us to accept its relevance in the digital library and information environment. She traces the development of the concept in the literature and reviews the impact of information and communication technology (ICT) on libraries and collections. She concludes that while the form and location of material has changed and will continue to change, the principles of selecting material to meet current and future use remain valid. Maggie Fieldhouse takes a complementary approach. Reviewing how the processes of collection management have changed in a digital environment, she draws on examples from the literature to illustrate the ways in which activities such as selection, acquisition and serials management have evolved. She identifies some of the trends that have influenced the role of collection managers and considers developments that should be heeded if libraries and their collections are to continue to be relevant.

Part 2   Trends in the development of e-resources

Part two is the heart of the book. It consists of three chapters and two case studies, all of which are characterized by the sense of being at a tipping point. Whether the issue is the inexorable switch from paper-based serials to electronic collections in learning institutions or the arrival and consolidation of e-books in public libraries, there is a sense that commentators and practitioners alike are being presented with ever-moving targets.

E-books illustrate how content has changed dramatically from flat pages to highly interactive, dynamic multimedia, hyperlinked text. This has impacted on how we view books, moving away from replication in print to a new model where content is not bound to specific containers. Today's users of resources expect access instantly and they want to share and socialize in the virtual world. The value of content to those users is therefore more than the original text and includes the context that is provided around it, based on social interaction and sharing. This is having a major impact on how e-books are constructed, how we view them and, more fundamentally, on how we define what an e-book is. The contributors to this section of the book have faced real challenges in making sense of these fast-moving developments in a collection development context and in pinning the situation down to the here-and-now. As the case studies on e-books in particular highlight, it is proving to be a challenge for information professionals to make definitive statements and draw firm conclusions about future development strategies.

David House's chapter introduces this section with an overview of electronic resources in UK further and higher education. He traces the development of the hybrid library and the impact of key policy initiatives in the UK, which encouraged library and information professionals to look into the future. He also notes, however, that those reports and initiatives from the 1990s assumed that libraries would remain the principal providers of academic information within institutions and how this situation has changed and is changing, particularly with regard to user expectations. He outlines the key role that JISC and JISC Collections have played with regard to e-journals, open access, e-books and digitization projects. He concludes that while the traditional role played by the academic library is now being challenged, the role of the library and information professional is ever more important in understanding user needs and ensuring that information is 'findable and deliverable'.

As several contributors point out, online journals are the most mature of the electronic formats and, as such, they provide us with insight into the challenges currently being faced by information professionals. Jane Harvell uses online journals as a funnel to explore new ways of delivering and discovering content in a university collection and the implications this has for the library's relevance and the information professional's skills. Her critique suggests a 'new normal' in which we will have to be forever flexible, adapting our skills to encompass licence reading, statistical interpretation, technical authentication issues and copyright law, as well as marketing these skills very visibly. In other words, it is about rethinking our whole approach to collection development.

E-book provision in libraries is gaining ground – in academic libraries in particular. In his case study of the University of Liverpool, Terry Bucknell traces the library's early tentative steps into e-book provision through to their current definitive strategy, predicting that the bulk of the library's book acquisitions will soon be electronic. While taking us through the University of Liverpool's journey, Terry also explores some of the key topical issues around e-book acquisition, including cataloguing, usage, digital rights management (DRM) and patron driven acquisition (PDA).

Essex County Council's Public Library Service was a pioneer with regard to e-books.

Martin Palmer is closely involved in the development of innovative services in Essex and in his case study he describes the e-book pilot project which took place in 2004 and the ensuing developments. In his chapter he toys with the question of whether the concept of collection development can be applied to the digital book world and explores the issues around suppliers, formats, platforms, DRM and so forth. He cuts a logical path for us through this complex world, concluding that those responsible for collection development in public libraries will need to use a wider range of criteria than in the past to inform their collection development policy (CDP) but that adopting a clear and rational policy is just as necessary as it ever was.

Digital formats present us with unprecedented challenges for capturing and preserving information and making it accessible for future generations. The world is perhaps only just waking up to this 'vexed proposition' but in Bradley Daigle's view now is the time to be strategic about it. He argues that we need to apply the same attention to digital material that we have done in the past to preserve and manage physical collections. He explores the concepts of stewardship and curation in a digital context and outlines a framework for a stewardship policy, through a carefully crafted set of questions. He argues that the key to success for successful stewardship is clarity around organizational goals and collaboration with colleagues and that efforts invested now will reap rewards in the future.

Part 3 Trends in library supply

Library supply, until quite recently, was a relatively straightforward and often genteel activity, fostered through relationships built up over years between libraries and their commercial suppliers. Various factors, including fundamental changes in the book trade and increasing volumes of material available in digital form only – much of this accessible free of charge – have combined to change this relationship forever. The chapters in this section explore this transformation.

David Ball examines how academic librarians are now managing their suppliers and, in particular, how they have had to adapt to learn and adopt the discipline of procurement. He outlines the standard procurement cycle, highlighting the importance of a well written specification as the basis for sound supplier selection. He goes on to explore the development of library purchasing consortia and their success in driving down costs in the academic marketplace and improving quality of service. He concludes by reflecting that the role of the academic librarian will be reversed – rather than collecting the output of the world's scholars and making it available to institutional users, the task in the future is to make the institution's output available to the world. This is a very different perspective on collection development.

Diana Edmonds discusses the background to outsourcing, a process that has revolutionized approaches to collection management in public libraries. Outsourcing and procurement go hand in hand and she explains how, to meet demands to cut spending, suppliers are commissioned and contracted to select, prepare and deliver books, audiovisual and other materials to standards and profiles specified by libraries, ready to go on the shelves. She also explores the extent to which some local authorities have further embraced these ideas by outsourcing the management of library services, not just their collections, to specialist companies as cost-cutting measures.

Developments in 'open access', a relatively new phenomenon, are set to change the face not only of library supply, but also of academic publishing and research access, for ever. The development of open access journals and Institutional Repositories (IRs) means that research material can be collated and accessed without the selection and mediation activities traditionally practised by information professionals. Open access therefore has the potential to change this aspect of collection development in radical ways.

David Brown begins his chapter on the 'open access' movement by addressing the question of why it is important. His answer highlights two key factors. First, that it makes it possible for research output to reach a much wider audience than has hitherto been the case, having been largely confined to research or academic library users, and second, that open access business models make little or no demands on library acquisition budgets. These two factors have significant implications for the role of research libraries in the future and for the nature of their collections. He goes on to explore the different and emerging open access models, examining the practical, commercial and ethical issues raised in each case. Although he wisely resists the temptation to forecast which – if any – of the models will be most widely adopted in the near future, he presents a convincing case for open access dissemination as the dominant means of scholarly communication for the future.

The growth and development of IRs can be viewed as a tangible and practical application of open access. Josh Brown argues that IRs present information professionals with an opportunity to extend their field of practice. He explores the diverse nature of IRs and, while identifying the challenges they present, he offers us practical advice on maximizing their potential. These include three steps to encourage collection growth, which require approaches and skills not always associated with collection development – such as advocacy, legal expertise, technical innovation and building closer relationships with the research community. His chapter is, in itself, an advocating voice for IR development and for using collection development skills in new and interesting ways.

Part 4   Making and keeping your collection effective

However comprehensive a library collection is, unless it works for your users it is an increasingly unaffordable luxury. Wendy Shaw argues that a cohesive collection development policy is still necessary, in the same way that a business needs a business plan. She describes what a collection development policy is and, using a well established framework, offers guidance on how to develop and implement a policy, highlighting extracts from existing library policies from around the world to illustrate the principles.

The other four contributors to this final section are practitioners, working in academic libraries and representing both sides of the Atlantic. Their perspectives differ but they all share a passion for demonstrating the value of collections, whether through effective marketing or by using information literacy (IL) to help users make appropriate judgements. The need to embed teaching and training alongside collection development is the binding theme.

Tracy Mitrano and Karrie Peterson show how the researchers and scholars of today are much less dependent on librarians to access the information they need and how that in itself brings its own set of challenges – to the scholars and librarians alike. They focus, however, on the opportunities this situation presents, exploring the ways in which IL tools can be embedded in information resources.

Ruth Stubbings discusses the importance of electronic information to the functioning of modern societies. She argues that policy makers have tended to ignore questions around IL, concentrating instead on access and use issues. Libraries, likewise, spend large amounts of money on information and must ensure that users can use them effectively. She goes on to explore some of the existing approaches to IL and ways to put them into practice.

This section ends with a case study of the Brighton and Sussex Medical School (BSMS) library, written by Jil Fairclough. The case study shows how 'outreach' has been replaced by 'inreach' – being embedded in the daily work of the institution – and how the librarian must operate as an integral member of the management team, as well as being teacher and product expert.

The book is aimed at library and information students and new practitioners but it is also relevant for those practitioners who have been round the block a few times. We hope that the new perspectives on the concepts and processes of collection management, introduced here by our contributors, will encourage you to think carefully about your resources – which may be held locally or remotely, in print, digitized or born-digital format – and about ways of ensuring their relevance in the digital age.

Part 1

The concept and practice of collection development

1

The concept of collection development in the digital world

Sheila Corrall

Introduction

The concept of collection development is central to the professional practice of librarianship, since the whole notion of a library is fundamentally associated with the idea of a collection, to the extent that the words 'library' and 'collection' are almost synonymous. Other terms such as 'information centre' 'learning centre' or 'discovery centre' are often used now instead of 'library' and terms such as 'information resources' may be substituted for 'library collections'. However, the activities and processes traditionally associated with collection development are still essential to the effective functioning of contemporary library information, learning and knowledge services, even though they may look and feel quite different to their historical counterparts. Our concern here is to explore the concept of *collection development* in the digital library and information environment and in particular to examine how thinking and practice in this vital area of library and information management have developed and changed in response to advances in digital technologies. What are the similarities and differences between collection development yesterday and today? Investigating such questions should help to prepare us for dealing with the collections of tomorrow.

The chapter therefore starts by examining a few definitions of the library as a collection to demonstrate the centrality of collection development to library and information professionals. Next, it moves on to the more problematic issue of collection development as a concept, showing how professional discourse on the subject has suffered from confused terminology. It then uses a convenient four-phase framework to review the impact of information and communication technology (ICT) on libraries, concentrating on its effects on collections and their development. The final part of the chapter returns to academic and practitioner conceptions of collection development in digital environments, concluding with a set of questions for reflection on the future of collection development.

The library as a collection

Dictionaries, glossaries, encyclopedias and other reference works within and beyond our professional field generally define a library primarily as a collection (of books and other materials) and rarely mention services in their definitions, or only as a supporting element. The focus on the collection as the defining characteristic of a library has continued into the digital age. Thus the continually updated *Online Dictionary for Library and Information Science* (Reitz, 2010) defines a library as 'A collection or group of collections of books and/or other print or nonprint materials organized and maintained for use (reading, consultation, study, research, etc.)' and then elaborates the definition by explaining that 'Institutional libraries, organized to facilitate access by a specific clientele, are staffed by librarians and other personnel trained to provide services to meet user needs.'

Harrod's Librarians' Glossary and Reference Book and the *International Encyclopedia of Information and Library Science*, respectively define a library as 'A collection of books and other literary material kept for reading, study and consultation' (Prytherch, 2005, 416) and 'A collection of materials organized for use' (McGarry, 2003, 371).

The ALA Glossary of Library and Information Science offers an older but more comprehensive definition of a library that links the important dimension of 'access' to the library and its collection:

> A collection of materials organized to provide physical, bibliographic, and intellectual *access* to a target group, with a staff that is trained to provide services and programs related to the information needs of the target group. (Young, 1983, 131)

Another later ALA publication offers a more modern conception of a library that interprets access as explicitly including materials in *other* collections:

> Libraries and information centers contain bibliographic materials, provide access to such materials, and supply services derived from those materials. These services are usually not based solely on materials actually present in a library's collection, but increasingly are enriched by access to materials in other collections. (Soper et al., 1990, 65)

From the same period, Buckland (1989, 220) provides a usefully concise definition of 'collections' as 'selections of materials deployed logistically to facilitate access to those materials for particular groups of users', which shifts the emphasis slightly by suggesting that collections are really a *means* to an *end*, rather than an end in themselves.

Nevertheless, the activities associated with creating organized and accessible collections remain central to the work of library and information professionals in all sectors, but how they are carried out and how they are conceived have changed significantly as digital technologies have transformed the information resources that are the focus of such efforts.

The concept of collection development

Collection development and the related term 'collection management' have been defined and described in different ways by academics and practitioners in the field over the years. Despite the confusions and ambiguities evident in the literature, we can identify several recurring themes. Collection development is particularly associated with the selection and/or acquisition of library materials (which can also include the 'de-selection' or 'de-acquisition' of stock), while *collection management* is generally seen as a broader term covering the whole range of activities involved in managing access to information resources.

Hendrik Edelman's seminal paper of 1979 is widely cited in the literature and a good starting point for discussion. He notes that in the USA, book selection in academic libraries had been a neglected subject in the literature, particularly when compared to the literature on book selection in public libraries. He explains the relationship between 'collection development', 'selection' and 'acquisition' as a hierarchy and defines *collection development* as follows:

> Collection development is a planning function. A collection development plan or policy describes the short- and long-term goals of the library as far as the collections are concerned, taking them into account and correlating them with the environmental aspects such as audience demand, need, and expectation, the information world, fiscal plans, and the history of the collections. From the collection development plan flows the budget allocation in broad terms.
>
> (Edelman, 1979, 34)

Edelman (1979) explains that *selection* is the next level, which implements the goals of collection development, using pre-defined criteria and methods; and *acquisition* then implements the decisions of selection and gets the material into the library. He also notes that the three levels naturally interact and may overlap. Gorman and Howes's book of 1989 provides a similarly clear and logical interpretation, complementing Edelman's (1979) triad by explaining the relationship in terms of the questions each process is intended to answer:

> In the hierarchy of [collection development] policy → selection → acquisitions, three questions are asked and answered in a sequence: why? what? how?
>
> (Gorman and Howes, 1989, 28)

Table 1.1 summarizes this initial conception of the field, bringing together Edelman's (1979) and Gorman and Howes's (1989) points and relating them to levels of strategic thinking.

Table 1.1 *The collection development hierarchy*		
Collection process	*Relevant question*	*Management level*
Collection development	Why?	Strategy
Selection	What?	Tactics
Acquisition	How?	Operations

As indicated above, the library environment has become more complex in recent decades, which has affected professional thinking on collection development and resulted in terminological problems. The following examples illustrate the divergence of opinion on the subject, drawing on professional glossaries, practitioner ideas and academic commentary. Fuller discussion of the relationship between collection development and collection management is provided by Ameen's (2006) review.

Prytherch (2005, 151) defines collection development as

> The process of planning a stock acquisition programme not simply to cater for immediate needs, but to build a coherent and reliable collection over a number of years, to meet the objectives of a service.

and sees maintenance as part of collection management, which he defines as

> The organization and maintenance of library stock, starting from collection development principles, keeping the needs of users a priority and considering alternative means of document and information supply to supplement local holdings. (p.152)

Prytherch (2005) thus presents collection development as a more *strategic* activity that is *operationalized* through the collection management function.

More typical is the widely cited definition provided by Cogswell (1987, 269) that describes collection management as

> The systematic management of the planning, composition, funding, evaluation and use of library collections over extended periods of time, in order to meet specific institutional objectives.

Writing in the academic library context, Cogswell (1987) cites the need to expand how we think about collection activities beyond selection and acquisition to access (in the form of resource-sharing), maintenance and preservation as an argument for *replacing* the word 'development' with 'management' when describing the collections process in a library. His conception of collection management includes *both* operational and strategic aspects of the process and he identifies eight functions that constitute this process:

- planning and policy making
- collection analysis
- materials selection
- collection maintenance
- fiscal management
- user liaison
- resource sharing
- programme evaluation.

The breadth of Cogswell's (1987) conception of collection management is shown by the activities that he proposes for the user liaison function of collection management, which include bibliographic instruction, online searching and reference service. However, in practice, although all these activities are clearly collection-based, they are not generally seen now as part of the collection management process, but as significant *services* provided by libraries.

Others also see collection management as a concept that has evolved from and replaced collection development, that is, as a mature version of an earlier concept, though not necessarily as broadly conceived as Cogswell (1987). Thus Soper et al. (1990, 66) state:

> The concept of collection development, or materials acquisition, has been evolving recently to that of collection control, or collection management. This concept encompasses the design of a process for selecting bibliographic materials to meet a library's needs, goals, objectives, and priorities . . . Collection management also includes the processes of making materials accessible and of analyzing materials to see if they meet the goals and objectives of a library and its users.

It is not completely clear where Gorman (2003) sees the boundaries between collection development and collection management: he notes that the two terms are sometimes used synonymously, but argues on the one hand that collection development is 'a specific *subset* of the broader activity of collection management' and on the other hand that collection management 'has *replaced* the narrower "collection building" and "collection development" of former decades' (Gorman, 2003, 81). He stresses that collection management is a more comprehensive term, 'covering resource allocation, technical processing, preservation and storage, weeding and discarding of stock, and the monitoring and encouragement of collection use'. Elsewhere, he links a growing preference for the latter term not only with a broader scope, which also includes systems development and new technology, but also with a paradigm shift, 'from discrete institutional collections to a wider library world' in the networked environment (Gorman, 1997, x).

However, researchers and practitioners continue to use the term collection development and the argument for replacing it with collection management is inconclusive; practitioners generally differentiate staff *development* from staff *management*, so there is no reason why we should not continue to differentiate developmental and managerial aspects of our work with collections.

The impact of information technology

The impact of digital technologies on collection development is multifaceted and can be traced back over five decades. Libraries were typically early adopters of computer systems within their organizations in the 1960s and they have continued to fulfil a leadership role with their development of access to networked resources and web-based services in the 1990s and into the 21st century. ICT has affected the development and management of collections operationally, tactically and strategically. The next section briefly reviews key themes in the history of library exploitation of computers/ICT in relation to other environmental influences to show how conceptions of collection development have evolved in the shift towards an increasingly digital world.

The three phases identified by Lynch (2000) in his survey of 40 years of library automation are used here as a convenient framework for the period up to the end of the 20th century, together with an additional fourth phase taking us into the first decade of the 21st century. Lynch (2000) identifies a significant shift in library use of ICT during the period under review, which he characterizes as moving from the *modernization* achieved by *automation* of library routines, through *innovation* accomplished by *experimentation* with new capabilities (such as end-user self-service access to electronic information resources), to the *transformation* represented by the *digitization* of library materials (including both the conversion to digital formats of existing stock and the routine acquisition of new content as electronic media). With the benefit of hindsight, Lynch's third phase has been relabelled here as a period of *transition*, on the basis that the transformation did not really take place until a critical mass of digital content was not only available, but also accessible, to the majority of libraries, which arguably did not occur – at least in the UK – until the new century.

This shift from collections as predominantly print-based materials to collections as increasingly electronically delivered content has not only radically changed the character of the materials collected by the library, but has also fundamentally altered the nature of the library itself and raised strategic questions about the boundaries of both services and collections. The switch from local collections to networked information has accelerated in the 21st century with the emergence of Web 2.0 technologies that are particularly associated with social media and notions of user-generated content. They have opened up more options for libraries and highlighted their role in not just supporting users but building communities. This latest phase emphasizes *personalization* and *socialization* of services and resources through collaboration both with other service providers and especially with service users. Table 2.2 summarizes the key themes discussed in the subsections that follow.

Table 2.2 *Digital technology developments and collection development issues*

	Digital technology developments	Collection development issues
late 1960s–1970s	automation, modernization, computer-based operations	library housekeeping, bibliographic utilities, COM catalogues, retrospective conversion, microform masters, self-renewing/no-growth library
1980s–early 1990s	experimentation, innovation, computer-based services	library management, Conspectus methodology, OPACs, access vs holdings/ownership, end-user searching, just-in-time information
late 1980s–1990s	digitization, transition, computer-based content	integrated systems, licensing consortia, full-text databases, multimedia products, resource discovery, virtual/digital/hybrid library
2000s–	collaboration, transformation, network-based collections	ERM systems, federated search, open access, institutional repositories, digital asset management, data curation

Modernization – computer-based operations

In the late 1960s and early 1970s, libraries introduced computers to improve the efficiency of day-to-day operations, particularly circulation and cataloguing, although other areas of work were also affected, such as dial-up access to mediated abstracting and indexing databases. The description of early library automation systems as library *housekeeping* systems underlines their perceived operational role. Shared cataloguing systems were a key development during this time. In the late 1960s the Library of Congress started to make its catalogue records available in machine-readable form to both individual libraries and library co-operatives/bibliographic utilities. As a prominent example of the latter, the Ohio College Library Center (OCLC, later the Online Computer Library Center) was formed in 1967 with a primary goal 'to develop a computerized sharable online bibliographic database to increase productivity and decrease the costs of processing for its members' (Trochim, 1982, 2). Libraries were thus able to obtain catalogue cards from external databases for local use, instead of producing them in-house.

Access to bibliographic data from other institutions also supported retrospective conversion of library catalogue records to machine-readable form and in addition facilitated resource sharing through interlibrary lending. This was especially important in view of the exponential growth in published output that occurred during the 1960s and raised awareness of the need for interlibrary co-operation in relation to collection development (Kohl, 2003). The computer-based catalogues that gradually replaced card catalogues were typically computer-output microform (COM) using microfilm cassettes or microfiches. Microfilm was an important medium for libraries during this period as it was seen as a cost-effective format for specialist material and official publications, as well as forming the basis of institutional and national strategies for the preservation of library collections, which became recognized as a major concern during the 1960s and 1970s because of the embrittlement of acid-based paper introduced in the 19th century (Kohl, 2003). A *National Register of Microform Masters* was established by the Library of Congress in 1965 and served as the model for other countries.

Several commentators identify the 1960s and 1970s as the period when the term 'collection development' started to be widely used and the area of work became recognized as a professional specialism, citing the launch of journals such as *Collection Management* (1976), *Library Acquisitions: Practice and Theory* (1977) and *Collection Building* (1978) as evidence. The complexity of the task in a world of increasing publication output and diverse formats, but with steady budgets, was viewed as justification for moving beyond the selection of materials to the development of collections in other ways, including resource sharing (Johnson, 2004; Kohl, 2003). Another key factor influencing thinking during this period was the costs of the space and buildings needed to house library collections. The University Grants Committee in the UK took a firm line on this issue in a seminal publication known as the *Atkinson Report* (University Grants Committee, 1976), which proposed the concept of the 'self-renewing library' in which new acquisitions would be offset by the equivalent volume of withdrawals.

The concept of the 'self-renewing', 'no growth' or 'steady-state' library was highly controversial and it was widely discussed by university librarians in the USA, UK and Australia at conferences and in the literature in the late 1970s; the books edited by Gore (1975) and Steele (1978) are prime examples. Critics argued that the concept was based on flawed assumptions, namely that knowledge becomes outdated at the same rate as it is created, that future use of publications can be accurately predicted and that scholars seek material as isolated elements rather than in relation to other work; more specifically, they contrasted the typical linear sequence of bibliographical research in natural sciences with the less predictable process of humanities research, likened to an 'ever-widening ring of references, citations, leads and discoveries' (Dowd, 1989, 67). It is important to note here that these arguments relate particularly to *research* libraries: smaller academic (university and college) libraries, school, public and many special libraries have generally operated on the basis of regular de-selection of items, recognizing that withdrawal of out-of-date or little-used material improves the quality of a collection and makes it easier for users to find relevant material.

Innovation – computer-based services

The 1980s and early 1990s coincided with growth in the use of the internet, personal computers and e-mail. Libraries migrated to more sophisticated modular-based library *management* systems covering a wider range of functions, including interlibrary loans (ILL) alongside the now commonplace modules for acquisitions, cataloguing, circulation and serials, although separate systems were often used for ILL. The key development at this time was end-user or public access computing, represented by online public access catalogues (OPACs) and databases designed for end-user searching, coupled with developments in local and wide area networking. The former enabled networked access to individual library and consortial union catalogues; the latter were initially accessed via dedicated customized computer workstations or CD-ROMs loaded on individual machines or networked across the organization. Self-service searching involved a substantial change in professional work from conducting searches for clients to training users as searchers. It had a significant impact on the instructional role of library and information services, leading to the development of purpose-designed computer-based training suites, in addition to the installation of many more individual workstations and computer clusters in libraries.

Access and specifically the concept of access to information and knowledge resources as an alternative strategy to *ownership* of library materials emerged as a critical issue in collection development in the early 1990s. The shift from ownership to access has also been likened to moving from a 'just-in-case' to a 'just-in-time' model of information provision. In practical terms, in the 1990s, this generally meant relying less on acquisition of stock and more on ILL or document supply. Writing from an American perspective, Brin and Cochran (1994) note that such discussion can be traced back to the 1970s, but became the subject of many more articles from 1989 onwards, citing papers offering general overviews and particular viewpoints, as well as treatment of specific aspects or reference to the concept while discussing other issues. In the UK, published case studies indicate that the debate was often described as access vs holdings, rather than ownership (Baker, 1992; Corrall, 1993), but the issues were the same; Crawford and Gorman (1995, 133) also use the phrase 'access vs collection', arguing strongly that the discussion should not be about access vs collection, but about finding the right balance between access *and* collection.

The antecedents here obviously included the zero-growth self-renewing library recommended by the *Atkinson Report* cited above (University Grants Committee, 1976), but additional impetus came from another UK government body, the Library and Information Services Council for England (LISC), which issued three seminal reports on the future development of library and information services during the 1980s, covering all sectors (not just universities). The LISC FD2 report, *Working Together within a National Framework* (Department of Education and Science, 1982), is significant as one of the first explicit attempts to articulate a strategy enabling libraries to fulfil their respective roles against a backdrop of severe financial constraints and proliferating information resources. The report concluded that:

> Libraries and information services should move more purposefully from a mainly 'holdings' strategy requiring the accumulation of large stocks towards a mainly 'access' strategy in which emphasis is placed on the efficient procurement of material and information as required . . . Emphasis needs to be placed on obtaining, from whatever source, quick and accurate answers to today's questions, using printed, electronic or other media or personal contacts as circumstances demand.
>
> (Department of Education and Science, 1982, 25)

FD2 explicitly links the access model with technological developments, anticipating that the development of databases combining bibliographic citations with the full text of articles and electronically mediated document delivery services would facilitate a rebalancing between the traditional storehouse role of the library and its newer 'gateway' role. The case studies from the universities of Arizona, Aston and East Anglia all identify rising literature prices and inadequate library budgets as key drivers, and technology as a critical enabler of the access strategies described (Baker, 1992; Brin and Cochran, 1994; Corrall, 1993).

Another significant contribution to the access movement during this period was the development by the US-based Research Libraries Group of the Conspectus methodology for collection evaluation. Designed to support collaborative collection development and resource sharing (particularly interlending), the tool was intended to provide a composite picture of existing collection strengths and current collecting intensities arranged by Library of Congress subject fields, using a numerical scale ranging from 0 (= out of scope) to 5 (= comprehensive collection). Predicated on the notion that 'all libraries are linked in a great chain of access' (Stam, 1983, 21), the methodology was adopted not only in North America, but also in the UK (Matheson, 1989) and Australia (Henty, 1991), although take-up in the UK was patchy, with better coverage of Scotland and Wales than

England (apart from the British Library). However, although conceptually attractive and potentially useful as a local management tool, the cost-effectiveness of Conspectus was a concern and its value in supporting collaborative collection building and resource sharing became questionable with the widespread availability of library catalogues on the web (Clayton and Gorman, 2002).

Transition – computer-based content

Overlapping with the phase above, in the late 1980s and particularly from the early 1990s, electronic library services progressed from citation databases to full-text content. Early examples included electronic versions of traditional print reference works provided on CD-ROMs, such as the *Encylopaedia Britannica*. In addition there were new electronic resources that had no printed counterparts, notably *Encarta*, a digital multimedia encyclopedia produced by Microsoft from 1993 (initially on CD-ROM, but later as a web-based product and in DVD format). The real breakthrough came with full-text primary material in digital form, such as the historic literature collections launched by Chadwyck-Healey (e.g. the *English Poetry Full-Text Database* launched in 1992) and full-text electronic journals, which had a lengthy gestation period experimenting with different formats. By the mid-1990s they were available variously as online pay-as-you-go titles on a cost-per-access basis, CD-ROM document delivery systems and networked e-journals, the last category amounting to only around 100 titles by the mid-1990s (McKnight, 1993; Woodward and McKnight, 1995).

Another key development during this period was national, university and public library involvement in the digitization of their own holdings for both access and preservation purposes. These were typically special collections, often facilitated by external project funding. For example, the Library of Virginia's Digital Library Project included records, correspondence, newspapers and photographs related to Virginia's history and culture. (Roderick et al., 1997). In the UK, the Electronic Libraries (eLib) Programme was launched in 1994 as a result of the *Follett Report* from the Joint Funding Councils Libraries Review Group (JFCLRG, 1993). This was a massive development programme, representing a significant investment of public funding in innovation for academic libraries: the first two of the three phases cost £15 million and the projects extended well beyond digitization, with programme strands also covering access to network resources, digital preservation, electronic document delivery, electronic journals, electronic short-loan projects, images, large-scale resource discovery, on-demand publishing, pre-prints, quality assurance, supporting studies, training and awareness (eLib, 2001; Rusbridge, 1998). The first usage of the term 'hybrid library' is generally attributed to Chris Rusbridge, Director of the eLib programme, who explained that

> The name hybrid library is intended to reflect the transitional state of the library, which today can neither be fully print nor fully digital. (Rusbridge, 1998)

The hybrid library strand of the programme aimed to integrate technologies, systems, resources and services, including access to 'legacy' print materials, 'transition' (digitized legacy) resources and new (born-digital) resources, such as e-journals, e-books, databases and data sets in many formats (bibliographic, full text, image, vector/map, audio/video, statistical and numerical). eLib contrasted with the US Digital Libraries Initiative, which was mainly a computer science *research* programme, in contrast to the UK library service *development* programme (Rusbridge, 1998). There were other important national and international collaborative developments: in the UK, the Higher Education Digitization Service (HEDS) was set up as a result of eLib (Tanner, 1997); in the US, the JSTOR (Journal Storage) organization was formed in 1995 to digitize journal backruns and the National Digital Library of Theses and Dissertations (now the Networked Digital Library of Theses and Dissertations) was established in 1996 at Virginia Tech University (Kohl, 2003).

New commercial document delivery services such as EBSCOdoc, Faxon Finder and UnCover also emerged in the 1990s, supporting the shift from holdings to access as a solution to periodical price inflation and library budget cuts: some offerings were marketed as combined Current Awareness Services with Individual Article Supply, known as CASIAS products (Brunskill, 1997; Kohl, 2003). As the volume of full-text electronic content increased, web-based collections or *aggregations* of electronic resources began to appear as an alternative to title-by-title subscription. Such resources included sets of journals, conference proceedings, data files and government publications, grouped by publisher, function or topic. All this added to the growing complexity of the information landscape for libraries and prepared the ground for the much larger 'bundles' of titles that eventually arrived, known generally as 'Big Deals' and usually acquired through licences, which were increasingly negotiated through regional consortia or national initiatives (Bley, 1998; Kohl, 2003; Roberts, Kidd and Irvine, 2004; Walters et al., 1998).

Investment in UK public libraries came later, but was equally significant: the People's Network was a £170 million project to create ICT learning centres in all 4,300 service points, funded through the government's New Opportunities Fund (NOF). The public library initiative was intended to complement programmes already under way in higher and further education, the health sector (the National Electronic Library for Health) and the central government UKOnline portal (Woodhouse, 2001). A substantial part of the funding (£50 million) was allocated to the NOF-digitize programme, launched in 1999, which awarded 154 grants, ranging from £14,000 to £4 million, to 37 consortia (including partnerships with national and university libraries) and 34 individual projects, to produce

> a digital learning materials foundry of well over 1 million images, tens of thousands of audio and video clips, innumerable pages of text and many hundreds of new learning packages on topics as diverse as biscuits, voluntary work, migration, biodiversity, football, contemporary art, music and photography, reading, etc.   (Woodhouse, 2001)

Transformation – network-based collections

From 2000 onwards the proliferation of licensed electronic content, especially e-journals, led to the development of electronic resource management systems (ERMS) to automate and streamline the processing of acquisitions by library staff and the presentation of content to library users, in many cases replacing the labour-intensive compilation of title-by-title listings on library web pages, which in some institutions were duplicated in their OPAC. The growing complexity of the library systems marketplace is shown by the different providers of such systems, which included individual libraries, library consortia, library systems vendors and subscription agents/aggregators (Collins, 2008). Other systems that libraries might be using now to manage access to digital content – in addition to their existing *integrated* library system – include a digital object or digital asset management system (DOMS or DAMS) for locally produced content, an information retrieval portal or federated search engine for cross-searching of databases (Hakala, 2004) and a virtual learning environment (VLE, also known as a learning or course management system), typically used by academic libraries to manage access to electronic course readings or 'e-reserves' and to information literacy tutorials (Black, 2008).

VLEs offer the potential to personalize the delivery of electronic information resources to users. Academic staff and students can automatically be given access to the courses, modules or units for which they are registered, together with the resources associated with the course, such as digitized versions of key texts and subject-specific electronic resource guides with links to relevant websites. However, they have created challenges for libraries, as access to the course websites within VLEs is generally controlled by academic staff, who do not always recognize the need to integrate library resources with their teaching materials. In some cases they have developed their own collections of electronic resources for students, in effect setting up mini online departmental libraries, often without checking the copyright position. In contrast, some librarians have carried on delivering course-related material via separate websites because they have not been given access to the VLE system (Corrall and Keates, 2011; MacColl, 2001).

The 'open access' movement to widen access to scholarship became a significant driving force during the first decade of the 21st century, manifested in new campaigning organizations and several formal declarations of commitment. Driven by the continuing escalation of journal subscription costs, the movement was also a natural evolution from open source software and reflected the frustrations around access to information having become more restricted at a time when the web was opening up resources in other areas. According to Suber (2003, 92)

> Open-access literature is defined by two essential properties. First, it is free of charge to everyone. Second, the copyright holder has consented in advance to unrestricted reading, downloading, copying, sharing, storing, printing, searching, linking, and crawling.

The two main strategies used to achieve open access are for researchers – or others working on their behalf, such as librarians – to deposit or 'self-archive' their outputs in individual, discipline-based, institutional, consortial or national repositories (Peters, 2002) and for publishers to create 'open-access journals', based on alternatives to the traditional subscription-based model, for example, by charging authors fees for publishing. The movement has been controversial and has generated a significant amount of literature on the issues arising, much of which predictably is freely available (see Bailey, 2010).

Institutional repositories have been defined as 'digital collections capturing and preserving the intellectual output of a single or multi-university community' (Crow, 2002, 4) and libraries have typically taken a lead role in establishing and developing them, generally in collaboration with IT and other services (Rieh et al., 2007). The term 'digital asset management' is particularly associated with efforts to manage all the important digital content of an organization or institution, moving significantly beyond the research outputs (e.g. journal articles, conference papers and doctoral theses) that are typically the starting-point for an institutional repository, to a broader range of material. There is often a focus on multimedia resources, including image, sound and video files, which could include not only teaching and learning materials, but also the workflows of scientific simulations, the data supporting scholarly papers and recordings of research symposia, musical and theatrical performances, public lectures and talks (Hilton, 2003; Joint, 2009; Lynch, 2003).

Much of the library literature on institutional repositories has concentrated on the role of subject/reference/liaison librarians, but repository development and management is essentially a collection development and management issue, where existing policies and practices in areas such as content selection, metadata creation, access management and collection evaluation need to be applied or adapted in line with strategies established for redefining the scope of the collection to meet institutional needs in the digital environment (Connell and Cetwinski, 2010; Genoni, 2004). The next challenge here is dealing with data: many academic libraries are already taking responsibility for managing access to publicly available numerical and geographical digital data sets, just as they used to acquire statistical series in hard copy; in addition, libraries are being encouraged to get involved with the management and curation of data generated by research projects within their institutions, by extending their repository services and engaging with virtual research environments (VREs) to facilitate the discovery, transfer, re-use and archiving of data (Hey and Hey, 2006; Voss and Procter, 2009; Walters, 2009).

Collection development in digital environments

Reflecting on the nature of librarianship in the 21st century, Michael Gorman (2000, 10, 11) offers a modern definition of the word 'collection', which he presents as a quadruple configuration that includes:

- tangible objects (books, and so on) that the library owns
- local intangible (electronic) resources owned and controlled by the library (CD-ROMs, and the like)
- tangible objects owned by other libraries, but accessible to local patrons by means of union catalogues and interlibrary lending schemes
- remote intangible resources not owned by the library but to which the library gives access.

The definition above incorporates several dichotomies: local and remote; owned and not owned, but accessible; tangible and intangible. An Association of Research Libraries Task Force also found that its members had 'expanded the traditional view and definition of collections' (ARL, 2002, 8). In addition to the examples given by Gorman (2000), the ARL (2002, 6, 8) report notes that 'libraries are engaging in digitizing and electronic publishing projects' and 'taking responsibility for born-digital collections (such as geospatial or numeric data sets, faculty or class websites) and developing tools for their management and use'. A more recent ARL report confirms growing involvement of libraries in data management, providing six detailed case studies as examples of emerging practice (Soehner, Steeves and Ward, 2010). Other significant activities include 'managing and servicing born-digital content that resides outside the domain of the library' (ARL, 2002, 6) through the development of knowledge management systems to preserve and make accessible the institution's intellectual capital; a notable example here is the Ohio State University Knowledge Bank (Branin, 2003).

The ARL (2002) report suggests that rather than being defined by ownership, future collections could simply be resources that the library *manages, services* or *preserves* on behalf of library users – regardless of their location (or content). The centre of gravity was shifting, with the focus of collection development moving from local to global resources, as envisaged by Billings (1996, 4):

> The local collection will evolve into one enhanced and extended by digital technologies and electronic information sources. Policies for managing – and sharing – national and global mega-collections will emerge from the construction of cooperative programs on a stage that far transcends concerns for building the local collection.

An international cross-sectoral survey of library collection managers similarly found that digital information developments had made them 'think differently about the meaning of collection development' and at a practical level had meant spending more time on consortia activities (Dorner, 2004, 272).

As Gorman (2000, 11) suggests, these conceptions of the collection could be modelled as a series of concentric circles 'beginning with the "traditional" collection of the local library' and expanding infinitely to include 'all the recorded knowledge and information in the world'. Lee (2000) argues that collection developers/information professionals view collections in terms of levels of *control* (e.g. ownership, lease, interlibrary loan, referral elsewhere and no availability), but information users view them in terms of access (e.g. immediate access, delayed access and no access – or even only in terms of immediate access or no access).

Writing specifically about *collection development* in the 21st century, Gorman (2003a, 459) reconfigures his four-part conception into a hierarchy where he claims that 'each level is less organized and harder to gain access to than its predecessor' as follows:

- locally owned physical documents

- physical documents owned by other libraries but available through ILL
- purchased or subscribed to electronic documents
- 'free' electronic documents.

The second part of his assertion is questionable, as electronic documents are often easier to access than physical documents, which may not be available at the time when the user wants them: e-reserves as electronic versions of book chapters and other recommended texts for students were developed precisely to solve the problem of many people trying to access the same texts at the same time; in addition, free electronic documents are often easier to access than purchased or subscribed documents, despite being less organized.

Another problem with Gorman's taxonomy is that it is not clear where physical documents held locally (i.e. within the organization or community to which the library belongs), but not owned by the library fit into the picture.

Building on her earlier work, Lee (2003) also proposes a concentric circles model of the information universe, but goes beyond Gorman's (2000, 2003a) conception by including researchers' personal collections in her model, which is based on interviews with academic staff and aims to reflect users' perspectives on the information environment supporting their research and teaching. Her model has three layers characterized as the 'immediate space', 'adjunct space' and 'outside space' and is interesting in including an aggregation of personal physical collections, personal digital resources and library electronic resources in the centre, while relegating the library's physical resources to the middle circle. Figure 1.1 (overleaf) adapts and extends Lee's (2003, 432) 'structure of users' information spaces' renaming the adjunct space as 'intermediate space' and introducing a few additional items to the 'immediate space' to provide a more comprehensive picture of the contemporary information environment.

The implications for collection development

Conceptual models such as Gorman's (2000, 2003a) and Lee's (2003) provide useful frameworks for thinking about information resources and collections, but cannot adequately capture the complexity of the contemporary information universe. In addition to electronic versions of traditional library materials, such as textbooks and reference works, newspapers and periodicals, theses and dissertations, archives and manuscripts, maps and photographs, music and film, there are web-based information resources with no direct print equivalents, including listservs (e-mail discussion lists) and chat rooms, blogs and wikis, where the content is not only *dynamic*, because it is being continually edited, revised and supplemented, but also *user-generated*, as people engage in continuous role-switching between information user and information producer. Previously distinct roles in the information supply chain have converged and diversified with individuals and institutions acting as publishers through their websites, and periodicals subscription agents becoming library systems suppliers; in addition, many academic libraries have become publishers of scholarly monographs, conference proceedings and peer-reviewed journals (Hahn, 2008).

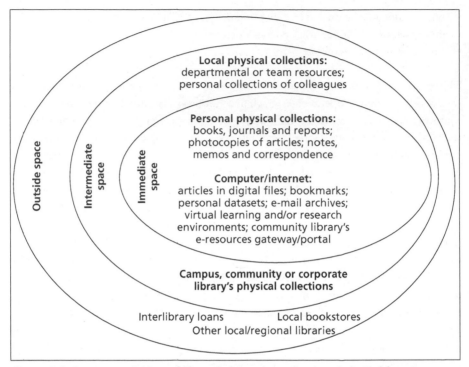

Figure 1.1 *A user-centric view of library/information collections (adapted from Lee, 2003)*

Buckland (1989) reviews the functional role of library collections, which he defines as three-fold: *archival* (retention and preservation), *dispensing* (availability and access) and *bibliographic* (organization and identification); he later added a fourth *symbolic* role, associated with rarity and status (Buckland 1995). Buckland (1989) first argues that the archival and bibliographic functions will continue to be important, but the dispensing role will shift from long-term to temporary local storage for electronic media. Moving on specifically to collection development, he then asks the fundamental question (Buckland, 1995, 157):

> What will collection developers do as local collections diminish in significance relative to networked electronic resources?

Drawing on McColvin's (1925) classic text on book selection for public libraries, Buckland (1995) argues the need to think differently about selection based on *demand* and selection based on *value*, which he refers to as *privileging* some works/documents over others, concluding that 'value-based privileging' will be more important than 'demand-based decisions' and will be implemented by providing customized access to the information universe for particular client groups, thus anticipating more recent discussion around *personalization* and *customization* of content through portals (e.g. Dempsey, 2003; Kalyanaraman and Sundar, 2006; Nichols and Mellinger, 2007; Shedlock et al., 2010).

Brophy (2007, 120–1) similarly confirms that selection should continue to be a central task for the modern library, but characterizes the role in slightly different terms, introducing concepts such as *sense-making, mapping* and *codifying*, which can be seen as contemporary interpretations of Buckland's (1989, 1995) bibliographic/advisory role:

> While libraries can act as the interface to this wealth of information, one of their most important tasks is to create order out of potential chaos. They do this by selecting and describing information sources which they will offer to their users . . . Within this understanding of the 'collection', the process of making sense of the information universe on behalf of users, partly by mapping and codifying it (including borrowing from the codification of others) and partly by selecting from it those parts which are likely to be of interest and are known, or likely, to be accessible, is critical.

Demas, McDonald and Lawrence, (1995) offer a more pragmatic view of collection development for the e-library, arguing the need to 'mainstream' electronic/networked resources by integrating them conceptually and operationally into collection development practice. Drawing on applied research and development at Cornell University, they describe the use of 'genre specialists', to develop expertise in different categories of resources (such as applications software, numeric files and multimedia materials); an Electronic Resources Council, to assess impact and co-ordinate activity across functional units; Internet Prospectors, an 'advance team' to develop strategies and policies for integration; and a five-level 'tiers of access' framework to match delivery mechanisms to anticipated demand. Many libraries established new teams and/or specialist positions to deal with new formats, but often as temporary structures to manage the transition (Dorner, 2004). Many libraries also used separate budgets for hard copy and electronic resources, which Gorman (2003a) rightly criticizes as inappropriate.

Demas (1998, 158) revisits Buckland's (1995) question about the role of collection development in the specific context of digitization, arguing that this is an area where the *art* of *value-based* selection – rather than the *science* of *demand-driven* selection – is needed to build 'a network of national and international digital libraries'. Demas (1998, 158) argues that market forces will deal with the high-demand material, but librarians need to develop 'rational, national co-operative plans' by collaborating with scholars in the *re-selection* of major parts of their collections for preservation and enhanced access within discipline-based intellectual frameworks. Lynch (1998) also calls for libraries to work together in developing co-ordinated national and international programmes to manage the transition to digital collections. He stresses the importance of moving beyond CD-ROMs as 'closed, bounded *artifacts*' to create resources that facilitate re-use and enhancement by the scholarly community over time, by integrating primary content 'into a web of commentary, criticism, scholarship, and instruction' and linking it to related content across institutional and geographical boundaries (Lynch, 1998, 140–1).

Evaluation and selection have emerged as key continuing roles for collection development in the digital world, but the information universe from which libraries can select and collect resources for their communities is far more diverse and dynamic than the print-based world. Several commentators have attempted to model the digital content landscape in order to help practitioners establish priorities for managing intellectual assets for their communities. Conway (2008) presents a complex multi-dimensional model that differentiates resources in a university context by source, structure, possession and rights. Dempsey (2003) describes a simpler 'collections grid' that divides materials into four categories on the basis of their *uniqueness* and *stewardship* (level of requirements for custodial care, such as metadata), which has been modified to cover collections in all types of libraries (OCLC, 2003). The OCLC (2003) model provides a useful graphic illustration of how the digital world has expanded the potential scope of collection development beyond the *published content* and *special collections* in the 'high stewardship' quadrants to include *open web content* and *institutionally produced content* that have generally been given 'low stewardship' attention. Thinking about the relative uniqueness of different resources may lead practitioners to change their priorities, spend less time on 'commodity content' and devote more effort to the unique resources within their communities.

Revolution or evolution?

Many commentators have stressed the transformation of libraries and their collections over the past 20 years. However, a few, notably Michael Gorman (2003b, 8), challenge this interpretation, arguing instead that library collections 'have grown and *evolved* over a long period', with each new development representing an 'evolutionary step' – not a 'revolution'.

Other commentators, including Brophy (2007), Buckland (1995), Demas (1998), Lynch (2000) and Moss (2008), have argued that the changes in the information universe demand that libraries *return* to and strengthen their traditional practice of *value-based selection*, to help their user communities navigate and make sense of the diversity and complexity of the new information universe. Demand-driven acquisition will also be important, but may in future be associated less with medium- to long-term collection development and more with short-term document delivery. The format and location of the material has changed (and will continue to change) but the principles of selecting material to meet current and future user needs still apply. More significantly, library and information professionals are increasingly applying their knowledge and skills in a wider context through participation in regional, national and international consortia and collaborative initiatives, recognizing that collection development for the future must look beyond traditional locally based collections to the development of large-scale global collections accessible to researchers and lifelong learners around the world, irrespective of their location.

Questions for reflection

- Is the concept of collection development relevant in the digital world?
- Do we need to adopt new terminology for the new information universe?
- How can libraries acquire the expertise to evaluate specialist resources?
- Should libraries shift their focus from local to global collections?
- Should libraries give higher priority to locally generated content?

• How should libraries deal with freely available internet resources?

References

Ameen, K. (2006) From acquisitions to collection management: mere semantics or an expanded framework for libraries? *Collection Building*, **25** (2), 56–60.

ARL (2002) *Collections & access for the 21st-century scholar: changing roles of research libraries, a report from the ARL Collections & Access Issues Task Force*, ARL Bimonthly Report, 225, www.arl.org/bm~doc/main.pdf.

Bailey, C. W. (2010) *Transforming Scholarly Publishing through Open Access: a bibliography*, Houston, Digital Scholarship, www.digital-scholarship.org/tsp/w/tsp.html.

Baker, D. M. (1992) Access Versus Holdings Policy With Special Reference to the University of East Anglia, *Interlending & Document Supply*, **20** (4), 131–7.

Billings, H. (1996) Library Collections and Distance Information: new models of collection development for the 21st century, *Journal of Library Administration*, **24** (1/2), 3–17.

Black, E. L. (2008) Toolkit Approach to Integrating Library Resources Into the Learning Management System, *Journal of Academic Librarianship*, **34** (6), 496–501.

Bley, R. (1998) NESLI – the National Electronic Site Licence Initiative, *VINE*, **28** (1), 34–7.

Branin, J. J. (2003) Knowledge Management in Academic Libraries: building the Knowledge Bank at the Ohio State University, *Journal of Library Administration*, **39** (4), 41–56.

Brin, B. and Cochran, E. (1994) Access and Ownership in the Academic Environment: one library's progress report, *Journal of Academic Librarianship*, **20** (4), 207–12.

Brophy, P. (2007) *The Library in the Twenty-First Century*, 2nd edn, Facet Publishing.

Brunskill, K. (1997) The Issues Surrounding the Provision of CASIAS Services in Libraries, *Interlending & Document Supply*, **25** (2), 57–63.

Buckland, M. (1989) The Roles of Collections and the Scope of Collection Development, *Journal of Documentation*, **45** (3), 213–26.

Buckland, M. (1995) What Will Collection Developers Do? *Information Technology and Libraries*, **14** (3), 155–9.

Clayton, P. and Gorman, G. E. (2002) Updating Conspectus for a Digital Age, *Library Collections, Acquisitions, & Technical Services*, **26** (3), 253–8.

Cogswell, J. A. (1987) The Organization of Collection Management Functions in Academic Research Libraries, *Journal of Academic Librarianship*, **15** (4), 268–76.

Collins, M. (2008) Electronic Resource Management Systems (ERMS) Review, *Serials Review*, **34** (4), 267–99.

Connell, T. H. and Cetwinski, T. (2010) Impact of Institutional Repositories on Technical Services, *Technical Services Quarterly*, **27** (4), 331–46. Preprint available at http://hdl.handle.net/1811/38978.

Conway, P. (2008) Modeling the Digital Content Landscape in Universities, *Library Hi Tech*, **26** (3), 342–54.

Corrall, S. M. (1993) The Access Model: managing the transformation at Aston University, *Interlending & Document Supply*, **21** (4), 13–23.

Corrall, S. and Keates, J. (2011) The Subject Librarian and the Virtual Learning Environment:

a study of UK universities, *Program*, **45** (1), 29–49.

Crawford, W. and Gorman, M. (1995) *Future Libraries: dreams, madness & reality*, American Library Association.

Crow, R. (2002) *The Case for Institutional Repositories: a SPARC position paper*, Scholarly Publishing and Academic Resources Coalition, www.arl.org/sparc/bm~doc/ir_final_release_102.pdf.

Demas, S. (1998) What Will Collection Development Do? *Collection Management*, **22** (3/4), 151–9.

Demas, S., McDonald, P. and Lawrence, G. (1995) The Internet and Collection Development: mainstreaming selection of internet resources, *Library Resources and Technical Services*, **39** (3), 275–90.

Dempsey, L. (2003) The Recombinant Library: portals and people, *Journal of Library Administration*, **39** (4), 103–36.

Department of Education and Science/Office of Arts and Libraries (1982) *The Future Development of Libraries & Information Services 2: working together within a National Framework*, Library Information Series No. 12, HMSO.

Dorner, D. G. (2004) The Impact of Digital Information Resources on the Roles of Collection Managers in Research Libraries, *Library Collections, Acquisitions, and Technical Services*, **28** (3), 249–74.

Dowd, S. (1989) Alexandria Revisited: another look at space and growth, *Collection Building*, **9** (3–4), 65–92.

Edelman, H. (1979) Selection Methodology in Academic Libraries, *Library Resources & Technical Services*, **23** (1), 33–8, http://alcts.ala.org/lrts/lrtsv23no1.pdf.

eLib (2001) Electronic Libraries Programme, *The Projects*, Bath: UKOLN, www.ukoln.ac.uk/services/elib/projects/.

Genoni, P. (2004) Content in Institutional Repositories: a collection management issue, *Library Management*, **25** (6–7), 300–6.

Gore, D. (ed.) (1975) *Farewell to Alexandria: Solutions to space, growth and performance problems of libraries*, Greenwood Press.

Gorman, G.E. (1997) Introduction. In Gorman, G. E. and Miller, R. H. (eds), *Collection Management for the 21st Century: a handbook for librarians*, ix–xv, Westport, CT: Greenwood Press.

Gorman, G. E. (2003) Collection Management. In Feather, J. and Sturges, P. (eds), *International Encyclopedia of Information and Library Science*, 2nd edn, 81–3, Routledge.

Gorman, G. E. and Howes, B. (1989) *Collection Development for Libraries*, Bowker Saur.

Gorman, M. (2000) *Our Enduring Values: librarianship in the 21st century*, American Library Association.

Gorman, M. (2003a) Collection Development in Interesting Times: a summary, *Library Collections, Acquisitions, & Technical Services*, **27** (4), 459–62.

Gorman, M. (2003b) *The Enduring Library: technology, tradition and the quest for balance*, American Library Association.

Hahn, K. L. (2008) *Research Library Publishing Services: new options for university publishing*, Association of Research Libraries, www.arl.org/bm~doc/research-library-publishing-services.pdf.

Hakala, J. (2004) Resource Description in a Heterogeneous System Environment, *Library Collections, Acquisitions, & Technical Services*, **28** (3), 275–82.

Henty, M. (1991) Conspectus in Australia: the view from the bridge, *Australian Library Review*, **8** (2), 107–13.

Hey, T. and Hey, J. (2006) E-science and its Implications for the Library Community, *Library Hi Tech*, **24** (4), 515–28.

Hilton, J. L. (2003) Digital Asset Management Systems, *Educause Review*, **38** (2), 52–3, http://net.educause.edu/ir/library/pdf/ERM0327.pdf.

Johnson, P. (2004) *Fundamentals of Collection Development and Management*, American Library Association.

Joint, N. (2009) Practical Digital Asset Management and the University Library, *Library Review*, **58** (2), 89–96.

JFCLRG (1993) Joint Funding Councils Libraries Review Group, *Report* [Follett Report], Higher Education Funding council for England, www.ukoln.ac.uk/services/papers/follett/report/.

Kalyanaraman, S. and Sundar, S. S. (2006) The Psychological Appeal of Personalized Content in Web Portals: does customization affect attitudes and behavior?, *Journal of Communication*, **56** (1), 110–32.

Kohl, D. F. (2003) Collection Development in the ARL Library. In Drake, M. (ed.), *Encyclopedia of Library and Information Science*, 2nd edn, 570–84, Dekker.

Lee, H.-L. (2000) What is a Collection? *Journal of the American Society for Information Science and Technology*, **51** (12), 1106–113.

Lee, H.-L. (2003) Information Spaces and Collections: implications for organization, *Library & Information Science Research*, **25** (4), 419–36.

Lynch, C. (1998) The Role of Digitization in Building Electronic Collections: economic and programmatic choices, *Journal of Library Administration*, **22** (3/4), 133–41.

Lynch, C. (2000) From Automation to Transformation: forty years of libraries and information technology in higher education, *Educause Review*, **35** (1), 60–8, http://net.educause.edu/ir/library/pdf/ERM0018.pdf.

Lynch, C. (2003) Institutional Repositories: essential infrastructure for scholarship in the digital age, *ARL Bimonthly Report*, **226**, 1–7, www.arl.org/resources/pubs/br/br226/br226ir.shtml.

Matheson, A. (1989) Conspectus in the United Kingdom, *Alexandria*, **1** (1), 51–9.

MacColl, J. (2001) Virtuous Learning Environments: the library and the VLE, *Program*, **35** (3), 227–39.

McColvin, L. (1925) *The Theory of Book Selection in Public Libraries*, Grafton.

McGarry, K. (2003) Libraries. In Feather, J. and Sturges, P. (eds), *International Encyclopedia of Information and Library Science*, 2nd edn, 371–4, Routledge.

McKnight, C. (1993) Electronic Journals – Past, Present . . . and Future? *Aslib Proceedings*, **45** (1), 7–10.

Moss, M. (2008) The Library in the Digital Age. In Nicholas, D. and Rowlands, I. (eds), *Digital Consumers: reshaping the information profession*, 69–91, Facet Publishing.

Nichols, J. and Mellinger, M. (2007) Portals for Undergraduate Subject Searching: are they worth it? *Portal: Libraries and the Academy*, **7** (4), 481–90.

OCLC (2003) *Collections Grid*, Dublin, OH: OCLC Online Computer Library Center, www.oclc.org/reports/escan/appendices/collectiongrid.htm

Peters, T. A. (2002) Digital Repositories: individual, discipline-based, institutional, consortia, or national, *Journal of Academic Librarianship*, **28** (6), 414–17.

Prytherch, R. (comp.) (2005) *Harrod's Librarians' Glossary and Reference Book: a directory of over 10,200 terms, organizations, projects and acronyms in the areas of information management, library science, publishing and archive management*, 10th edn, Ashgate.

Reitz, J. M. (2010) *ODLIS: online dictionary for library and information science*, Santa Barbara, CA: ABC-CLIO, www.abc-clio.com/ODLIS/odlis_A.aspx.

Rieh, S. Y., Markey, K., St. Jean, B., Yakel, E. and Kim, J. (2007) Census of Institutional Repositories in the U.S.: a comparison across institutions at different stages of IR development, *D-Lib Magazine*, **13** (11/12), www.dlib.org/dlib/november07/rieh/11rieh.html.

Roberts, M., Kidd, T. and Irvine, L. (2004) The impact of the current e-journal marketplace on university library budget structures: some Glasgow experiences, *Library Review*, **53** (9), 429–434.

Roderick, E., Taylor, J.M., Bourd, S. and Courson, G. (1997) The Library of Virginia's Digital Library Project, *Library Hi Tech*, **15** (3–4), 56–62, 89.

Rusbridge, C. (1998) Towards the Hybrid Library, *D-Lib Magazine*, **4** (7/8), www.dlib.org/dlib/july98/rusbridge/07rusbridge.html.

Shedlock, J., Frisque, M., Hunt, S., Walton, L., Handler, J. and Gillam, M. (2010) Case Study: the Health SmartLibrary experiences in web personalization and customization at the Galter Health Sciences Library, Northwestern University, *Journal of the Medical Library Association*, **98** (2), 98–104, www.ncbi.nlm.nih.gov/pubmed/20428276.

Soehner, C., Steeves, C. and Ward, J. (2010) *E-Science and Data Support Services: a study of ARL member institutions*, Washington, DC: Association of Research Libraries, www.arl.org/bm~doc/escience_report2010.pdf.

Soper, M. E., Osborne, L. N. and Zweizig, D. L. (1990) *The Librarian's Thesaurus*, American Library Association.

Stam, D. H. (1983) Think Globally – Act Locally: collection development and resource sharing, *Collection Building*, **5** (1), 18–21.

Steele, C. (ed.) (1978) *Steady-State, Zero Growth and the Academic Library: a collection of essays*, Bingley.

Suber, P. (2003) Removing Barriers to Research: an introduction to open access for librarians, *College & Research Libraries News*, **64** (2), 92–4, 113, expanded preprint available at www.earlham.edu/~peters/writing/acrl.htm.

Tanner, S. (1997) The Higher Education Digitization Service: managing the conversion to electronic formats, *Serials*, **10** (3), 352–6.

Trochim, M. K. (1982) *Academic Library Resource Sharing through Bibliographic Utility Program Participation: report to the Office of Libraries and Learning Technologies*, Washington DC: United States Department of Education, Office of Educational Research and Improvement, www.eric.ed.gov:80/PDFS/ED227853.pdf.

University Grants Committee (1976) *Capital Provision for University Libraries: report of a Working*

Party, HMSO.

Voss, A. and Procter, R. (2009) Virtual Research Environments in Scholarly Work and Communications, *Library Hi Tech*, **27** (2), 174–90.

Walters, T. O. (2009) Data Curation Program Development in U.S. universities: the Georgia Institute of Technology example, *International Journal of Digital Curation*, **3** (4), 83–92, www.ijdc.net/index.php/ijdc/article/viewFile/136/153.

Walters, W. H., Demas, S. G., Stewart, L. and Weintraub, J. (1998) Guidelines for Collecting Aggregations of Web Resources, *Information Technology and Libraries*, **17** (3), 157–60.

Woodhouse, S. (2001) The People's Network and the Learning Revolution: building the NOF digitise programme, *Ariadne*, **29**, www.ariadne.ac.uk/issue29/woodhouse/.

Woodward, H. and McKnight, C. (1995) Electronic Journals: issues of access and bibliographical control, *Serials Review*, **21** (2), 71–8.

Young, H. (ed.) (1983) *The ALA Glossary of Library and Information Science*, American Library Association.

2
The processes of collection management

Maggie Fieldhouse

Introduction

In the previous chapter, Sheila Corrall discusses the concept of collection development. This chapter will consider, with particular reference to academic libraries, the processes of collection management that have developed over time as technology and publishing models have changed.

On a practical level, collection management encompasses a wide range of activities: selection and acquisition, budget allocation and management, serials and electronic resource management and access control, stock evaluation, weeding, storage and preservation, as well as liaison with users, managers, suppliers and publishers and collaboration with other institutions. Promotion and marketing activities are increasingly becoming associated with collection management and are discussed by Mitrano and Peterson, Stubbings and Fairclough in Part Four of this volume. Collection managers are also responsible for the quality of both bibliographic and electronic records and the use of appropriate metadata to describe resources accurately to facilitate access. These activities are not the domain of any specific library sector, although the extent to which they are developed will be influenced by organizational policies and strategies.

This chapter will consider the core activities of collection management and identify how the digital age has transformed the processes underpinning library resource provision from the relevant literature. Its purpose is to update the established practices described in the standard textbooks by Johnson (2009), Clayton and Gorman (2006), Evans and Saponaro (2005) and Jenkins and Morley (1999), by referring readers to the wisdom of those authorities whose knowledge withstands the test of time. The chapter concludes by focusing on the issues raised and identifies some points for further reflection.

Policy and strategy

Collection development and management have become synonymous with each other and a strategic approach to the meeting of users' information needs emerged during the 1980s and 1990s. Gorman, in his introduction to *Collection Management for the 21st Century: a Handbook for Librarians* (Gorman and Miller, 1997), identifies a growing preference for the phrase collection *management*, rather than *development*, as the fundamental activities of collection building, selection and acquisition, began to involve wider issues such as budgeting, relegation and stock withdrawal, managing new resource formats, storage, preservation, performance measurement, technology and resource sharing. Branin (1994) noted that, as early as 1981, Paul Mosher identified the trend towards collection management[1] calling for a more managerial approach to matching resources and user needs. By 1993 Mosher was, according to Branin, also urging librarians to manage the convergence between print and electronic systems effectively.

To reinforce this change, collection or stock development policies were formulated by libraries to meet organizational strategies, and address issues raised by the transition from print to online resources as well as demonstrate prudent management of resource budgets. Breaks (1999), Cox (2003) and Cole and Usherwood (1996) provide a historical perspective on the introduction and value of such policies, while Evans and Saponaro (2005, 49–68), Clayton and Gorman (2006, 16–36), Johnson (2009, 72–82) and Shaw, in Part 4 of this volume, offer practical advice on the creation and updating of collection management policies.

This strategic approach led to the more rigorous management of processes to address growing budget constraints, due to spiralling costs and the phenomenal growth in journal publishing. The tasks of selection and acquisition also came under scrutiny in order to ensure that resources relevant to users' needs were provided within shrinking budgets.

Selection

Historically, library collections were developed to meet the perceived and potential needs of users. Stueart (1980, 4) noted that stock selection for university libraries was the task of academics, and for public libraries was the responsibility of 'cultured' members of the community. This resulted in collections that might once have been assumed to meet the needs of the local user community, but as a result of global access to online library catalogues via the internet, inadequacies in library collections have been exposed to the scrutiny of all.

Stock selection has traditionally been a key function of collection development, but questions arise about who influences the activity: should librarians dictate what resources are available, or should user preferences have priority? The selection and acquisition of materials might depend on many factors including:

- the value and relevance of content
- book reviews
- publisher standing
- author reputation
- accessibility
- cost.

Other methods of selection include usage statistics, ILL requests and user suggestions.

Because good practice in resource selection requires an understanding of the information needs of the community the library serves, it could be argued that librarians should take responsibility for identifying appropriate resources, being in a position to respond to demographic changes and research trends and keep up to date with the environment in which the organization exists. More important, they know what is relevant to the collection, the quality and accuracy of its content, its potential use and what resources are accessible elsewhere. They are aware of the collection's strengths and weaknesses, how to identify and evaluate resources and who to select from. They also understand the often complex roles of agents and suppliers. Public libraries often depend on stock profiles supplied to vendors, who match publications with expressed needs and provide materials on approval. For a discussion of the benefits and disadvantages of approval plans in academic libraries, see Fenner (2004). User-purchase suggestion schemes supplement librarian-led selection, and studies of users' information-seeking behaviour indicate trends towards user or patron-driven selection and acquisition, especially in respect of electronic books and journals (Peters, 2001; Nixon, Freeman and Ward, 2010).

The processes of selection are considered in depth by Clayton and Gorman (2006, 73–118), Johnson (2009, 103–18), and Evans and Saponaro (2005, 69–98), but the big question for collection managers is the extent to which electronic resources such as books and journals will impact on selection and acquisition in the future.

Licensing, access and economic models for electronic books have yet to reach maturity. The complexities of the market are illustrated in the case histories in Part Two which discuss the challenges for the selection and acquisition of e-books in an environment in which publishers offer one-off purchase, subscription or rental models. The JISC National e-books Observatory Project[2] (JISC, 2009) sought to evaluate the use of e-books in higher education in the UK and investigate publishers' concerns about loss of print sales. No conclusive evidence to uphold these concerns was found, although librarians felt that the e-books market was overly complex, with inappropriate business models, complicated licences and high prices.

The impact of the digital environment on the selection and acquisition of serials is discussed later in this chapter.

Acquisition

The acquisition of library resources, which involves ordering, receipting, preparing items for the shelves and providing access to electronic information, has also been transformed by technological developments. Manual order creation has largely been supplanted by downloaded bibliographic records and Electronic Data Interchange (EDI).[3] Agents and vendors now dominate the supply chain and librarians have to contend with pricing models and negotiating licensing terms and conditions. Suppliers may be contracted to provide shelf-ready books, relieving library staff of routine tasks such as labelling and security tagging. In many cases classification numbers, or shelf marks, are assigned by suppliers according to schedules provided by the library.

Acquisitions, a technical services function once considered to be a backroom operation, is now very much incorporated into the business of libraries as service providers. Acquisitions librarians work as part of a team, liaising with other members of library staff to provide relevant resources in a timely manner. The negotiation of pricing models, access rights and licensing agreements with vendors, agents and publishers are critical activities, discussed in Dunham and Davis's review of acquisitions literature between 2004 and 2007 (Dunham and Davis, 2009). Horava (2010) explores how acquisitions work is changing in the digital environment, while List and Chadwell (2011) consider some of the challenges for collection managers in the next five years.

One significant issue is access to, rather than ownership of, information. The ever-growing amount of content held in publisher-, vendor- or aggregator-owned databases, which libraries gain access to by signing up to licensing agreements rather than outright purchase, raises serious questions about the sustainability and preservation of library collections to provide long-term access to materials that have been acquired from library budgets. Ball (2005) considers the implications of electronic resource licences, such as publishers' and aggregators' monopolies over content and the associated loss of control by libraries while Kane (1997) discusses the dilemmas of ownership vs access for librarians. The trend towards access, rather than ownership, means that acquisition is increasingly a just-in-time, as opposed to just-in-case, activity led by users or patrons. Patron-driven access models for electronic books and serials are becoming an attractive alternative to the Big Deals,[4] which are considered later in this chapter, and bundles that have enabled increased access to scholarly information and attempted to reduce the impact of high publishing costs. While publishing and access models for e-books are far from standardized, Sharp and Thompson (2010) discuss purchasing models for e-books, while Pan, Byrne and Murphy (2009) and Hodges, Preston and Hamilton, (2010) consider the challenges e-books pose for academic libraries. Schell, Ginanni and Heet (2010) discuss the advantages and drawbacks of pay-per-view (PPV) models for journal subscription and e-book acquisition.

Gifts, donations and exchanges can be a valuable means of acquiring out-of-print items and filling gaps in collections, but can pose dilemmas for collection managers. They must be assessed for relevance to the collection and processing donated items can be time-consuming. Large collections may contain material that is of little value and it is worth ensuring that such items may be disposed of by the library if it accepts the donation. Some gifts may come with specific conditions attached, such as retention or keeping a collection together, which may be unacceptable. A specific donations, or gifts policy, either contained within the collection management policy, or published as a separate document, which states the terms on which gifts are accepted helps to address political considerations, such as the 'valuable' collection offered by a notable person. Clayton and Gorman (2006, 130–134), Johnson (2009, 125–7) and Evans and Saponaro (2005, 242–4) offer advice on handling exchanges and gifts, both solicited and unsolicited.

The processes of acquisition are discussed in detail by Chapman (2000), Clayton and Gorman (2006, 118–39), while Holden (2010) provides an up-to-date guide to acquisitions work.

Budgets

Budget management has been a major challenge since the early 1990s. Ford (1999) identifies increasing demands on library budgets from document delivery services, copyright and licensing fees to electronic products (together with the associated hardware and software), and online searching. Ford also explores the wide range of factors that determine budget allocation formulae, identifying the typical problems and pitfalls that can entrap the unwary.

The struggle to stretch library budgets to keep pace with spiralling costs and the rapidly increasing number of publications, whilst maintaining expenditure at levels sufficient to provide adequate resources to meet the needs of users, is a continuing theme. Financial constraints, further exacerbated by the economic recession of 2008/9 have prompted strategic reviews of budget allocation models and concerns about unsustainable expenditure on resources (Dinkins, 2011; Kaay and Zimmerman, 2008; Goulding, 2009). The Association of College and Research Libraries Planning and Review Committee (ACRL, 2010) identify static materials budgets and the effect on staff recruitment and retention, collection building, access to resources and service development as issues. The value of the Big Deal and its sustainability are being called into question (Taylor-Roe, 2009; Best, 2009; Cleary, 2009; Cryer and Grigg, 2011). Sykes (2010) discusses the prospects for UK university library budgets, noting problems such as journal price inflation, finding funding for special initiatives and identifying alternative income sources.

The principle of budgeting is to ensure the fair distribution of money to meet users' needs and to ensure timely expenditure. To achieve this, when money is, in real terms, diminishing, librarians can employ a number of strategies to maximize budgets, such as reducing expenditure on books to meet the increasing costs of subscriptions, entering into co-operative or consortial purchasing agreements, and reviewing access, for example, to journal content, by adopting PPV schemes. However, such measures do not come without penalties and the implications for libraries include:

- less comprehensive collections
- collections owned by information providers
- reducing support for some collections to maintain it for others
- finding new revenue streams
- reducing overheads, such as staffing costs.

Other options for maximizing budgets include evaluating open access journals and revising budget allocations, a strategy described by Steele (2008).

Budget models and fund allocation can be politically sensitive and will depend on any number of variables, such as the number of users, teaching and research priorities, and historic expenditure:

- *Lump sum budgets* are based on previous allocations plus an amount to cover inflation, or increased demand for resources.

31

- *Formula-based budgeting* is transparent and enables expenditure to be managed according to specific criteria, but can be inflexible.
- *Needs-based budgeting* supports core collections by top-slicing amounts to cover, for example, general reference or electronic resources. It can also reflect demand for teaching materials, or specific formats.
- *Zero-based budgeting* is founded on the principle of predicting the year's spend, based on essential and desirable resources and projects. While this reflects expenditure needs, unexpected currency fluctuations and cost increases can be problematic.

Whichever model is adopted, it would be sensible to bear in mind how expenditure relates to the library's objectives as stated in the collection management policy. Budget models are explored in some detail by Ford (1999) while Evans and Saponaro (2005, 277–94), Johnson (2009, 83–96) and Clayton and Gorman (2006, 140–59) offer useful discussions of the principles of budget allocation.

Budget planning is essential to accommodate annual subscriptions for serials and standing orders and maintain appropriate levels of committed and spent funds. To avoid any possibility of cuts, it is prudent to monitor expenditure to ensure that the allocation is exhausted at the end of the financial year.

Serials management

In terms of library collections, the management of serials has undergone the most radical transformation and their selection and administration has been transformed by electronic publication and the Big Deal, aggregated packages of electronic journal content licensed by vendors to institutions for the cost of subscriptions to journal titles, plus a premium to include wider content. The implications of Big Deals for collection managers are discussed in more detail by Harvell in Part 2.

Historically, titles would be selected according to their impact factor,[5] academic recommendation or affinity to a learned organization. Individual subscriptions would be taken out with publishing bodies and issues checked in manually. Because of limited print runs, missing copies would have to be chased within a short space of time to ensure continuity of holdings. Print subscriptions were typically managed on a title-by-title basis and obtained from publishers. The very fact of ownership meant they occupied significant amounts of shelf space, and were frequently bound by volume in order to preserve them. Access to content was by means of annual indexes, bibliographies and abstracting services.

The revolution in serials management began in the 1990s, when full-text electronic journals began to encroach on the periodicals scene. Despite obstacles posed by licensing terms and pricing models, librarians began to be able to offer remote access to vast quantities of content by negotiating terms with publishers.

The bewildering array of pricing models resulted in a complex situation: free electronic versions with print subscriptions, electronic only (on which VAT was payable), print subscription plus an additional payment for electronic access (again liable to VAT) are just a few examples. Other factors affecting pricing in the UK included the institution's JISC banding, the number of users, the number of simultaneous users and the number of sites accessing the resource. For academic collection managers, the complexities of agreeing definitions of concepts such as sites (campus? building?) users (guests? visiting academics?) and use restrictions with publishers posed significant challenges. These issues, and the increasing role played by e-journals in the UK, are discussed by Kidd (1998).

Current licensing agreements, which provide a standard approach to access to online content are the result of two developments in the UK: The Pilot Site Licence Initiative (PSLI), supported by the Higher Education Funding Council for England (HEFCE) and the JISC-funded National Electronic Site Licence Initiative (NESLi). These initiatives sought to address problems of access and authentication, multiple interfaces and archiving. NESLi introduced the concept of the managing agent, whose role was to negotiate value for money deals for electronic journals with publishers and define a model site licence to standardize definitions which spawned the Big Deal. For collection managers, such agreements, which are often time-limited, provided clarity and stability in what had been a volatile market. Bley (2000) and Harwood (2000) consider the benefits of NESLi, while Borin (2000) provides a useful review of both initiatives. The significance of licensing agreements is discussed by Richards (2001) and Ball (2005), who also considers the implications of the Big Deal and the role of publishers and vendors. For the UK higher education sector, other agreements are negotiated by Eduserv CHEST,[6] and JISC,[7] which undertakes licensing and procurement activities on behalf of the academic community.

In this environment new skills are necessary to manage access to, rather than the acquisition of, journal content and the impact of the tensions between managing print and electronic journal provision on the working practices of serials librarians has been discussed by Duranceau (1997). An awareness of publishing trends and developments in open access is essential to keep abreast of an ever-changing market. Skills such as licence negotiation, IT troubleshooting, statistical analysis and an understanding of business and pricing models are fundamental.

The current economic climate means that collection managers also have to contend with static budgets, which, increasingly, cannot be stretched to accommodate the Big Deals which devour a significant proportion of resource allocations. Restricted cancellation options and the imposition of penalties erode the librarian's freedom to manage their journal collections effectively. Questions about the future of the Big Deal have been raised by Frazier (2001), Best (2009) and Bergstrom (2010).

The explosion of electronic journal titles has resulted in new management systems to provide administrative support and effective access for users. The Digital Library Federation's Electronic Resource Management Initiative (ERMI), sought to simplify the tasks of processing licence agreements and administrative activities by bringing together librarians, publishers and vendors to define standard specifications. Library management system providers and serials agents, such as Ex Libris, Innovative Interfaces, Serials Solutions and EBSCO offer electronic resource management (ERM) tools to manage aspects such as licences, bibliographic data, link resolvers, A–Z listings, subscription and cost data, renewals and usage statistics. Bevan et al. (2001) offers a case study of e-journals management at Cranfield University. Ellingsen (2004) and Collins and Grogg (2011) discuss ERM functionality, noting the need for interoperability with other systems.

The measurement of e-journal usage to assess cost effectiveness and value for money, introduces a need for comparable and consistent data. The COUNTER project, an international initiative involving librarians and publishers[8] was established in 2002 to set standards for measuring and reporting e-journal usage. The SUSHI protocol[9] was added to the COUNTER standard in 2007 to facilitate the automated harvesting and consolidation of usage statistics from different vendors. The COUNTER and SUSHI protocols are discussed by Pesch (2007) and updated in Pesch (2008), while Jones (2009) provides a comprehensive discussion of issues in electronic journal and resource management.

The emergence of electronic resources and the increase in publishing rates to the point where economically, libraries can no longer sustain comprehensive journal collections have impacted on serials publishing models by introducing more informal routes. As well as electronic journals, collection managers must engage with open access publishing, which has led to the building of institutional repositories and strategies for self-archiving publications.

Open access offers two routes to publishing:

- The green route, or self-archiving, allows articles or e-prints, which may also be published in journals, to be deposited in an institutional or subject repository.
- The gold route, which is a means of publishing articles in open access journals, which are free to access, have no copyright or licensing restrictions and offer peer reviewed content. Publication costs are borne by the author, their employing or funding organization.

In Part 3, David Brown takes a detailed look at open access models and their importance for scholarly communication while Josh Brown considers the implications of institutional repositories for collection managers.

Co-operative collection development and consortia

Naylor, in 1999, made cautious predictions about consortial approaches to purchasing, stock management and preservation, suggesting that while collaborative purchasing is becoming a necessity, collection description levels are too generalized and the costs of preservation too high to render collaborative approaches to stock management cost effective (Naylor, 1999, 277–80).

Collaborative purchasing is one aspect of co-operative collection development, often considered to increase benefits by reducing costs and ensuring comprehensive subject collection. Resource sharing, interlibrary loans, bibliographic record exchange, reciprocal borrowing and assigned subject specialization also contribute to the concept. However, co-operative collection development, which attempted to reduce duplication in libraries, has run a rocky path, and there are many issues which can cause initiatives to founder. Political conflicts between local and wider needs, logistical problems and ideas that collaboration will provide something for nothing are potential pitfalls (Evans and Saponaro, 2005, 339–58). A notable failure was the Farmington Plan, launched in 1948 but abandoned in 1972, the victim of constantly changing institutional needs and a lack of recognition that local needs will be prioritized (Edelman, 1973).

In 2002, a Center for Research Libraries (CRL) sponsored survey identified 89 co-operative projects, mostly centred in the US although 20% featured participation by Australian and UK libraries (Haar, 2003). Many came into being in the 1990s, when consortia focusing on the purchase of electronic databases began to emerge. Print-based co-operative collection development initiatives, such as the Research Library Cooperative Program, involving California-Berkeley, Stanford and Texas-Austin universities and aiming to jointly build and share research collections in Latin American Studies continue to flourish (Haar, 2003). Other projects included the Triangle Research Libraries Network (selection of non-electronic monographs and/or serials) (Antelman and Couts, 2009), the California Digital Library and OhioLINK (shared electronic purchasing or licensing), PORTALS, a co-operative formed of libraries in the Portland Oregon area (serials weeding, co-operative purchasing) (Rohe, O'Donovan and Hanawalt, 2000) and PANDORA (National Library of Australia), which addressed access, storage and preservation (Shelton, 2003).

Consortial purchasing has met with some success in the UK and the USA. Collins' review of the serials literature 2008–9 considers the value of consortia deals in journals pricing (Collins, 2011), while Kinner and Crosetto (2009) provide a comprehensive analysis of activity in the USA, including the benefits offered by the well established OhioLINK network.[10] Ball (2000, 2003) describes periodicals and electronic resource purchasing in the UK and Kidd (2009) considers SHEDL, the Scottish electronic resource collaborative initiative.

Gorman (2000, 241–306), Evans and Saponaro (2005, 339–56), Clayton and Gorman (2006, 52–72), Shreeves (2003) and Johnson (2009, 264–303) describe approaches to collaborative collection development, resource sharing and co-operation.

Issues pertaining to access, storage and preservation were being addressed by the Consortium of University Research Libraries (now Research Libraries UK (RLUK)). The UK Research Reserve (UKRR) is a collaborative distributed national research collection which provides access to a shared collection of printed research journals. UKRR makes low-use, but still important, research material accessible cost effectively and allows libraries to de-duplicate print journal holdings of a title if two copies are held by other UKRR members (Wright and Crawford, 2008; Boyle and Brown, 2010). JSTOR,[11] was conceived in 1995 as a shared digital archive of journal content which would enable institutions to free up valuable space. It has become an established scholarly resource and in 2009 became part of ITHAKA,[12] a not-for-profit organization dedicated to exploiting information and networking technologies to preserve knowledge to support the academic community.

The development of shared services is beginning to emerge as a potential solution to library and collection management. In the UK, JISC[13] is exploring resource discovery and the Society of College, National and University Libraries (SCONUL)[14] is investigating how shared services might benefit the management of electronic resources. EDUCAUSE is also encouraging collaboration to promote open access to knowledge (Goldstein, 2007).

Stock evaluation: retention and disposal

Library hygiene is an important element of collection management as overcrowded shelves full of outdated texts will not attract or please users. Collection evaluation, also referred to as collection assessment or review, helps to keep stock relevant and up to date, increase its visibility, make the most of valuable shelf space and maximize reshelving rates. In the days when collection building and development were a priority, stock evaluation was neglected as an irrelevant, time-consuming and potentially controversial activity.

Collection evaluation includes the weeding, or deselection of stock, the relegation of low-use material to on-site or off-site storage and the disposal of items that contain outdated or harmful content (e.g. medical or legal textbooks), lack relevance or are in poor condition. Caution is advisable as, in some subjects, historical publications or different editions of a title can be a valuable research resource. Weeding academic library stock should therefore be a consultative process and criteria for the disposal of unwanted items should be defined in a collection management policy, to avoid misunderstandings. Weeding can be a risky undertaking; it has been known for users to find discarded items on sale in second-hand bookshops and return them (sometimes indignantly) to the library. Materials for disposal may be candidates for book sales, offered to dealers or exchange programmes, recycled or consigned to landfill.

Evaluation methods may be:

- quantitative and user oriented, based on circulation statistics or in-house use
- collection-centred and qualitative, based on currency, relevance, condition and duplication, or multiple copies.

Often a combination of both methods is used to identify candidates for relegation or disposal. Relegation may depend on the availability and cost of suitable secure storage.

Agee (2005) describes three approaches to evaluation: user centred, physical assessment and assessment of specific subject support. Slote's seminal text, which remains the most authoritative source on the subject, provides practical advice on weeding methods (Slote, 1997). Evans and Saponaro (2005, 295–338) offer comprehensive insights into evaluation and deselection, while Clayton and Gorman (2006, 160–86) discuss the reasons for evaluation and appropriate procedures.

Preservation

Preservation is very much a part of collection management if library materials are available for as long as they are needed. For printed materials, factors such as environmental conditions (e.g. humidity, lighting levels), handling, pest control, binding and rebinding, and repair programmes contribute to the conservation of stock. Supervised access, or provision of surrogate items such as photocopies (subject to copyright restrictions), microforms or digitized versions of texts may be appropriate in the case of fragile materials.

A preservation policy, which may be separate from, but linked to, the collection management policy, provides a clear statement of intent in respect of the acquisition and retention of library resources. The preservation implications of purchasing a paperback, rather than hardback version of a text are self-evident, and other materials, such as newspapers, raise issues about the preservation of content over form. The problems of acid paper, which causes brittleness and yellowing, derives from the introduction of wood pulp, rather than cloth, as a basis for paper production in the mid 1800s. Mass deacidification programmes have been widely undertaken by libraries such as the Library of Congress,[15] New York Public Libraries (Pilette, 2004) and the British Library.[16] Approaches to preservation are discussed in Gorman and Shep (2006) and Feather (2004), while the Preservation Directorate at the Library of Congress[17] and the British Library's Preservation Advisory Centre[18] provide a wealth of information. Summaries of preservation issues for collection managers can be found in Williams (1999), Elkington (1999), Gorman and Miller (2000), Williams (2000) and Evans and Saponaro (2005, 357–83).

Digital preservation or curation are increasingly important issues. Collection managers have in the traditional environment, been in control of the physical resource life cycle and preservation, whereas with electronic sources, control has shifted to suppliers and publishers. The tensions between access, ownership and the persistence of electronic content have been challenging collection managers since the mid 1990s. With the trend for reference and other information to be published electronically, the preservation of born-digital resources and web archiving are expanding fields. In the UK, JISC[19] has focused on programmes to ensure the sustainability of digital and online materials, while the Digital Curation Centre[20] offers advice on their organization and preservation. In the USA, librarians and publishers are working together on projects such as LOCKSS[21] (Lots of Copies Keep Stuff Safe) and CLOCKSS[22] (Controlled LOCKSS, which releases content no longer available from a publisher) to preserve e-content. PORTICO[23] permanently archives electronic journals, books and digital collections.

Disaster planning

Disaster planning stemmed from events such as the 1966 floods in Florence, 9/11, the 1992 burning of the National Library in Sarajevo, the Prague floods of 2002, the Sri Lankan tsunami in 2004 and Hurricane Katrina in 2005.

Tragedies on this scale are, fortunately, not everyday occurrences, but leaking pipes and floods can and will happen from time to time. Calzonetti and Fleischer (2011) stress the value of being prepared to deal with a disaster and the importance of having a disaster management plan in place which assesses potential risks, includes contact addresses, designates disaster management teams, identifies salvage priorities and sets out service continuity arrangements. The M25 Consortium of Academic Libraries offers a detailed model, with templates, for developing a disaster control plan[24] and the International Federation of Library Associations and Institutions (IFLA) provides a selected list of useful resources.[25]

Fleischer and Heppner (2009) provide a useful summary of the disaster planning process. The aftermath of Hurricane Katrina has been well documented (Fialkoff, 2006; Clareson and Long, 2006; Topper, 2011; Wilson, 2010).

Conclusion

It is clear that in the digital age, the processes of collection management are in a state of flux. E-books and e-journals shift responsibility for selection and acquisition from librarians to users, who now have the power to influence the purchase of monographs, and publishers, aggregators and vendors, who bundle titles together to provide access to vast quantities of content, but limit cancellation options. The internet, Google and Google Scholar are used by academics and students alike for information seeking, bypassing the resources identified by and paid for from hard-won (and hard-pressed) budgets by librarians who have assessed them for authority, quality and currency. The expectations of digital natives who, with the constant availability of vast quantities of freely accessible online 'stuff', display very different relationships with information, knowledge and learning than scholars hitherto, have to be accommodated, if not met. The dis-intermediation of the library is seen as a real threat and complacency is an unaffordable luxury for collection managers, who must be proactive and innovative in raising the library's profile, for example by using Web 2.0 technologies to promote new resources and services. In a world of wikis, blogs and social networking, where self-publishing is simplicity itself and a search-engine mentality dominates, the role of the collection manager can be called into question.

As we have seen, budgets are stretched to the limit, not only because of the exponential growth in and associated cost of publications but also due to economic recession, which publishing models such as open access may help to redress. Although library budget models and the proportional spend between staff and resources can be reviewed, there is surely a point where staffing levels can be cut no further if services to those users who still venture through the library's doors are to be maintained. The potential for the increases in tuition fees to change the higher education system in the UK is, at present, a matter of speculation but is a ball that collection managers need to keep their eyes on.

Digital preservation is another area in which collection managers need to keep a watching brief. The digitization of collections held by universities, national libraries and archives simplifies access to teaching and research resources, and harnessing these for the benefit of students and researchers is a role that collection managers are well equipped to fulfil.

Pedagogic theories underlying teaching strategies will undoubtedly develop: evidence-based and resource-based learning and the introduction of virtual learning environments (VLEs) have, for example offered new opportunities for providing access to library resources and keeping abreast of trends in teaching methods should be on the collection management librarian's professional development agenda.

You might like to consider what the future holds for libraries and their collections by thinking about issues such as:

- How well do the processes of collection management meet the demands of the digital environment?
- Will maintaining hard copy collections and dealing with gifts and donations continue to be core activities for collection managers?
- How can shrinking budgets be maximized to sustain adequate library resources?
- What impact will digital preservation have on the management of library collections?
- Are traditional library skills adequate to promote resources and services to users?

References

ACRL Research Planning and Review Committee (2010) 2010 Top Ten Trends in Academic Libraries: a review of the current literature, *College and Research Libraries News*, **71** (6) 286–92.

Agee, J. (2005) Collection Evaluation: a foundation for collection development, *Collection Building*, **24** (3), 92–5.

Antelman, K. and Couts, M. (2009) Embracing Ambiguity . . . or Not: what the triangle research libraries network learned about collaboration, *College and Research Libraries News*, **70** (4), 230–3.

Ball, D. (2000) Library Purchasing Consortia: the UK periodicals supply market, *Learned Publishing*, **13** (1), 25–35.

Ball, D. (2003) Public Libraries and the Consortium Purchase of Electronic Resources, *Electronic Library*, **21** (4), 301–9.

Ball, D. (2005) Signing Away Our Freedom: the implications of electronic resource licenses, *Acquisitions Librarian*, **17** (35/36), 7–20.

Bergstrom, T. (2010) Librarians' Fix: economics of the big deal, *Serials*, **23** (2), 77–82.

Best, R. D. (2009) Is the 'Big Deal' dead?, *The Serials Librarian*, **57** (4), 353–63.

Bevan, S., Nieminen, S., Hunn, R. and Sweet, M. (2001) Replacing Print with E-Journals: can it be done?: a case study, *Serials*, **14** (1), 17–24.

Bley, R. (2000) NESLI: a successful national consortium, *Library Consortium Management: an international journal*, **2** (1), 18–28.

Borin, J. (2000) Site License Initiatives in the UK: the PSLI and NESLI experience, *Information Technology and Libraries*, **19** (1), 42–6.

Boyle, F. and Brown, C. (2010) The UK Research Reserve (UKRR): machinations, mayhem and magic, *Interlending & Document Supply*, **38** (3), 140–6.

Branin, J. (1994) Fighting Back Once Again: from collection management to knowledge management. In Johnson, P. and MacEwan, B. (eds), *Collection Management to Knowledge*

Management: issues in an electronic era, American Library Association, xi–xvii.

Breaks, M. (1999) Management of Electronic Information, *IATUL Proceedings (New series)*, **9**, www.iatul.org/doclibrary/public/Conf_Proceedings/1999/breaks.doc.

Calzonetti, J. A. and Fleischer, V. (2011) Don't Count on Luck, be Prepared: ten lessons learned from the 'great flood' at the University of Akron's Science and Technology Library, *College and Research Libraries News*, **72** (2), 82–5.

Chapman, L. (2000) Acquisitions: the emerging electronic paradigm. In Gorman, G. E. (ed.), *Collection Management*, Library Association Publishing.

Clareson, T. and Long, J. S. (2006) Libraries in the Eye of the Storm: lessons learned from Hurricane Katrina, *American Libraries*, **37** (7), 38–41.

Clayton, P. and Gorman, G. E. (2006) *Managing Information Resources in Libraries: collection management in theory and practice*, Facet Publishing.

Cleary, C. (2009) Why the Big Deal Continues to Persist, *Serials Librarian*, **57** (4), 364–78.

Cole, N. A,.and Usherwood, R. C. (1996) Library Stock Management Policies, Statements and Philosophies, *Public Library Journal*, **11** (5), 121–5.

Collins, M. (2011) Serials Literature Review 2008–9: embracing a culture of openness, *Library Resources and Technical Services*, **55** (2), 60–80.

Collins, M. and Grogg, J. (2011) Building a Better ERMS, *Library Journal*, **136** (4), 22–6, 28.

Cox, J. (2003) Establishing a Collection Management Policy in a Hybrid Library Context, *SCONUL Newsletter*, **30** (Winter), 26–30.

Cryer, E. and Grigg, K. S. (2011) Consortia and Journal Package Renewal: evolving trends in the 'big package deal'?, *Journal of Electronic Resources in Medical Libraries*, **8** (1), 22–34.

Dinkins, D. (2011) Allocating Academic Library Budgets: adapting historical data models at one university library, *Collection Management*, **36** (2), 119–30.

Dunham, B. S. and Davis, T. L. (2009) Literature of Acquisitions in Review 2004–7, *Library Resources and Technical Services*, **53** (4), 231–42.

Duranceau, E. F. (1997) Beyond Print: revisioning serials acquisition for the digital age, *The Serials Librarian*, **33** (1), 83–106.

Edelman, H. (1973) The Death of the Farmington Plan, *Library Journal*, **98** (8), 1251–3.

Elkington, N. (1999) Preservation and Collection: management: ties that bind. In Jenkins, C. and Morley, M. (eds), *Collection Management in Academic Libraries*, 2nd edn, Gower.

Ellingsen, M. (2004) Electronic Resource Management Systems, *LIBER Quarterly*, **14** (3/4), 313–21.

Evans, G. E. and Saponaro, M. Z. (2005) *Developing Library and Information Center Collections*, 5th edn, Libraries Unlimited.

Feather, J. (2004) *Managing Preservation for Libraries and Archives: current practice and future developments*, Ashgate.

Fenner, A. (2004) The Approval Plan, *The Acquisitions Librarian*, **16** (31), 227–40.

Fialkoff, F. (2006) No Katrina Fatigue Here, *Library Journal*, **6**, April, www.libraryjournal.com/article/CA6317218.html.

Fleischer, S. V. and Heppner, M. J. (2009) Disaster Planning for Libraries and Archives: what you need to know and how to do it, *Library & Archival Security*, **22** (2), 125–40.

Ford, G. (1999) Finance and Budgeting. In Jenkins, C. and Morley, M. (eds), *Collection Management in Academic Libraries*, 2nd edn, Gower.

Frazier, K. (2001) The Librarians' Dilemma: contemplating the costs of the 'Big Deal', *D-Lib Magazine*, **7** (3), www.dlib.org/dlib/march01/frazier/03frazier.html.

Goldstein, P. J. (2007) IT Collaboration: multi-Institutional partnerships to develop, manage, and operate IT resources, *EDUCAUSE ECAR Research study*, www.educause.edu/ECAR/ITCollaborationMultiInstitutio/161735.

Gorman, G. E. (2000) (ed.) *Collection Management*, Library Association Publishing.

Gorman, G. E. and Miller, R. H. (1997) *Collection Management for the 21st Century: a handbook for librarians*, Greenwood Press.

Gorman, G. E. and Miller, R. (2000) Changing Collections, Changing Evaluation. In Gorman, G. E. (ed.), *Collection Management*, Library Association Publishing.

Gorman, G. E. and Shep, S. J. (2006) *Preservation Management for Libraries, Archives and Museums*, Facet Publishing.

Goulding, A. (2009) Credit Crunch: the impact on libraries, *Journal of Librarianship and Information Science*, **41** (3), 3–6.

Haar, J. (2003) Assessing the State of Cooperative Collection Development: report of the Working Group to map current cooperative collection development projects. In Shreeves, E. (ed.), *The New Dynamics and Economics of Cooperative Collection Development*, Haworth Information Press.

Harwood, P. (2000) NESLI: an agent for change or changing the agent?, *The Electronic Library*, **18** (2), 121–6.

Hodges, D., Preston, C. and Hamilton, M. J. (2010) Resolving the Challenge of E-books, *Collection Management*, **35** (3), 196–200.

Holden, J. (2010) *Acquisitions in the New Information Universe: core competencies and ethical practice*, Facet Publishing.

Horava, T. (2010) Challenges and Possibilities for Collection Management in a Digital Age, *Library Resources and Technical Services*, **54** (3), 142–52.

Jenkins, C. and Morley, M. (1999) *Collection Management in Academic Libraries*, 2nd edn, Gower.

JISC (2009) JISC National e-Books Observatory Project: key findings and recommendations, www.jiscebooksproject.org/reports/finalreport.

Johnson, P. (2009) *Fundamentals of Collection Development*, 2nd edn, American Library Association.

Jones, W. (ed.) (2009) *E-journals Access and Management*, Routledge.

Kaay, A. and Zimmerman, P. (2008) The Development and Application of a Unique Percentage-based Allocations Formula at the University of Windsor, *Library Collections, Acquisitions, and Technical Services*, **32** (2), 92–6.

Kane, L. T. (1997) Access vs Ownership: do we have to make a choice?, *College and Research Libraries*, **58** (1), 58–66.

Kidd, T. (1998) Electronic Journals: their introduction and exploitation in academic libraries in the United Kingdom, *Serials Review*, **24** (1), 7–14.

Kidd, T. (2009) Collaboration in Electronic Resource Provision in University Libraries: SHEDL, a Scottish case study, *New Review of Academic Librarianship*, **15** (1), 97–119.

Kinner, L. and Crosetto, A. (2009) Balancing Act for the Future: how the academic library engages in collection development at the local and consortial levels, *Journal of Library Administration*, **49** (4), 419–43.

List, C. and Chadwell, F. A. (2011) What's Next for Collection Management and Managers?, *Collection Management*, **36** (2), 79–88.

Naylor, B. (1999) Collection Management for the 21st Century. In Jenkins, C. and Morley, M., *Collection Management in Academic Libraries*, 2nd edn, Gower.

Nixon, J. M., Freeman, R. S. and Ward, S. M. (2010) Patron-Driven Acquisitions: an introduction and literature review, *Collection Management*, **35** (3), 119–24.

Pan, R., Byrne, U. and Murphy, H. (2009) Nudging the Envelope: the hard road to mainstreaming UCD Library e-book provision, *Serials*, **22** (3), S12–S21.

Pesch, O. (2007) Sushi: what it is and why you should care, *Computers in Libraries*, **27** (4), 6–8.

Pesch, O. (2008) An Update on COUNTER and SUSHI, *The Serials Librarian*, **55** (3), 366–72.

Peters, T. (2001) Some Issues for Collection Developers and Content Managers, *Collection Management*, **25** (1), 137–53.

Pilette, R. (2004) Mass Deacidification: a preservation option for libraries, *IFLA Journal*, **30** (1), 31–6.

Richards, R. (2001) Licensing Agreements: contracts, the eclipse of copyright and the promise of cooperation, *The Acquisitions Librarian*, **13** (26), 89–107.

Rohe, T. A., O'Donovan, P. and Hanawalt, V. (2000) Cooperative Collection development in PORTALS, *The Acquisitions Librarian*, **12** (24), 89–101.

Sharp, S. and Thompson, S. (2010) 'Just in Case' vs 'Just in Time': e-book purchasing models, *Serials*, **23** (3), 201–6.

Schell, L. E., Ginanni, K. and Heet, B. (2010) Playing the Field: pay-per-view e-journals and e-books, *The Serials Librarian*, **58** (1), 87–96.

Shelton, C. (2003) Best Practices in Cooperative Collection Development, *Collection Management*, **28** (3), 191–222.

Shreeves, E. (2003) (ed.) *The New Dynamics and Economics of Cooperative Collection Development*, Haworth Information Press.

Slote, S. (1997) *Weeding Library Collections: library weeding methods*, 4th edn, Libraries Unlimited.

Steele, K. (2008) Trying to Thrive: making do without making waves, *The Bottom Line: Managing Library Finances*, **21** (1), 17–19.

Stueart, R. D. (1980) Introduction. In Stueart, R. D, and Miller, G. B. (eds), *Collection development in libraries: a treatise: Foundations in Library and Information Science. Vol 10, Part A*. JAI Press.

Sykes, P. (2010) 'I Tell you Naught for your Comfort': budgetary prospects for academic libraries over the next few years, *Serials*, **23** (1), 6–11.

Taylor-Roe, J. (2009) 'To Every Thing There is a Season': reflections on the sustainability of the 'big deal' in the current economic climate, *Serials*, **22** (2), 113–21.

Topper, E. F. (2011) After Hurricane Katrina: the Tulane recovery project, *New Library World*, **112** (1/2), 45–51.

Williams, R. (2000) Weeding library collections. In Gorman, G. E. (ed.), *Collection Management*, Library Association Publishing.

Williams, S. (1999) Stock Revision, Retention and Relegation in US Academic Libraries. In Jenkins, C. and Morley, M., *Collection Management in Academic Libraries*, 2nd edn, Gower.

Wilson, V. (2010) Public Libraries Can Play an Important Role in the Aftermath of a Natural Disaster, *Evidence Based Library and Information Practice*, **5** (3), 59–61.

Wright, N. and Crawford, J. (2008) Supporting Access to the UK's Research Collection: the UK Research Reserve project, *Interlending & Document Supply*, **36** (4), 210–12.

Notes

1 Mosher presented the Keynote Address at the first Advanced Collection Management and Development Institute held in Stanford, California, July 6–10, 1981.

2 www.jiscebooksproject.org/.

3 EDI enables the electronic transfer of documents, such as book orders, between organizations.

4 The Big Deal emerged in the late 1990s in an attempt to address the spiralling costs of journals. Big Deals are online aggregations of journals offered by publishers as a one-price, one size fits all package. Price increases are capped for an agreed period.

5 Journal impact factors are a measure of the frequency with which the 'average article' in a journal has been cited in a given period of time. http://thomsonreuters.com/products_services/science/free/essays/impact_factor/.

6 www.eduserv.org.uk/lns/agreements.

7 www.jisc-collections.ac.uk/.

8 www.projectcounter.org/.

9 SUSHI stands for the Standardized Usage Statistics Harvesting Initiative, a NISO standard (Z39.93) see www.niso.org/workrooms/sushi/.

10 www.ohiolink.edu/.

11 http://about.jstor.org/.

12 www.ithaka.org/.

13 http://rdtf.jiscinvolve.org/wp/implementation-plan/.

14 http://helibtech.com/SCONUL_Shared_Services.

15 www.loc.gov/preservation/resources/deacid/index.html.

16 www.bl.uk/blpac/pdf/enemy.pdf.

17 www.loc.gov/preservation/.

18 www.bl.uk/blpac/index.html.

19 www.jisc.ac.uk/whatwedo/topics/digitalpreservation.aspx.

20 www.dcc.ac.uk/.

21 http://lockss.stanford.edu/lockss/Home.

22 www.clockss.org/clockss/Home.

23 www.portico.org/digital-preservation/.

24 www.m25lib.ac.uk/m25dcp/.

25 www.ifla.org/en/preservation-and-conservation/useful-resources.

Part 2
Trends in the development of e-resources

3
An overview of e-resources in UK further and higher education

David House

Introduction

In October 2010, the British Library staged a debate on the motion 'Is the physical library redundant in the 21st century?' The outcome was predictably inconclusive, given that the debate was taking place in the UK's most prestigious physical library building. It did, however, underline the fact that the widespread availability of digital technology has already changed the nature of libraries in a relatively short space of time. In the space of little more than a decade, the potential scope of library collections has been dramatically expanded, and the facility to replicate and deliver information to users has been transformed. At the same time, the coherence and organization of library collections has been challenged by the organic growth and pervasive use of digital material available through the internet, providing immediate access to information from the desktop or mobile phone, and raising for some the question of whether libraries will maintain their role of guide and gatekeeper.

In terms of collection development, the conventional discussion of 'holdings' and 'access' has necessarily shifted, since most of the digital content sought and used by colleges and universities is hosted on remote servers – either provided by the original owner or publisher, or at a recognized data centre – but that content needs to be presented to library users alongside the continuing print collection. However, the library will normally wish to assure itself that the digital material will continue to be available on a permanent basis. Though the material is not physically held, it nevertheless forms part of the library's collection, rather than an external information source. For the foreseeable future, mainstream library collections are likely to be hybrid, and librarians will face challenges in presenting a coherent view of their collections to users.

Development of the hybrid library

In general, technological advances frequently work on a 'push' basis, where the technology uncovers a possible approach and the search for applications and appropriate business models then begins. This approach can be seen in the development of commercial e-books and in the rollout of digital versions of newspapers, now beginning to withdraw behind pay walls in order to protect revenue streams. The case of academic publishing and scholarly communication in the UK is a little different in that early development was very much a function of expressed user need and community investment.

One of the first acts of the HEFCE when it was established in 1992 was – jointly with the equally new funding bodies for Scotland, Wales and Northern Ireland – to commission a review of library provision. The review group was charged with making recommendations on the future needs for library and information provision in higher education against a background of growing student numbers and the emerging potential of information technology. The group's final report, known as the *Follett Report* (HEFCE, 1993), made a series of recommendations – some for immediate funding and some for further work. A major chapter of the report focused specifically on information technology and articulated a vision of what the higher education information landscape might be like within a decade. It urged investment in networking, in retrospective digitization, in e-journals and data sets and in the development of navigational tools. It expected much of the follow-up work to be undertaken on behalf of the funding bodies by JISC, which already had responsibility for the Joint Academic Network, a high-speed computer network linking 150 sites, including access to over 100 library catalogues.

In a period of relatively generous resourcing, three major initiatives emerged from the *Follett Report*. JISC was funded to launch a multi-stranded electronic libraries (e-Lib) programme, while the funding bodies themselves entered into arrangements with four major journal publishers to establish a National Pilot Site Licence Initiative and a firm start was made on a digitization programme.

The e-Lib programme ran for five years, during which time some £20m was invested in around 60 projects, linked within a single framework and led by an overall project director. The programme took forward the majority of Follett recommendations. Formal reviews of the programme (ESYS, 2001; Duke and Jordan, 2006) highlighted some weaknesses, largely to do with the large number of small projects which made up the early stages of the programme, but much of the work undertaken within the programme has clearly shaped current provision. Models were developed for e-journals, on-demand teaching materials, navigation and resource discovery, and the management of hybrid libraries. The operational period of the e-Lib programme coincided with the rapid development and rollout of the world wide web, not directly foreseen by the *Follett Report*. Many strands of work in the e-Lib programme were therefore accelerated, including the dissemination of project results.

The Pilot Site Licence Initiative brought together four publishers (Academic Press, Blackwell Publishing, Blackwell Science, Institute of Physics) who, in return for a lump sum payment from HEFCE, were to provide an agreed set of journals in print and electronic form, with unlimited access within institutions. The initiative, which ran from 1996 to 1998, was judged successful, and its successor scheme – the National Electronic Site Licence, or NESLi2[1] – now operates on a larger scale, with the full cost transferred to subscribing institutions.

The first phase of a digitization programme began in 1994, with £10m funding for six projects, covering newspapers, medical journals, parliamentary papers, sound recordings and news film. These projects were of significant value in terms of content and also useful test beds for developing of technical standards and devising satisfactory partnership agreements between the HE sector and commercial partners.

Current context

The *Follett Report* (HEFCE, 1993) examined the future needs of libraries, and its recommendations were couched in terms which expected libraries to remain the principal or sole providers of academic information resources within institutions. Though their role remains significant, the development and widespread use of the internet has transformed user expectations over the last decade and a half. The use of digital services is commonplace in most aspects of daily life, and the information infrastructure within which we live is quite different from that of a decade ago. The emergence of Google, Amazon, iTunes and Facebook has had a huge impact on the social and commercial world and that impact has spread into the world of further and higher education in a variety of ways.

Students in further and higher education are now able to engage with learning in a variety of modes and places, accessing resources (including their teachers) through mobile telephones and portable laptops, using public networks as well as their institutional access. Experience of other forms of internet transaction leads to expectations of instant access, personalized information and prompt feedback.

Some studies of the 'net generation' suggest that information-seeking behaviour of those born after 1993 is fundamentally different from that of older users. A major study commissioned by the British Library and JISC, however, finds that the changes are common to professors and lecturers, who all exhibit a strong tendency towards shallow, horizontal, 'flicking' behaviour in digital libraries (CIBER, 2008). The instant availability of information delivered to the desktop has led to a culture of quick skimming and power browsing through titles, contents pages and abstracts. Evidence on how much is actually read is scant.

The ubiquitous availability of digital technology has led inexorably to greater integration of information resources of all kinds into the workflow patterns associated with teaching, learning and research. It is common for colleges and universities to promulgate e-learning policies and strategies. Indeed, most were encouraged or required to do so by their respective funding bodies. Both the Department for Education and Skills (2005) and the HEFCE (2005) published e-learning strategies, though neither had ever felt it necessary to publish a teaching and learning strategy. The Learning and Skills Council, responsible for funding sixth-form and further education colleges, required its institutions to lodge an Information and Learning Technology Strategy as a condition of releasing funding for the purchase of a virtual learning environment (VLE). The almost universal use of the VLE in both further and higher education requires learning materials to be embedded within the digital curriculum space, rather than housed in a separate collection.

Parallel with the rise of e-learning, digital developments have transformed the way in which much research is conducted, as well as the way in which the results of research are communicated. E-research typically involves shared access to large data sets and the use of advanced computational tools for data analysis. Many projects are collaborative and iterative, involving the modelling of complex systems, with approaches first adopted in science and technology now being used in the humanities and social sciences. The very nature of the scholarly enterprise is being transformed, with information flows embedded within research activity and influencing its outcome, rather than simply reporting results at the conclusion of a project. As researchers have come to share information and data with one another more freely, so the tendency has increased to view research information as publicly owned, with a consequent move towards open and instant access.

Earlier discussions of the prospects for the digital library generally focused on the question 'what impact is this technology likely to have on the library?' The way in which everyday working practices have been significantly transformed across teaching, learning and research means that the question we now face is rather 'what impact is this technology having on academic activity, and what is the revised role of the library in teaching and research?'

E-journals

The point has now been reached where all significant peer-reviewed journals in the fields of science, technology and medicine are available in electronic form, as are the majority of highly regarded journals in the arts and social sciences. For the most part, both print and electronic forms of the same title are published, though the number of electronic-only journals continues to increase. Expectations that the obvious advantages of digital delivery would lead to the rapid decline of demand for printed versions have not so far been realized. In part, this stems from the reluctance of academics to support cancellation of print versions, seeing the electronic version as supplementary to the print version, rather than replacing it. For their part, librarians have some concerns about the long-term preservation of electronic journals, for which generally they will not hold source files. Many publishers have not yet reconciled themselves to business models which exclude print sales, which have hitherto provided their major income stream through a fairly straightforward subscription model.

The major subscription agents (such as EBSCO and Swets), who have long served the academic library world, have been quick to adapt their services to the digital environment, offering complete packages covering identification of titles through ordering, renewals, cancellations, invoicing and usage statistics. Their ability to provide an integrated service covering both print and electronic journal subscriptions has been a positive advantage for libraries seeking workflow efficiencies. At the same time, individual publishers have developed their own services, with many of the most important academic publishers now preferring to deal directly with major library customers and consortia, offering deeply discounted deals rather than list prices and resolving issues of access and authentication, thus diminishing the role of subscription agents.

The national site licence initiative, NESLi2, managed by JISC Collections[2] is a major resource-sharing initiative which offers libraries access to over 7000 journal titles from 17 major academic publishers. The portfolio of titles has been determined through consultation with users, and the financial saving to the sector has been estimated at more than £10m per year. An extension of this principle to small and medium-sized publishers (NESLi2 SMP) brought a further 900 journals from 22 publishers into the scope of the arrangements. The negotiating and licence experience of JISC Collections can also be deployed for specific regions or sectors. For example, the higher education institutions in Scotland have come together to form the Scottish Higher Education Digital Library (SHEDL).[3] This initiative makes the content of almost 2000 journals available to all researchers and students in Scottish higher education, thus eliminating differential access arising from local purchasing decisions.

Teachers and researchers now have an unprecedented level of access to the knowledge contained in scholarly articles. Investigations by the Research Information Network (RIN) show that within a broadly static level of total expenditure by university libraries on content between 2003 and 2008, there was an increase of over 40% in spending on e-journals (e-only or e+print), set against a decline of 20% in spending on print-only journals. Measured in terms of titles, rather than cash, the shift to e-only was even greater. The increased selection of journal titles available led to a spectacular growth in the number of full-text article downloads, which more than tripled at the research-intensive Russell Group institutions and doubled at the post-1992 institutions. The research shows a high level of correlation between the level of downloads and generally accepted measures of research success, such as income from research grants and contracts, PhDs awarded, articles published and number of citations (Research Information Network, 2011).

The move to e-journals has been the basis for two contrasting trends. The first is the move to treating the individual article as the entity, rather than the journal issue. There were, of course, precedents for this in the print world, in the form of pre-prints, off-prints and document supply, but the ability to identify and purchase just one article direct from a publisher is now routinely offered to personal customers through publishers' websites and by some aggregators, such as ingentaconnect. The second trend is for publishers to offer libraries apparently heavily discounted rates to take large bundles of journals in electronic form, throwing in less heavily used titles alongside those which they judge to be essential purchases. Librarians and their users have been tempted by these 'big deals', since they offered additional journals to researchers at what appeared to be marginal cost, though there are now clear signs that the price increases demanded by major publishers are outstripping the willingness of libraries to pay. Publishers have strengthened their position further (if a monopoly can be strengthened) by insisting on long-term contracts of three to five years, and basing the price of the whole deal on an individual library's historical print expenditure.

The imperative to publish in high-status journals remains exceptionally strong and shows no sign of abating as preparations are made for the next version of a research assessment exercise – the Research Excellence Framework[4] – which will be completed in 2014 and be based on research outputs for the period 2008–13. Bibliometric information will play a greater part than in previous exercises as funders seek to assess not simply the quantity and quality of completed research, but its actual and likely impact. Against such a background, publishers of 'must have' journals have been in a strong position to impose challenging price increases. Since government policy has been one of gradually concentrating research resources on a smaller number of institutions, publishers have few opportunities to extend their customer base in home markets, so have sought to increase income by raising prices for existing customers. At a time of severe reductions in both teaching and research income, university libraries will no longer be in a position to accept such increases and a major initiative is currently under way, led by Research Libraries UK (RLUK),[5] to prepare contingency plans if the next round of licence renewals does not deliver affordable deals. Maximizing the use of free online journals and relying on sparing use of pay-as-you-go downloading of individual articles are strategies which are likely to be adopted.

Open access

As digital technologies have become ever more widely available, there have been two driving forces towards open access models of information delivery. One has been a general community expectation that material on the web is, or should be, 'free', and a variation of this which asserts that scholarly communication is the property of the academy, and not of commercial partners or predators. Indeed, the argument can be taken further to propose that since most academic research is partly or wholly funded by public funding, the outputs of that research should be available to all who seek them and not just to those within scholarly communities. The other is a more focused concern by academic communities that they are the producers of research outcomes and scholarly literature, and they also serve as peer reviewers, providing a major free service to publishers. They therefore seek an escape route from the dilemma outlined earlier, whereby they are forced to pay ever-increasing prices to access the collective record of their endeavours, and to re-use it in their teaching and research. The costs of peer review across the UK have been estimated at £165m per year; a sum which is broadly equal to the total sum spent by UK higher education institutions on print and electronic journal subscriptions (Research Information Network, 2008).

Some passionate advocates of open access have a vision of a world without commercial publishers. That prospect seems distant, not least because the reputational position of scholars is closely linked to high-quality journals and to the continued existence of journal titles, rather than to individual articles lodged in institutional repositories. Current models of open access in which payments are made by authors or their funders (the 'Gold' model) provide a foundation for an extended period of transition from print to electronic, while versions of the alternative 'Green' model, or free open access, show few signs of causing the widespread financial failure of journals as predicted by publishers' bodies.

E-books

In the world of general commercial publishing, the e-book has begun to assume huge importance. Global corporations have moved into the territory (Amazon, Google, Sony, Barnes and Noble), and sales of e-books have increased rapidly, against a background of falling sales of printed paperback and hardback books. The Association of American Publishers figures for February 2011, for example, show e-book sales increased by 202.3% against February 2010, with adult hardback and paperback books 34.4% lower on the same basis. Debates about competing formats, digital rights management, pricing policies and piracy are well under way, carrying echoes of similar concerns in the music and film industries.

The appetite of further and higher education for digital learning materials, supporting open, distance and blended learning, suggests that market opportunities for e-books would be strong and uptake rapid. In practice, availability and take-up has been markedly slower than in the field of e-journals, particularly in the incorporation of e-books into library collections or VLEs. From the publishers' perspective, there has been understandable nervousness about possible perturbations in markets for core textbooks, where sales to individual students have traditionally accounted for 70–90% of total sales. At the other end of the publishing spectrum, print runs for scholarly monographs have become so modest that any development which might reduce sales has been viewed with great caution. Academic users of e-books, meanwhile, appear to be more inclined to consult e-books when they are provided through a college library service rather than to contemplate outright purchase.

JISC Collections commissioned work from the CIBER group at University College London to investigate patterns of use of a selected range of course textbooks in e-format in four disciplines (business and management, medicine, engineering and media studies). The final report of the project (CIBER, 2008) highlighted significant usage levels and positive reactions, with respondents generally using the electronic text for looking up facts and extracting data rather than lengthy continuous reading, for which a print version would be preferred. Access from off-campus was an important advantage, though restrictions on downloading to portable devices were criticized. Librarians saw the availability of e-textbooks as easing major pressures on short-loan collections, but were concerned about costs, business models and licensing restrictions. Importantly, the project could identify no significant impact on the volume of print sales; print and electronic versions of the same text appeared to be providing complementary functions.

A further project at JISC Collections has provided a core collection of e-books for the further education sector. Initial funding for the initiative was provided centrally, recognizing that FE library systems were not universally well funded, and this was used to establish a collection of around 3000 titles across a range of disciplines, which are being freely used by over 350 colleges for an initial five-year period up to 2014. Over 13 million pages had been viewed by March 2011, and plans were being made to add further titles. It may take some creative thinking to establish a sustainable financial model to retain and develop this collection once the initial project funding comes to an end.

Though e-textbooks have not been widely used in further education previously, there is a well established practice of using and sharing electronic resources, generally mounted on a VLE platform. Learners have come to expect learning materials to be rich materials, with multi-media adjuncts and interactive tools, and a straightforward replica of a printed textbook is not always an attractive learning resource.

Major aggregators have seized opportunities to develop supply chains for the sale of e-books, with Ebrary (now part of Proquest) and MyiLibrary being prominent. Typically, such aggregators offer whole collections of titles for purchase, enabling libraries to build holdings quickly. Individual publishers have also embraced the 'collection' approach, including major players such as the Cambridge University Press, Oxford University Press and Springer, and learned societies such as the Royal Society of Chemistry. This is a further instance of bundling, which offers librarians an instant approach to collection building, but may result in the purchase of lower priority items, in a way which would not have been contemplated in print-only circumstances.

Customization of a collection can be offered, either by an individual publisher (e.g. the environmental chemistry subset of the Royal Society of Chemistry collection) or by an aggregator. This allows libraries to deselect strands of a collection not relevant to their academic profile, or material which is already in stock. A good example of customization is seen in the collaboration by four universities with the Royal College of Nursing to define and procure a core electronic collection of recommended reading for nursing students, much of whose education takes place off-campus for extended periods (Ball, Beard and Newland, 2007).

One feature of the pre-electronic world – the fact that a high-street bookseller or a library supplier would supply any book from any publisher – has not been carried forward into the digital world. Aggregators enter into non-exclusive contractual arrangements with publishers, and make the content of those publishers available on their platform. There are therefore overlaps and underlaps in the world of e-book supply, on a constantly shifting basis. Both Cambridge University Press and Oxford University Press, previously offering only their own publications directly to customers, have announced plans to develop their e-books platforms (Cambridge Books Online and Oxford Scholarship Online) to offer items from other scholarly publishers.

Aggregators who have developed large databases of e-books are in a position to make those databases available to institutional customers for integration into an online catalogue. The catalogue then presents information both on material purchased or licensed by the library and material available for viewing or download. This offers the library user the ability to link to an item not currently held, to browse an item for a limited time, or to 'borrow' an item on a pay-per-view basis. If an item is viewed more than an agreed number of times, then the book is automatically purchased and added to the library's permanent collection. A pilot project carried out at King's College London, in partnership with e-Book Library over a six-week period generated 9669 free browses, 5089 short-term loans and 3292 downloads, with 195 purchases triggered by a fourth loan request. This demand-led approach to acquisition was strongly favoured by users, and was judged cost effective by staff, though it requires a fresh approach to financial monitoring and management (Holmes, 2011).

Digitization programmes

Alongside the move towards digital resources for current book and journal provision, there has been a major thrust towards the digitization of earlier material, in order to maximize access to scholarly material which was not born-digital. Core areas addressed have included back runs of journals and newspapers, early printed books and collections of still and moving images. In the UK, initiatives have been largely steered by JISC and the British Library, with significant involvement from individual universities and research bodies. In the USA, parallel work has been led by the Library of Congress, with important contributions from ITHAKA and the Internet Archive.

This work takes place against a background of strident attempts by Google to create an extensive international digital library by – to put it bluntly – digitizing first and discussing permissions later. A recent court judgement in the USA has once again interrupted this project, where concerns focus principally on items which are in copyright but out of print. Whatever the reservations of librarians and rights holders, it is inevitable that many library users will turn to Google as a first port of call.

The JISC Collections portfolio[6] includes a range of resources which are available without charge to all UK further and higher education institutions. Major collections include 19th Century British Newspapers, British Library Archival Sound Recordings and collections of parliamentary papers from 1688 to 2004. These are supplemented by further important collections to which subscription charges apply, including English books from 1473 to 1900 and major back files of journals. In many cases, JISC Collections has purchased material for use in perpetuity, or simply made hosting arrangements for the delivery of materials digitized through its parent body, JISC. Importantly, decisions about funding digitization programmes or purchasing digitized materials are made through a process of consultation with the relevant educational communities.

Institutions themselves are the owners of much valuable content and many have embarked upon digitization programmes of their own. Good examples can be seen on library websites at the universities of Exeter and Oxford and at SOAS (School of Oriental and African Studies). The digitization of treasures in special collections and archives serves both to widen access to them and to preserve the originals.

Enthusiasm for digitization has, however, led to a plethora of individual projects, with only limited attempts at co-ordination. Many of JISC's current activities are therefore aimed at encouraging the development of broader approaches. One way of achieving this is to provide consolidated platforms, so that users no longer have to access (and pay for) multiple platforms for related material. From mid-2011, the JISC eCollections service will host content JISC has already purchased on three platforms[7] – JISC Journal Archives, JISC Historic Books and JISC Mediahub. JISC Journal Archives will bring together the files of over 1000 journals, enabling cross-searching and full-text access. JISC Historic

Books will offer similarly integrated access to the contents of Early English Books Online, Eighteenth Century Collections Online and the British Library's 19th Century Books from the British Library Collection. JISC Mediahub will bring together three vital resources – Newsfilm Online, Film and Sound Online and Digital Images for Education.

On a broader front still, JISC has taken the lead in establishing the Strategic Content Alliance, which brings together major organizations in the public sector involved in the creation, management and exploitation of digital content. The members of the alliance – JISC, the British Library, the BBC, the Museums, Libraries and Archives Council, and the Wellcome Trust – are committed to co-ordinating activity in order to maximize return in investment and ease of use.

Digital preservation

The increasing pace of digital developments, not only in the realms of scholarly discourse but also in public policy, the creative industries and cultural heritage, raises obvious concerns about the long-term curation and preservation of that information. One area of major concern to the academic world – though not necessarily to those concerned with mainstream library collections – is that of raw research data. This covers observational data (gathered from satellites, telescopes or demographic surveys), experimental data (such as that derived from clinical trials) and complex computational data. The growth in the volume of such data may well exceed the growth in storage capacity, which brings into sharp focus the need for careful planning of what is to be preserved, and at what cost.

The territory of digital preservation has been carefully surveyed by the Blue Ribbon Task Force. This US-led group (but with UK participation) has set out a range of high priority actions required if sound and sustainable models of preservation are to be developed. The group recognizes that the information environment continues to change rapidly and that decisions on preservation will always be made under conditions of uncertainty (Blue Ribbon Task Force, 2010). In the UK, JISC Collections has funded a specific study of archiving solutions for e-journals (Morrow et al. 2008).

There are both technical and curatorial issues involved in preservation discussions. The curatorial issues include determining who takes responsibility for archiving (publisher, user, consortium, third party), what is to be archived and how it is accessed, and how the costs and benefits are assessed. The technical issues include ensuring that changes to software and formats do not mean that material which has been preserved is no longer useable.

The JISC Collections report (Morrow et al. 2008) compares six e-journal archiving programmes, all of which were relatively new, and all of which had advantages and disadvantages. The programmes were assessed against four scenarios:

- cancellation of a title by the library, but access to back issues required
- e-journal no longer available from publisher (title discontinued, or sold)
- publisher has ceased operation, and access to servers is no longer possible

- catastrophic failure of publisher's operations/servers.

Each library needs to undertake its own risk assessment in the light of its own circumstances and priorities, and in light of the extent to which the material held by a particular archiving programme matches its holdings, both in title holdings and date ranges.

Looking forward

As the information world moves ever more boldly towards a digitally dominated environment, the traditional model of the academic library faces a range of challenges. Its role as a central physical store of information has been overtaken by user expectations of information delivered directly to their desktop or mobile device, and users generally have become unwilling to accept delays and barriers. The days of happily waiting a week or two for an ILL are long past; even the fact that electronic access to one item may be free and open whilst a similar item requires subscription and payment can be a significant source of frustration.

There remains uncertainty as to whether we are in a transition period, in which print and electronic resources will co-exist for a period before most academic material is available in e-only versions, or whether the hybrid model will continue indefinitely. There are examples of the virtual cessation of print collections – at the engineering libraries at Stanford and Cornell, for example, as well as at Wellington College, where 80% of the library's books are being disposed of to create space for a 'research and innovation centre' stocked with tablet computers, e-book readers and armchairs.

Across the arts and social sciences, large legacy print collections will continue to remain essential repositories. Although digitization programmes will continue to make selected key resources available electronically, there will remain a large rump of material to be preserved and consulted in the traditional manner. Indeed, it is a major concern that the process of digitization is somewhat random, with a large number of players making independent decisions, leading to a fragmented picture of national and international provision. The challenge for libraries and librarians is to make sense of this hybrid landscape. Conventional professional practice has served well through a print era which has seen the library sit unchallenged at the centre of the information landscape, with librarians particularly skilled at building comprehensive collections delivered with the aid of settled publishing practices, legal deposit and national bibliographies and strong shared cataloguing systems. The electronic world is less coherent, and the role of the library as information provider and broker is as one of a number. Information resources are more closely embedded within teaching, learning and research, requiring librarians to develop ever-closer links with learning technologists, research managers and web and intranet managers. The volume of information available is greater than ever, though users may often be more concerned with quality and relevance rather than quantity and be little concerned with whether that information is delivered from a local collection or a distant host. The library profession has excelled at focusing on ensuring that information is available through sound collection development. It now has to place greater attention on ensuring that information is actually findable and deliverable, through significant emphasis on electronic resource management systems and ever greater understanding of user needs and preferences.

References

Ball, D., Beard, J. and Newland, B.(2007) eRes: Innovative E-learning with E-resources. In Jezzard, H. (ed.) *Online Information 2007: proceedings*, Incisive Media.

Blue Ribbon Task Force (2010) *Sustainable Economics for a Digital Planet: ensuring long term access to digital information*, Blue Ribbon Task Force.

Duke, J. and Jordan, A. (2006) *Impact analysis of the JISC funded elib programme*, JISC.

CIBER (2008) *Information Behaviour of the Researcher of the Future*, CIBER.

Department for Education and Skills (2005) *Harnessing technology: transforming learning and children's services*, Department for Education and Skills.

ESYS (2001) *Summative evaluation of Phase 3 of the eLib Initiative: final report*, ESYS.

HEFCE (1993) *Joint Funding Councils' Libraries Review Group: report*, HEFCE.

HEFCE (2005) *HEFCE Strategy for e-learning*, HEFCE.

Holmes, G. (2011) Letting patrons choose, *CILIP Update with Gazette*, April, 31.

Morrow, T. et al. (2008) *A Comparative Study of E-journal Archiving Solutions: a JISC funded investigation*, JISC Collections.

Research Information Network (2008) *Activities, Costs and Funding Flows in the Scholarly Communications System in the UK*, Research Information Network.

Research Information Network (2011) *E-journals: their use, value and impact – final report*, Research Information Network.

Notes

1   www.jisc-collections.ac.uk/nesli2/.
2   JISC Collections is the trading company established by JISC in 2006. See www.jisc-collections.ac.uk for a description of its products and services.
3   http://scurl.ac.uk/WG/SHEDL/index.html.
4   www.hefce.ac.uk/research/ref/.
5   www.rluk.ac.uk.
6   www.jisc-content.ac.uk.
7   www.jisc.ac.uk/contentalliance.

4
Supporting online collections: the role of online journals in a university collection

Jane Harvell

Introduction

In recent years there has been a considerable and significant shift towards delivering, accessing and storing scholarly content in an online format. We have witnessed the mass proliferation of subscribed and freely available digital content across all formats traditionally collected by academic libraries. Crucially, empirical data on user behaviour demonstrates that in almost all subject areas there is an ever-increasing preference for retrieving content online. In fact, the availability of an instantly accessible format for information is now expected and presumed by most scholars and students, as noted in the USA-based 2009 *Annual Faculty Survey*: 'Faculty attitudes suggest that a tipping point has been passed for journal current issues, and, with certain narrow exceptions, that print editions of current issues of scholarly journals are rapidly becoming a thing of the past'. (Schonfeld and Housewright, 2010, 1).

The model for providing online access to journals is the most mature in respect of online content and has led the way in offering solutions to the challenges information professionals now face. This publication format will be explored in more detail here. It must be acknowledged, however, that many of the methods and philosophies of collecting, budgeting, storing and providing access apply to all online information formats, including books, data and journals currently held in academic libraries.

This chapter will outline the issues involved in managing the shift from print to online, discuss the challenges and explore some of the solutions we are considering and working with in academic libraries today. A number of these solutions anticipate the future for collections and the chapter will consider what this means for the information profession.

Delivering content
The seduction of the 'Big Deal'

Over the past ten years the widespread take-up of the nationally and regionally negotiated publishers' 'Big Deals' for online content have had an enormous impact on the size and nature of journal collections in Higher Education (HE) libraries globally. In the UK many of the 'Big Deal' negotiations are carried out by JISC Collections, through its NESLi2 initiative.[1] These deals, which are essentially single subscriptions to a 'bundle' of journals from a publisher, have been widely subscribed to by institutions of all shapes, sizes and budgets. Virtually all the major commercial publishers now have a negotiated NESLi2 licence that provides online access to the majority of their journal content (give or take a few new titles or recent portfolio acquisitions), and they have proved very popular for a number of reasons. The recession has meant that budgets have gradually become tighter as a result of an abundance of requests to support new courses and expanding areas of research with no extra money. Additionally, there is increasing pressure on academics to publish, feeding an ever-growing portfolio of scholarly journal titles which are in turn requested for purchase by libraries to support research and learning. These deals have presented librarians with quick and affordable solutions. As a consequence of this, the volume of online journal content available to users of HE libraries has increased dramatically as some of these NESLi2 deals provide access to literally hundreds of titles. The added attraction with these deals is the inclusion of the online historical back-files. Subscribers are thus acquiring widespread access to important current content as well as gaining the added bonus of being able to retrieve previously unavailable and substantial historical content and archives included in the subscription price for the deal. Not only have the NESLi2 deals increased access to content exponentially, they can be incredibly good value for money. In some notable cases it has been cheaper to move to a NESLi2 deal and acquire all the content of a journal publisher online than it is to sustain a number of single subscriptions.

Negotiation

In the UK, licences for NESLi2 deals are now negotiated on behalf of HE and FE by JISC Collections. As part of this co-ordinated and collective approach to negotiation, representatives from all institutions (usually the e-resources or journals librarian or similar) are kept informed of progress on a secure, password controlled website. Representatives are asked to submit an annual 'letter of intent', which indicates subscribers' potential interest in proposed deals, to support the negotiation process. The resulting agreements (varying in complexity from publisher to publisher) are made available to representatives via the website.

Under NESLi2 the makeup of every offer and licence negotiated by JISC for the HE and FE community in the UK is unique, as they depend very much on the nature and size of the publisher. For example, some of the deals require that a legacy print spend is maintained – meaning that even if the deal agreed involves a move to online only, the subscription represents the cost of the existing single subscriptions plus an additional amount to cover the rest of the portfolio of content offered. All have slightly different clauses and licences that require careful consideration of the cost and coverage. However, the clear benefit here is the understanding that the deal has been negotiated by a third party (JISC Collections). So, whoever is carefully weighing up the offer is doing so with the knowledge that this is probably the best price available to them for acquiring online content from this publisher in the UK.

The Research Information Network (2010a), in its explanation of publisher pricing strategies, notes that the variation in pricing policies is further exacerbated as publishers cannot confer on pricing or on standardization of pricing. It points out that 'such discussions would constitute a breach of competition law in the UK and other EU states, anti-trust law in the USA, and similar laws in most jurisdictions' (Research Information Network, 2010a, 20).

The reductions in library budgets and difficult economic outlook, along with the 'ever changing licensing and service models from publishers and vendors' mean that librarians 'struggle to maintain and expand accessibility in an increasingly complex environment' (Lawson, 2010, 137). However, in the UK we are beginning to see the Big-Deal negotiations with publishers falter as a direct result of smaller resource budgets (Taylor-Roe, 2009). Yet requests for new titles and access to information from faculty and students do not stop. Looking for coping strategies, Kidd (2010) explains that the basis of the NESLi2 consortium is one of opting in; that is, negotiations result in an offer of a deal for a particular publisher, which individual libraries can decide to take up or not. Although the 'letter of intent' aids the process, this is obviously not the optimal way of negotiating large deals, as neither party knows how much money is actually 'on the table'. Kidd presents the successful Scottish Higher Education Digital Library[2] (SHEDL) as an example of a 'shared service' model that could be replicated and adopted as a way of partially coping with the funding problems of the next few years.

Online historical content

In addition to the impact that the NESLi2 deals have had on journal collections by vastly increasing the amount of content online, the number of back-file titles offered by publishers for purchase has grown enormously. These are generally acquired as 'one-off' items separately from subscriptions and are not subject to any changes that could take place with the current subscription. They can be purchased 'in perpetuity' in a number of ways – in subject groups, as individual titles in date clusters or as a complete archive of a journal title. In a world where users expect instant access to data and, increasingly, archival information, these permanent and sustainable online acquisitions are very attractive to libraries.

Despite the shift towards online back-files, many libraries will still be left with extensive legacy print journal collections to manage. With pressure on space in many institutions, some librarians have seen the solution to their problem as being the disposal or relegation of print journals that overlap with online content. To do this responsibly, information professionals need to ask a number of questions:

- At what point does online content become sustainable enough for us to consider withdrawal (permanent or otherwise) of the print version?
- When the content is available as part of a subscription, what happens if the subscription is cancelled?
- How far do you trust a 'trusted service' such as JSTOR to sustain access?

Cooper and Norris (2007) detail a thorough and systematic process for identifying and logging print journal content for withdrawal at Imperial College, using criteria for assessing sustainable resources. Additionally, they indicate that they have armed themselves with two insurance policies which offer protection against future loss of access to valued journal content. These are involvement in the UK Research Reserve Project (UKRR)[3] and membership of Portico (Cooper and Norris, 2007, 209). The UKRR Project is a UK Higher Education Funding Council (HEFCE) funded initiative that aims to create a 'collaborative distributed national research collection' managed by a partnership between the Higher Education sector and the British Library. It enables those libraries that join to de-duplicate their print journal holdings of a title if two copies are held by other UKRR members, 'ensuring continued access to low-use journals, whilst allowing libraries to release space to meet the changing needs of their users'. Funds are made available to support libraries with this work and the substantial costs involved in undertaking the selection, checking and ethical disposal of this material. There are currently 29 members of UKRR, and it has a target of releasing 100 km of shelf space by the end of 2013. Quite clearly a post-UKRR research world in the UK will see greater collaboration between institutions in order to provide (and maintain) access to legacy print journal content.

It is fair to say that the UK is fortunate in having this co-ordinated project for the withdrawal of print journals which ensures that there are three accessible copies of a title (including those held by the British Library). Other countries are not so lucky. The USA, for example, with its decentralized HE system, has seen 'few co-ordinated efforts to manage collections at a system-wide level to accomplish community preservation goals' (Schonfeld and Housewright, 2009, 5). From their report we can clearly see that tackling the issue of co-ordinating the preservation of print in the USA is important in managing a consultative and sustainable move to online only access to journal content. A number of initiatives have attempted to manage collaborative collecting and preservation but have proved difficult to develop and sustain. There have been some successes but these have largely occurred for government information: the Federal Depository Libraries Program[4] co-ordinated by the Government Printing Office, the National Network of Libraries of Medicine[5] co-ordinated by the National Library of Medicine, and a number of comparable federal initiatives.

The other key 'insurance policy' identified by Cooper and Norris (2007) is participation in Portico,[6] the international e-journal preservation and archiving service. This, along with similar initiatives' LOCKSS (Lots of Copies Keep Stuff Safe)[7] and CLOCKSS (Controlled LOCKSS),[8] provide an important additional layer of security by sustaining and assuring long-term access to electronic content. Portico is a US-based subscription preservation service with over 100 publisher members. LOCKSS and CLOCKSS are digital preservation tools developed at Stanford University, which enable the local archiving of journal content. In the UK, the LOCKSS Alliance is hosted by EDINA.[9]

Open access

Alongside this growing preference for online access, the bundled deals and increased availability of back-files, the open access movement is beginning to impact on and challenge what we see as the traditional functions of the librarian, the journal collection and the traditional scholarly communication model. There are currently two chief methods for offering material via open access. The open access Gold model, as employed by BioMed Central and the Public Library of Science (PLoS) titles (and others), requires the researcher to pay the publisher to print their article, which is then free for all to access. The Green open access model involves scholars publishing in conventional subscription journals and self-archiving their final peer-reviewed (or not) papers in an institutional repository (IR) or in a central or subject-based repository such as arXiv[10] or PubMed Central.[11] Both models challenge the traditional role of the information professional as research material can be accessed for research and teaching purposes without having been mediated, for the most part, in any way by the librarian. This raises the question as to whether we add these open access journal titles to our 'collection'. The Directory of Open Access Journals (DOAJ)[12] lists many but not all titles, and can easily be linked to from the traditional library catalogue, but as the DOAJ grows this will become a more significant issue.

Without doubt the model for scholarly communication is changing as it shifts online. As Woodward (2010) states in her guest editorial to the first open access issue of the *New Review of Academic Librarianship*: 'The role of librarians in championing open access through the setting up and populating of institutional repositories (IRs) and undertaking advocacy campaigns within their institution is having an impact' (Woodward, 2010,1).

For this and many other reasons it is crucial that librarians ensure they play a central role in the open access movement, for this method of scholarly publishing has the potential to impact profoundly on the scholarly communication landscape – and on our collections and our funding. Some publishers offer discounts on submission if the institution has an enhanced subscription to the title. For example, moving to a more expensive institutional subscription to the open access OUP title *Nucleic Acids Research* from a standard subscription rate will secure substantially discounted publication charges for authors of that institution. Such precedents will inevitably result in requests to librarians to enhance subscriptions, which would in turn have an impact on the resources budget. We therefore need to question whether libraries should consider using their subscription budgets to support research output. Additionally, funds are occasionally made available from a central institutional budget to cover Gold open access fees. If senior university managers make an unsubstantiated link between the wider availability of open access material and the library needing fewer subscriptions then the implication for libraries could be that this central pot of money could be drawn from the library resources budget.

New models of delivery

Taking all this into account it seems obvious that we are now looking for what Henderson and Bosch (2010) call 'a new normal' for collecting scholarly content, 'one that requires varied approaches to services and collections'. Publishers are consulting and working more closely than ever with information professionals and library users to trial and develop new models of access for online information such as pay-per-view (PPV, where users pay for content as they need it) and patron-driven selection (where online material is purchased for the library collection when it is needed) for books as well as journals. Rapid changes in technology mean that it is crucial for both librarians and publishers to understand how researchers are working, what they need and how they are accessing it and which model is going to deliver this best.

Schell, Ginanni and Heet (2010) list several potential benefits for staff and users for these new models of delivery:

1 Users can access thousands more articles than previously available through traditional library subscriptions.
2 Cost-per-use for on-demand articles is dramatically cheaper than seldom used subscriptions.
3 There are no storage costs.
4 Evaluation by usage statistics is more precise.
5 They can serve as a valuable supplement to interlibrary loan (ILL) services.

(Schell, Ginanni and Heet, 2010, 87)

Their article recognizes that several obstacles still stand in the way of realizing the viability of on-demand access as a business model; but the authors believe 'the potential for growth is vast if publishers are willing to invest in improving their interfaces, accounting mechanisms and price points' (Schell, Ginanni and Heet, 2010, 88).

Anderson (2010) takes this a step further:

> The journal subscription is a left-over artefact of the print era, when the constraints of physical printing and distribution made it necessary to bundle articles together and ship them out as issues . . . the online environment, in which printing is unnecessary and distribution can be virtually instantaneous, requires neither bundling nor the purchase of unwanted articles in order to get the articles one needs. (Anderson, 2010, 42)

But why do we need the journal at all? If the value was placed on the article and not on the bundled journal format then there would no longer be any need for publishers to hold back from publishing finished articles as soon as they have been reviewed. If databases of research libraries such as the Mendeley[13] programme (which provides a collaborative, online space for researchers to work and access research papers) are successful, then providing access to scholarly information could be taken out of the hands of the institutional academic library completely. An alternative future scenario is that instead of an institutional journal collection, we use the British Library ILL service to access current articles online as a cheap and quick alternative to taking out new journal subscriptions and rely on the UKRR distributed journal collections for any print journal needs.

All these new models and potential methods of delivering content seriously challenge the traditional role of the academic library as a 'just-in-case' collection, as it moves towards becoming a 'just-in-time' provider. Again, for this reason it is important that information professionals take an interest in and are actively involved in future models for scholarly communication. Changes in this area have a fundamental impact on the essential skills needed to be an information professional in the 21st century in supporting users of scholarly content.

Discovering the content

A new infrastructure?

The considerable shift towards e-only has triggered a significant transformation in how academic libraries manage their storage, space and access needs for their online (journal) content. The complexities of offering a substantial portion of the library collection remotely raise a wide range of issues. There is an absolute expectation, reinforced by our strong and certain e-learning future, that material is easily and sustainably discoverable and accessible at all times from any device with an internet connection. All this has to be supported and sustained within the existing library infrastructure and resources.

Furthermore, as a result of this shift, information professionals have had to rapidly identify solutions to problems such as the gathering and storing of collection metadata by, for example, electronic resource management technology (open or otherwise) and composite-integrated cataloguing systems. In addition, the enormous speed of the shift to e-only has meant that multifarious (non-user centred) systems have sprung up that purport to provide the 'best' access to journals and their content. The profession is now taking stock and is consulting, commissioning and listening to the considerable evidence-based user behaviour studies now available.

User behaviour

Although costly, online journal subscriptions have met with huge success, not just with librarians but also with users (Research Information Network, 2009). The Centre for Information Behaviour and the Evaluation of Research (CIBER) has researched, written and presented extensively on user behaviour:

> There is a big risk of libraries being decoupled from their customer base as users migrate in number from the physical to the digital library, the former the province of the librarian and the latter now the province of the publisher. In the increasingly digital information environment, libraries are becoming increasingly anonymous (and unacknowledged) third parties, as users work ever more remotely and directly.   (Nicholas, 2008, 122)

Users are identifying scholarly material in a variety of ways, using freely available articles alongside subscription resources and expect a simple and straightforward route to it. In the same way that a considered strategic approach is taken to designing a library space for users of the building, it is important to listen and consult with users in order to offer them the most appropriate environment in which to work with the online content. Stone (2010) concludes that:

> Our job over the next five to ten years is to provide a way to access these valuable resources in an intuitive, easy-to-use, one-stop shop, and not to be afraid of running a continual beta test where new services and functions can be added as and when necessary…In addition, we must keep evaluating users' needs and reach out by adapting to fit their requirements, rather than expecting them to come to us, indeed our very future depends on it.
>
> (Stone, 2010, 156)

Revising our physical space

The knock-on effect of the move away from maintaining large print stocks has naturally resulted in prime space being released in public areas of library buildings. The transfer to online collecting has presented universities with an excellent opportunity to rethink what they offer in terms of space to support the learning experience, and many have taken the opportunity to reinvest in the library space and reinvent what we think of today as the academic-research library. 'Many new libraries are landmark buildings on campus, with a strong "sense of place", and they have facilitated a step change in support for learning, teaching and research in their institutions' (McDonald, 2010, 48).

Adapting skills

It is obvious that the shift to online is transforming the role of the information professional and there are numerous examples that illustrate how this is happening. It is evident from what has already been outlined that, in addition to conventional collection management skills, information professionals will need to acquire new expertise. These additional skills include a thorough understanding of such new 'back-room' tasks as licence reading, complex statistical interpretation and technical authentication issues to support mobile and other future forms of access. Transformations in technology and in copyright law will have a bearing on many of the new types of routine tasks and a core understanding of the issues and consequences of these will be central to the essential skill set of librarians in academic institutions.

We now need to recognize that the model for delivery of scholarly communication is never going to be static, and this will have a direct impact on how we prepare our budgets. We need to become more adept at building flexibility into our forecasting in order that we can move quickly to support whatever becomes the preferred method of acquiring scholarly content. As publishers and librarians work more closely together, engagement with cross-sectoral groups such as the United Kingdom Serials Group[14] (UKSG) and the North American Serials Interest Group[15] (NASIG) is crucial. They provide important developmental opportunities for librarians to engage with and understand the workings of publishers and all those involved in the serials supply chain and vice versa.

It is vital then that information professionals are considering a strategic approach to the online delivery of information that is based on the needs of their users. There is a problem here, though, as we are no longer able to observe our users *using* our collections in the online environment – their behaviour is hidden from us, and it is dangerous to assume we know how they are finding information, what they are finding and what they are missing. We must make full use of the reports and evidence available to us on patterns of behaviour and understand that there may be differences in approach by the subject divisions. This is illustrated by the series of case studies produced by the Research Information Network[16] (RIN) which examined the practices of a number of groups of researchers in particular research fields. However, each institution is different, and it is important to survey and work closely with the researchers and learners in your own institution. Find out how they work, what they expect and what obstacles are in the way to them finding and managing online information.

Visibility

Now more than ever we must find a way to be visible to the academics and students of our institutions. As well as the traditional teaching and awareness skills we need to acquire highly developed communication and liaison skills in order to fulfil (and manage) user expectations in respect of accessing information. We need to ensure that we are the professionals they turn to in order to keep their communities up to date with the fast-moving world of digital information. As the collections are no longer tied to the physical building, librarians must leave the libraries with which they have so long been identified in order to market collections effectively – both in the departments and in the online space.

This shift to online will present opportunities for librarians to play an invaluable role in supporting researchers and students. Not only should we be marketing our collections, we also need to market our own skills very carefully. We are perfectly positioned to act as information scholars within universities. The RIN report, *Research Support Services in UK Universities* (Research Information Network, 2010b) focuses on the tools and services researchers make use of in the course of the research life cycle. There is potential for librarians to play a significant role in supporting these services and offer much needed expertise and leadership within their institution. This could include leading on data management and curation, the co-ordinated awareness of publication channels, bibliometrics, copyright and intellectual property, digitization and open access (including institutional repositories).

All this, of course, requires a big shift in staffing structures as well as raising no small number of professional development issues. Currently the largest staffing resource in the library is the front-of-house operation, and this needs to alter. As the shift to self-service, longer opening hours, less material being borrowed and a move to supporting online formats progresses, we are beginning to see changes. Support is taken away from the static enquiry desk and moved to maintain the online space – supporting enquiry and marketing services such as Meebo, Ask a librarian, Twitter and Facebook or just generally working to ensure the online environment is available and responsive to the changing needs of the users.

Conclusions

This chapter has, inevitably, raised many more questions than answers, as much of the future of online information depends on an imagined future for technology. One such future is illustrated in the British Library *2020 Vision* document (2010) which states that the technology that underpins delivery of scholarly information 'will be in a constant state of beta'. The importance of technology in the delivery of scholarly information now suggests that we have to assume that, whatever the mode of delivery, scholarly communication will likewise in the future – always be in beta. For this prediction we will have to be highly adaptive and become proficient in continually modifying our core skill set to accommodate persistent changes.

However, there will be other challenges that will need to be addressed in this e-only information world besides technology. The funding crisis has already seen significant reductions in budgets available for purchasing material across all formats. Online access to journals (and e-books) can alleviate some of the problems but in a way that much of the responsibility of the selection is taken away from the librarian. The patron-driven e-book model has been wholeheartedly embraced both by librarians and users of libraries. Moving the responsibility for straightforward selection (and instant access) to the user at the point of need results in every purchased item being required and used. The online explosion of content has meant we have had to rethink our view of a library. It is no longer appropriate (save for a few notable examples such as national collections) to build up comprehensive collections of material that might never be used within an institution; demands on time and money have put a stop to this. Additionally, the concept of collection development needs to be totally re-examined. The range of available online information is so broad that our traditional policies in this area are becoming completely unfit for purpose. We have to adjust very quickly, rethink our skills and promote their value and impact to universities in order to ensure we continue to play a major role in the research and teaching process in HE.

Here are some points for you to reflect on:

- At what point do we stop trying to define what is our collection?
- Will online content become sustainable enough for us to consider withdrawal (permanent or otherwise) of the print version?
- What are the implications of open access publishing models for resource budgets?
- How do we develop appropriate skills for supporting online collections that are in a 'permanent state of beta'?
- Do we need to make a conscious decision to provide just-in-time rather than just-in-case collections?

References

Anderson, R. (2010) Scholarly communications: the view from the library. In Woodward, H. and Estelle, L. (eds), *Digital Information: order or anarchy*, Facet Publishing.

British Library (2010) *2020 Vision*, www.bl.uk/2020vision.

Cooper, R. and Norris, D. (2007) To Bin or not to Bin? Deselecting print back-runs available electronically at Imperial College London Library, *Serials*, **20** (3) 208–14.

Henderson, K. S. and Bosch, S. (2010) Budget Strains Force Radical Change, *Library Journal*, April, **7**, 15, www.libraryjournal.com/lj/ljinprintcurrentissue/884221-403/periodicals_price_survey_2010_seeking.html.csp.

Kidd, T. (2010) The View from the UK: the economic crisis and serials acquisition on an offshore island, *The Serials Librarian*, **59** (3) 384–93.

Lawson, K. (2010) Serials Collection Management in Recessionary Times: strengths, weaknesses, opportunities, and threat, *The Serials Librarian*, **59** (2) 137–46.

McDonald, A. (2010) Libraries as Places: challenges for the future. In McKnight, S. (ed.), *Envisioning Future Academic Library Services*, Facet Publishing.

Nicholas, D. (2008) If We Do Not Understand Our Users, We Will Certainly Fail. In Stone, G., Anderson, R. and Feinstein J. (eds), *E-Resources Management Handbook*, UKSG.

Research Information Network (2009) *E-journals: their use, value and impact. Phase one report*, www.rin.ac.uk/system/files/attachments/E-journals-report.pdf.

Research Information Network (2010a) *E-only Scholarly Journals: overcoming the barriers*, www.rin.ac.uk/system/files/attachments/E-only_report_for_screen_0.pdf.

Research Information Network (2010b) *Research Support Services in UK Universities*, www.rin.ac.uk/system/files/attachments/Research_Support_Services_in_UK_Universities_report_for_screen.pdf.

Schell, L. E.,Ginanni, K. and Heet, B. (2010) Playing the Field: pay-per-view e-journals and e-books, *The Serials Librarian*, **58** (1), 87–96.

Schonfeld, R. C. and Housewright, R. (2009) *What to Withdraw? Print collections management in the wake of digitization*, www.ithaka.org/ithaka-s-r/research/what-to-withdraw.

Schonfeld, R. C. and Housewright, R. (2010) *Faculty Survey 2009: key strategic insights for libraries, publishers, and societies*, www.ithaka.org/ithaka-s-r/research/faculty-surveys-2000-2009/Faculty Study 2009.pdf.

Stone, G. (2010) Resource Discovery. In Woodward, H. and Estelle, L. (eds), *Digital Information: order or anarchy*, Facet Publishing.

Taylor-Roe, J. (2009) 'To Everything There is a Season': reflections on the sustainability of the 'big deal' in the current economic climate, *Serials*, **22** (2) 113–21.

Woodward, H. (2010) Dissemination Models in Scholarly Communication, *New Review of Academic Librarianship*, **16** (S1) 1–3.

Notes

1   www.jisc-collections.ac.uk/nesli2.

2   http://scurl.ac.uk/WG/SHEDL/index.html.

3   www.ukrr.ac.uk.

4 www.fdlp.gov.

5 http://nnlm.gov.

6 www.portico.org/digital-preservation.

7 http://lockss.org/lockss/Home.

8 www.clockss.org/clockss/Home.

9 http://edina.ac.uk/lockss/index.html.

10 www.arxiv.org.

11 www.ncbi.nlm.nih.gov/pmc/.

12 www.doaj.org/.

13 www.mendeley.com.

14 www.uksg.org.

15 www.nasig.org.

16 www.rin.ac.uk/our-work/using-and-accessing-information-resources.

5

Electronic books in academic libraries: a case study in Liverpool, UK

Terry Bucknell

Outline and overview

Electronic books have taken much longer than electronic journals to be accepted into the mainstream of academic library collections. This chapter reviews the experiences of one UK academic library in developing its e-book collection, some of the impacts it has had on processes and workflows and the analysis that has been carried out. It outlines how this has helped us to understand what gets used and why, and what the most cost-effective methods are to build an e-books collection that meets user needs. Finally, the chapter considers some of the challenges that lie ahead.

A history of e-books at the University of Liverpool

The University of Liverpool (UoL) is a Russell Group (i.e. research intensive) University, founded in 1881, with about 17,000 FTE students. Its library occupies two buildings on either side of the university precinct. In common with most UK academic libraries it has transitioned its journal subscriptions from predominantly print, via combined print+online subscriptions for a time, to online-only where possible.

Although UoL Library had provided access to online products such as *Early English Books Online* and online reference works like the *Grove Dictionary of Music* and the *Oxford English Dictionary Online* since the early 2000s, its first steps in 'proper' e-books were tentative: a single biology textbook and six *Oxford Handbooks* in medicine, all acquired on subscription. The uptake was disappointing, though perhaps not too surprising given that there were only seven e-books among about two million print books in the library catalogue. The *Oxford Handbooks* were not renewed after the first year due to poor usage (though a subscription to twice as many titles was started again in March 2011) and the biology textbook continued for several years with a moderate level of usage until the publisher changed hands and the book ceased to be made available online.

In the autumn of 2005, the library started to support a cohort of online students, the vast majority of them based overseas, for whom the physical library was utterly irrelevant. An attempt was made to establish a critical mass of content in computing and business/management through a subscription to Safari.[1] The Safari model employs 'slots' which the library fills with books that typically occupy between 0.5 and 2 slots each. The library chooses which level of simultaneous users to pay for, and it can change its choice of titles every 30 days. This collection of e-books proved much more popular with users but library staff found that they did not have the time every month to review and update the collection. Furthermore, the pricing model meant that to expand its collection the library would have to pay twice: once to increase the number of slots, and once to increase the number of simultaneous users. After three years, with a collection that had changed little over that period, the subscription was cancelled.

By 2006 the budgetary situation at UoL Library was much improved and a substantial collection of e-books was sought. A subscription to ebrary Academic Complete[2] was started under terms negotiated by the Southern Universities Purchasing Consortium (SUPC) but made available to all UK HE institutions. Academic Complete suddenly provided a critical mass of over 30,000 e-book titles. Keyword searches of the library catalogue were likely to turn up some e-books, and uptake was very rapid with little promotion. In the first month, over 100,000 pages were accessed from over 4000 different books and nearly 7000 pages were printed. It was felt that part of the success of Academic Complete was because its e-books were provided on an unlimited simultaneous users basis, albeit with restrictions on the amount of content that could be copied or printed in a session.

The success of Academic Complete led to demand for e-books that were not included in that subscription package. To accommodate these demands, the library started buying single perpetual access titles also on the same platform, though these were often limited to single-user access. The hope was that all UoL's e-books could be offered on a single platform so that users would only need to learn how to use a single platform, and they would be able to search the full text of all UoL's e-books simultaneously. It quickly became apparent that this vision would not become the reality. Some requested titles were only available through other platforms so the library started purchasing single titles on Myilibrary[3] and Dawsonera.[4] The latter provides unlimited simultaneous access but limits the number of times that an e-book may be used per year.

By 2006 UoL had embarked upon a programme of enhanced library funding to improve the student experience and the quality of research and, to be honest, to boost its poor standing in national league tables of library spending per FTE student. But in a library where the culture was that books were selected by academics, rather than collections built by librarians, better funding meant that not all the funds had been spent by the end of the financial year. Purchasing e-book packages at the end of the financial year was an ideal solution to this 'problem': the 'goods' could be 'delivered' almost instantly and they could benefit a wide range of subject areas. The problem with this approach is that if a year-of-publication e-books collection is purchased in July of that year, then some of those titles will already have been purchased (in print and/or online) through an aggregator platform with Digital Rights Management[5] (DRM). To avoid such double-buying it is necessary to study the usage of purchased collections and to try to budget for the purchase of future collections at the start of each year.

By March 2011 UoL library was providing access to just over 200,000 contemporary e-books, comprising purchased e-book collections from 12 different publishers, single e-books purchased through three aggregators and two publishers, subscriptions to collections on three e-book platforms, and through some e-book content in other full-text aggregated databases that were dominated by e-journal content. In addition to all that contemporary material, access is available to over 300,000 digitized historical books. Thus e-books now account for about 20% of UoL's entire books collection, the print portion of which has taken 130 years to build; the online portion less than ten years.

Selection and acquisition processes

For single-title purchases, the priority is to provide users with a DRM-free version where possible. Where DRM cannot be avoided, the library will choose among its three preferred suppliers according to the available access model (single user, multi-user, maximum number of uses per year), the usability of the platform and cost. The library works with vendors to connect their systems to the library management system through EDI where possible. The JISC E-books Observatory Project (JISC Collections, 2009) found that librarians were looking for a one-stop shop to find and order e-books from multiple vendors, and UoL are starting to use SwetsWise[6] to fulfil this function.

UoL library maintains a wish list of potential collection purchases throughout the year and a group comprising the senior liaison librarians and the Electronic Resources Manager decides which ones to proceed with towards the end of the financial year. Some priority collections are ordered at the start of the year. Collection purchases usually require paper-based university purchase orders and licence agreements.

Subscriptions to e-book packages are subjected to the same annual review procedures as e-journals and databases, with usage being key to deciding whether a package justifies renewal.

Cataloguing and access processes

UoL uses separate e-book and print book catalogue records. These allow for ease of maintenance but may cause confusion for some users. The e-books portion of the UoL catalogue is available as a separate 'scope' so users can limit their search to e-books-only if they prefer.

Purchasing or subscribing to collections of e-books is highly efficient from a cataloguing perspective. Typically the vendor will offer a set of MARC (Machine Readable Cataloging) records, either through an administration site, as an e-mail attachment or through OCLC. Publisher-supplied records are sometimes of poor quality, sometimes even lacking URLs. Publishers have rarely had any prior experience of MARC records and tend to appreciate feedback about the standards that libraries expect. For example, it is becoming more common to see records with Library of Congress Subject Headings (LCSH) and tables of contents included. The Library Management System at UoL[7] has good facilities for ingesting and editing records in bulk, for example, inserting the Ezproxy[8] login string into the URL.

Regular MARC record updates are required for subscription collections or those that have been purchased before they are complete. Such updates are typically made available once a month, and for subscription packages may be accompanied by a list of records to be deleted (because publishers may choose to withdraw titles from collections). This can present some challenges to the publisher and the library. If the publisher just makes a complete, updated batch of records available then the library has to either load the complete batch, overwriting previous records and any edits made to them, or devise a means of limiting the set to just those records that the library does not yet have in its catalogue. It is better for the publisher to provide separate batches of new records as well as a file that contains multiple updates (a year's worth, for example) and a complete record set. That way, the library only needs to load the updates it requires, but if the library falls behind with its processing it can select the batches of records that it requires or opt for a full reload.

Single titles purchased through regular library book suppliers also tend to have good integration with library management systems, for example, sending payment information through EDI and FTPing MARC records directly into a staging area of the catalogue. Single titles purchased directly from the publisher may require much more labour-intensive processes, but even in the worst case the library can download a MARC record from its normal sources and augment it with the URL and other information it requires for e-book records.

Usage statistics for e-books

Launched in March 2002, COUNTER is an international initiative of librarians, publishers and intermediaries that sets standards to facilitate the recording and reporting of online usage statistics in a consistent, credible and compatible way. The first COUNTER Code of Practice, covering online journals and databases, was published in 2003. Release 1 of The COUNTER Code of Practice for Books and Reference Works (COUNTER, 2006) was published in March 2006 and is still in force as of April 2011. It specifies two full-text reports for e-books: Book Report 1: Number of Successful Title Requests by Month and Title (only for titles/platforms that are provided as a single file), and Book Report 2: Number of Successful Section Requests by Month and Title. A 'section' in Report 2 can be anything from a page to a chapter, depending on the platform. It is thus extremely difficult to try to compare usage on ebrary (a section is a page) with SpringerLink (a section is a chapter) with Palgrave Connect (books provided as single files). At UoL, COUNTER usage reports are collated and provided to all library staff through an MS SharePoint intranet site.

It should also be borne in mind that platforms with DRM tend to restrict (or prevent entirely) downloading and offline reading, whereas platforms that provide e-books as DRM-free PDFs (like almost all e-journal platforms do for journal articles) allow the user to download once and then read offline as much as they like. Only the initial download from such platforms will be reported in the COUNTER usage statistics, whereas on DRM-enabled platforms such re-readings will tend to be reported each time they occur.

Many e-book platforms also provide their own types of usage reports and these can be helpful to try to get an insight into user behaviour. For example, ebrary provides figures for the number of pages that have been copied or printed, and the percentage of the whole book that has been viewed, copied or printed; and IEEE Xplore provides a chapter-level report.

If the vendor provides files of metadata about its e-books using the same identifier (usually the ISBN) as the usage report, the identifier can be combined with the usage report to allow for analysis according to variables such as subject area, price, publication date or length of ownership. The library may be able to extract such information from the MARC records in its catalogue, and even extend this to circulation data for print copies of the same titles. However, the variability in ISBNs (print vs electronic, 10 digit vs 13 digit, hardback vs paperback and so on) make this much more challenging than for e-journals. Tools for combining spreadsheets in this way include the VLOOKUP function in Excel[9] and Google Fusion Tables.[10]

User attitudes towards e-books

In March 2010 the University of Liverpool carried out an online survey about e-books in association with Springer who provided a laptop in a prize draw to encourage participation. The results were made available as a white paper (Springer, 2010) and among the most notable were:

- 90% of students were aware that the library provided access to a large number of e-books. The figure was lower, but still substantial, for staff and researchers at 77%.
- Staff/researchers who did not use e-books said this was either because they were not aware of them (41%), they had no need for them (28%), they did not know how to use them or had technical problems (17%) or they preferred reading print books (11%).
- 68% of students and 53% of staff/researchers reported using e-books at least monthly.
- Of the staff and researchers who used e-books, 85% used them for research and 48% for teaching.
- 86% of respondents said that they used the library catalogue to search for e-books, compared to 48% for Google and 41% for Google Book Search.
- Only 9% of users printed from e-books and 5% copied and pasted; the rest read online (69%) or downloaded for offline reading (16%).
- Readers preferred print for the pleasure of reading, but e-books for currency and anytime-anywhere availability and for the ease of making copies.
- Most users appreciated that e-books are protected by copyright and that they should not share them with people outside the university. There was less certainty about whether it was OK to print and download e-books, but that is probably because the ability to do such things varies so much between platforms.

Digital Rights Management (DRM) and accessibility

One of the reasons why e-books have been slower than e-journals to gain acceptance is the issue of DRM. The books that libraries are most keen to acquire online are the core textbooks, but these are the very titles that publishers are least willing to license to academic libraries because they risk losing print sales to individual students or they open up the risk of piracy. In response, many e-books licensed to libraries are encumbered with DRM. DRM may:

- render pages one at a time
- limit the speed with which pages can be 'turned'
- limit the number of pages that can be copied or printed
- prevent downloading for offline reading
- restrict the device(s) on which the content can be read, or the duration for which it can be read.

The music industry appears to have learned the lesson that DRM can always be defeated by determined pirates, and the imposition of DRM serves only to annoy bona fide users. Increasingly, the book industry is coming around to this view too, as evidenced in the following interview with Tim O'Reilly:

> Let's say my goal is to sell 10,000 copies of something. And let's say that if by putting DRM in it I sell 10,000 copies and I make my money, and if by having no DRM 100,000 copies go into circulation and I still sell 10,000 copies. Which of those is the better outcome? I think having 100,000 in circulation and selling 10,000 is way better than having just the 10,000 that are paid for and nobody else benefits.
>
> People who don't pay you generally wouldn't have paid you anyway. We're delighted when people who can't afford our books don't pay us for them, if they go out and do something useful with that information.
>
> I think having faith in that basic logic of the market is important. Besides, DRM interferes with the user experience. It makes it much harder to have people adopt your product.
>
> (Bruner, 2011)

Most publishers who offer the e-books on their own platform now do so without DRM, yet they also offer the same titles via aggregators who impose DRM. The experience at the University of Liverpool is that users intensely dislike DRM. For example, a postgraduate geologist, after being informed about a new collection of e-books on a publisher's platform where the e-books are presented as simple PDF chapters, commented:

> I assumed it would be in the form of that 'orrible, oh so 'orrible e-book reader, copyright protected and only viewable on screen. I much prefer what the library is providing here – downloadable chapters in PDF format. . . . Great for the research community.

UoL library has recently become aware of an unintended consequence of the use of DRM: e-books that do not work with screen-reader software for visually impaired users. Although the software works with PDF files, and although the e-book platforms can produce PDF files, the DRM embedded in the files prevents the screen-reader software from working. In contrast, DRM-free PDFs from publisher platforms tend to perform reasonably well with screen-reader software. It is essential that e-book providers consider the full consequences of the DRM that they impose and try to find solutions that achieve their intended aims without reducing the usability of their content.

Analysis of e-book package usage statistics at University of Liverpool

In 2009 UoL Library undertook a study of the usage statistics for the Springer e-book collections that it had purchased on the SpringerLink platform (Bucknell, 2009). Some of the key findings of this and later analysis (Bucknell, 2011) were:

- About 40% of UoL's downloads from SpringerLink are e-book chapters (and 60% are e-journal articles). In the first month of each academic year the ratio switches to 60:40 in favour of e-book chapters. This presents a budgetary challenge: UoL's STM departments often allocate the vast majority of their library budget to journals, leaving very little for books (or e-books).
- E-books are a long-term investment: in 2010 the titles published in 2005 accounted for a significant proportion of the usage, and some 2005 titles were used for the first time in 2010, five years after publication. Table 5.1 shows that e-books have more longevity than e-journals. Of the 2007–2010 e-book chapters downloaded in 2010, 45% were published in 2007 or 2008, compared to 36% for e-journal articles. (SpringerLinks's Journal Report 5, full-text downloads by year of publication, groups year prior to 1997).

Table 5.1 *SpringerLink Usage Statistics*		
Year of publication	E-book chapters downloaded	E-journal articles downloaded
2007	21%	16%
2008	24%	20%
2009	31%	29%
2010	24%	35%

- Cost per download, the familiar tool for calculating the value of e-journal subscriptions, is much more problematic for e-book purchases. In the calculation for e-journal subscriptions, the cost of one year's subscription is divided by the usage of the journal in that year even though most of the usage is for articles paid for in previous years, and the future usage of articles paid for by the current year's subscription is not known. For e-book purchases, there is no previously purchased content to serve as a proxy for the usage of the paid-for content in future years. Thus, value can only be determined over a long time period (see Figure 5.1), or,

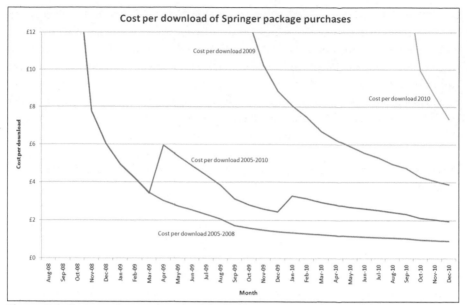

Figure 5.1 *Cost per chapter download for UoL's separate purchases of three Springer e-book collections (2005–2008, 2009 and 2010) and in combination*

equivalently, short-term value calculations should try to correct for unknown future usage.

- The proportion of each collection used obviously increases over time, but the pattern for each Springer collection was very consistent: after a year of ownership, 45% of the books had been used; after two years of ownership, 65% had been used. For individually selected titles on aggregator platforms, 80% had been used after a few months, but after 18 months there were still some titles that had not been used. However, the University of Leeds report that *all* their single purchase titles on aggregator platforms are used (Sharp and Thompson, 2010).

- There are some differences in the proportion of different subject collections that have been used. In one group of subjects about 70–75% had been used after two years; in other subjects about 60% had been used, and in Maths only about 45%. It is not yet clear whether ultimately all subjects will reach the same level of usage, but some subjects will just take longer to reach that level.

- The Springer collections at UoL conform to the Pareto rule: the best-used 20% of the collection accounts for 80% of the usage. However, UoL's use of single title purchases on aggregator platforms is even more concentrated: 80% of usage coming from just 15% and 11% of titles on two platforms. This is because just three titles on the first platform account for 21% of usage and a single title on the other accounts for 35% of usage. Looking at how usage is concentrated therefore tells you nothing about the overall usefulness or value of a collection.

- Of the Springer e-books that had been used, around a third had only had one, two or three chapters downloaded (so far). The proportions were only slightly less for single titles bought on aggregator platforms and of course those are bought at full price whereas a collection is bought at a discount off the total list price of the titles.

Patron-Driven Acquisition

In Patron-Driven Acquisition (PDA), a library partners with an e-book platform and loads the MARC records for all non-purchased titles (or a pre-selected subset of those titles) into the library catalogue. Usage is monitored in real time, and when a threshold level of usage occurs, a purchase (or a request for purchase) is initiated. The precise model, and the threshold, varies according to the platform. Often it is possible for one or more of the threshold usage events to generate 'rentals' or 'short-term loans' for a percentage of the purchase price, prior to a purchase being generated after a specified number of such rentals. Often the library can determine the number of such rentals: too low and books with just a transient interest will be purchased; too high and the library could end up buying books for much more than the purchase price because of a number of prior rentals on the same title. Libraries can also usually choose whether to mediate requests or to allow the process to be fully automatic.

At UoL, library funds were set aside for a PDA experiment but the decline of sterling against the euro and the US dollar at the start of the economic downturn meant that the earmarked funds had to be spent on higher than expected journal subscriptions instead. Nevertheless, usage statistics from purchased e-book collections have been used to assess what might have been spent under PDA. Such assessment can only be approximate because PDA models use real-time data, whereas sample modelling has to interpret and extrapolate from usage reports.

The modelling showed that PDA would usually prove to be more costly than buying a package. This is because, other than for core textbooks, most books are used consistently over time. A book may be used intensively for a short period but then never again (maybe a research monograph that really 'hits the spot' for the project of a particular group of final year students), or may be used a little every few months over an extended period (for example, a set of conference proceedings that several users occasionally require a single paper from). In both of those scenarios, a purchase may be triggered by PDA at full list price (or more if the model allows for rentals before purchase) whereas they could have been purchased in a collection at a discounted price.

This is borne out by the University of Iowa, one of the pilot sites for the ebrary PDA model. After two months, they had spent all the funds that they had deposited for PDA and spending was increasing, so they reviewed the titles that they had purchased, bought packages from three of the largest STM (scientific, technical and medical) publishers and then carried on with PDA operating on a much smaller pool of titles (Hames, 2011). Further analysis of UoL's Springer collections showed that if single titles had been bought, only those with more than six chapters downloaded could have been purchased for the same price as the collection. It is hard to envisage a PDA model that would provide the same level of access at lower cost.

Evidence-based selection

Both collection buying and PDA involve taking a gamble. When buying a collection the library does not know in advance how well the collection will be used, and hence whether it will represent good value. With PDA, it is only after titles have been bought that the library can determine whether there could have been a more cost-effective way of acquiring them. Evidence-based selection promises to remove the uncertainty inherent in other models. The library pays a modest upfront fee for access to all titles on a platform. At the end of the year the library can choose which titles to keep, up to the amount that it has already paid, or it can choose to retain access to a greater number of titles if it pays the difference.

UoL did something very much like this several years ago. In July 2007 it bought a large number of e-books from a publisher (at a heavily discounted price) and access was also granted to the publisher's other titles for a year. At the end of the year the best-used 580 titles were purchased. In the following year, 77% of those 580 titles were used, and 73% of them the year after. Only 61% of the titles were used in all three years. Of course the great unknown is how many of the titles that were not purchased after the first year would have gone on to be well used in years two and three. PDA would of course have purchased the required titles at the time they were needed, but would have done so at full price or more.

Evidence-based selection can still lead the library to buy books that are never used again (as can any other model), but it can provide the library with a low-risk and cost-effective way to experiment with the content on e-book platforms. It could reveal that regularly buying certain subject collections could be a good approach, or could give the library and vendor an evidence base for arriving at a mutually acceptable price for collections.

Current UoL strategy

At UoL library the current thinking is that e-books should be acquired through the following means:

1 Annual purchase of certain collections, where evidence of past usage or past purchasing patterns indicates that a collection would provide good value. Some of these might be part of combined e-journal/e-book licences.
2 Aggregated databases of e-book content (usually not front list titles) to give a critical mass at an affordable price.
3 Individually purchased titles, selected through normal means, on DRM-free publisher platforms where possible, but DRM-enabled platforms where necessary.
4 PDA to fill the gaps and spend the remaining budget, supplemented by additional collection purchases at the end of the financial year.

UoL has a Collection Management Policy in the final stages of ratification that states that e-books are the preferred format for acquiring books. However, it provides for print books where there are sound academic reasons for acquiring them. It is thus likely that within a relatively short period of time the bulk of UoL's books acquisitions will be electronic, just as has already occurred with journals. At present, the library books budget is split into departmental allocations through a funding formula. Plans are in progress to centralize the book fund to enable the annual purchase of certain key e-book collections, and to avoid having to modify the formula in light of university restructuring.

Concluding remarks

Until recently the provision of full-text e-resources in academic libraries has been centred around providing access to PDFs (and web pages) through a web browser on networked PCs. Now users expect to be able to access e-resources wirelessly through laptops, smart phones and tablet computers, and e-books through dedicated e-book readers too. Publishers are already beginning to offer e-books to library users in ePub format as well as in PDF and this trend will surely accelerate. There is also a burgeoning market in consumer e-books, led by the Kindle and Sony e-book readers, but it is unclear how much these will impinge on the academic library world. Amazon's announcement that (in the USA) library users will be able to borrow library-purchased Kindle e-books on the user's own Kindle or Kindle app (Amazon, 2011) was quickly followed by news that seven months into a study at the University of Washington, where computer science students were provided with Kindles for their study, 60% had stopped using them (Dudley, 2011).

Perhaps the licensing of single e-book chapters direct to students through services like Reference Tree[11] will become important. Will students pay for their own content if it is priced at a similar level to a song on iTunes or an iPhone app? Will academic departments bypass the library and pay for their students' content – on devices provided to each student to attract them to the institution? Can libraries work with such providers to offer students fast, affordable access to content that the library does not own? Can libraries generate income through revenue sharing through such services?

The proliferation of devices and apps could perhaps provide publishers with an additional income stream that would allow libraries to license core e-content at an affordable price. For example, the library could license an e-textbook that is a simple flat PDF fax of the printed book and the student could pay extra to access it in ePub format on their e-book reader, or as an enhanced e-learning app on their iPad. Or could the library-licensed e-book site include a link for the student to purchase a print-on-demand copy at a discounted price?

The future will doubtless be very different from the present, and it will be a challenge for libraries, publishers and intermediaries to find the solutions that work best for users while ensuring that each player in the supply chain brings sufficient value to the process to justify their continued existence.

References

Amazon (2011) *Amazon to Launch Library Lending for Kindle Books*,
   http://phx.corporate-ir.net/phoenix.zhtml?ID=1552678&c=176060&p=irol-newsArticle.
Bruner, J. (2011, March 25) *Tim O'Reilly on Piracy, Tinkering, and the Future of the Book*, Message

posted to http://blogs.forbes.com/jonbruner/2011/03/25/tim-oreilly-on-piracy-tinkering-and-the-future-of-the-book/.

Bucknell, T. D. (2009) The 'Big Deal' Approach to Acquiring E-books: a usage-based study, *Serials*, **23** (2), 126–34.

Bucknell, T. D. (2011) *Buying by the Bucketful* (presented at 2011 UKSG Conference, Harrogate), http://prezi.com/hgzl2iw2wuvh/.

COUNTER (2006) *The COUNTER Code of Practice – Books and Reference Works: Release 1*, www.projectcounter.org/cop/books/cop_books_ref.pdf.

Dudley, B. (2011) *Kindle So-so for Students, UW study concludes*, http://seattletimes.nwsource.com/html/technologybrierdudleysblog/2014937738_kindle_so-so_for_students_uw_s.html.

Hames, I. (2011) Patron-Driven Acquisition (PDA) and Other Trends in eBook Access (presented at 2011 ASA Conference, London), www.subscription-agents.org/system/files/Ian%20Hames%20ASA%202011.ppt.

JISC Collections (2009) *JISC National E-Books Observatory Project – Key Finding and Recommendations – Final Report*, http://observatory.jiscebooks.org/reports/jisc-national-e-books-observatory-project-key-findings-and-recommendations/.

Sharp, S. and Thompson, S. (2010) 'Just in case' vs. 'Just in time': e-book purchasing models, *Serials*, **23** (3), 201–6.

Springer (2010) *A Survey of eBook Usage and Perceptions at the University of Liverpool*, www.springer.com/cda/content/document/cda_downloaddocument/V7671+Liverpool+White+Paper+Part2.pdf?SGWID=0-0-45-1037538-0.

Notes

1 www.proquest.co.uk/products_pq/descriptions/safari_tech_books.shtml.

2 http://site.ebrary.com/lib/academiccompletetitles/home.action.

3 www.myilibrary.com.

4 www.dawsonera.com.

5 Digital Rights Management is an access control technology used by hardware manufacturers, publishers, copyright holders and individuals to limit the use of digital content.

6 www.swetswise.com.

7 Millennium from Innovative Interfaces Inc - www.iii.com/products/millennium_ils.shtml.

8 Ezproxy is extensively used by libraries to provide remote access to websites that authenticate users by IP address to allow users to login to bibliographic databases and other electronic resources that their library subscribes to.

9 http://office.microsoft.com/en-us/excel-help/results.aspx?qu=vlookup.

10 www.google.com/fusiontables/Home/.

11 www.reference-tree.com/.

6

E-book collection development in public libraries: a case study of the Essex experience

Martin Palmer

Introduction: the early days . . .

In 2002 Essex Libraries were asked by the Co-East partnership (a co-operative organization consisting of all the public library authorities in the east of England at that time) and Loughborough University to host a project funded by the LASER Foundation to investigate the feasibility of providing e-books in UK public libraries. This chapter outlines the project and uses the perspective of collection development to discuss the issues arising from it.

Context

It is true to say that – at the start of the project – the question of collection development was not among the highest priorities on the project's list of things to consider. This was partly because a number of what seemed to be more pressing questions had sprung to mind first – who might use such a service? What kind of device would they use? – but it was mainly because it was not entirely clear that the concept of collection development, as understood by librarians used to the well established patterns of the print industry, could realistically be applied to digital material.

Unlike the academic world, where a growing number of publishers – particularly of journals – had already seen that the digital approach offered an increasingly rewarding way forward, most mainstream publishers appeared to be either unaware of the potential, or – more usually – very nervous of what might happen to their content if made available to the wider world in such an apparently vulnerable format. Having seen what was beginning to happen to the recorded music industry, with peer-to-peer sharing of digital tracks decimating previously fairly resilient income streams, book publishers were perhaps understandably wary of suffering a similar fate.

As a result, the idea that the project would be able to demonstrate that public libraries could provide the same mainstream material digitally that their borrowers expected to find as a matter of course in print format began to look unlikely, to say the least. In fact, it soon became clear that such material – particularly for recreational reading – was very scarce indeed. It also quickly became equally clear that suppliers themselves were not exactly overabundant, and seemingly all based in the USA.

Suppliers

Not only were these organizations few in number, but the term 'supplier' also disguised the fact that these organizations were not quite the same kind of company as the long-established 'library suppliers' of print material. They certainly shared the same basic supply-chain role – acting as an intermediary between the publisher and the library and providing various value-added services – but the activities that each performed (inevitably, in light of the difference in types of product supplied) were very different. Nevertheless, the function they fulfilled was essentially very similar – to supply the product in a form readily usable by the public.

So, instead of 'processing' titles – jacketing, adding spine labels, and so forth – to make them shelf-ready, the suppliers of electronic resources provided the means by which the material could be easily accessed by library users. This usually meant the provision of a 'platform' of some kind – usually a website – to enable delivery, authentication and all the other processes required to manage the pathway between the publishers' content and the end-user.

The pathway for digital content was in turn very different from that for print material; librarians used to ordering any title of interest to their readers simply by tracing it as being 'in print' and forwarding the ISBN to their supplier would find that the process was not quite so straightforward for e-books. First, bibliographic control of e-material at this time was virtually non-existent, but more importantly, selection of titles was essentially limited to material listed in the supplier's catalogue. A title might well be available in digital format, but unless it was deliverable via the supplier's platform it would not be possible to provide it to the library user.

As if this were not disincentive enough, the long-term survival of these suppliers – on whom so much responsibility for content development had to be placed by libraries – was not always guaranteed. For example, when Essex was first beginning to look for suppliers at the start of its project, it seemed likely that NetLibrary, based in Boulder, Colorado, would have a potential role to play as it was one of the more established providers in the market, having been set up in 1998. However, by the autumn of 2001 it had been obliged to file for Chapter 11 bankruptcy, eventually being taken over by OCLC[1] in early 2002.

Essex eventually adopted OverDrive,[2] based in Cleveland, Ohio, and ebrary,[3] based in Palo Alto, California, as the suppliers for its project. The primary reason for these choices, unsurprisingly, was that they were able to provide content that was thought to be of interest and use to a UK public library audience. On the one hand, OverDrive had a reasonably extensive range of mainly recreational reading while on the other ebrary offered a collection of mainly more academic non-fiction.

Together, they seemed to provide a good range of material for the project which – regardless of the technology involved – would (hopefully, at least) minimize the likelihood of potential users complaining about lack of content. Also, despite being USA-based companies, they both featured a large amount of UK-sourced material.

Models

The two suppliers also offered the opportunity to explore different kinds of delivery and collection development. OverDrive's service, similar in many ways to the traditional lending library model, was based on the downloading of individual copies of particular titles to a computer for eventual transfer on to a handheld device if desired. As a result, it was necessary for librarians to select titles and numbers of copies from the OverDrive catalogue in exactly the same way that they would select for a print collection. On the other hand, the ebrary model used online access, allowing simultaneous use by all library members of all the titles available. At the time of the project, the usual method of selection for ebrary was to purchase an entire collection, paying for it by a subscription based on the number of active users.

There was, of course, another source of digital material available at this time, which was both free and fairly extensive in the form of Project Gutenberg,[4] the pioneering programme originally set up in 1971. However, although an excellent example of the power of the internet and collaborative working, the fact that the material available from Project Gutenberg was almost entirely in the public domain meant that it was felt to be of comparatively little use to the Essex project. Although classics such as Dickens and *Moby Dick* clearly have a part to play in any public library collection, they cannot be relied upon to attract an audience of any significant size, nor very much in the way of repeat business. Also, although the Gutenberg collection currently stands at around 33,000 titles, it consisted of only around 5000 at the time the Essex project started.

End-user technology

The one thing that both the OverDrive and ebrary services had in common was that they were both primarily designed to be used in conjunction with PCs/Macs or laptops, in other words generic, multifunctional devices, rather than proprietary e-book readers (although OverDrive's downloads could be transferred to compatible handheld devices as well).

This was especially important for the project as, at that time, there were no longer any dedicated e-book reading devices available to buy; the Franklin e-Bookman,[5] the Rocket Book[6] and similar readers had all recently become obsolete, and so it was necessary to find services that could be used on generic equipment such as PCs instead.

This 'convergence' approach to technology had a very liberating effect on the project's approach to collection development, as it meant that selection of material was not limited by the proprietary nature of any one specific device. However, as described later in this chapter, this question has returned to the fore more recently.

Project outcome

The outcome of the pilot project, which ran for 12 months from early 2004, was that it demonstrated that enough demand and benefit had been identified to justify incorporating both the OverDrive and the ebrary services into the mainstream offer provided by Essex libraries. For more details about the project generally, there are a number of articles and reports, including Dearnley, McKnight and Morris (2004) and McKnight, Dearnley and Morris (2008).

Since then, demand has continued to grow, and both services remain a key part of provision in Essex. It is possible, therefore, to compare and contrast the original and current experience of e-book provision in Essex to explore the present state of public library digital collection development.

Growth in suppliers

Six years on from the end of the original pilot project, it is clear that public library digital collection development has changed in at least one aspect, and that is the range of available suppliers, with an increasing number of companies entering the market.

OverDrive and ebrary have both consolidated their positions as major players, but they have been joined by many others. These include not only other adopters of the aggregator role such as Ingram,[7] but also some publishers supplying their material directly. This expansion is particularly interesting from a UK viewpoint as it also includes, for the first time, the appearance of British-based suppliers. Among these are Bloomsbury,[8] now joined by other publishers in Public Library Online,[9] Askews,[10] the traditionally print-based library supplier, who launched their service during 2010 and Dawsons.[11]

Similarly, the products offered have diversified to some extent, with e-audio now being an important feature of the range provided by suppliers such as OverDrive, or indeed the primary feature for others, such as W F Howes.[12]

However, one element which has not changed significantly is that of the models for supply and delivery. Most new suppliers have adopted one or other of the models offered by OverDrive and ebrary, downloads or online access or, as in the case of the service from Dawsons, a hybrid whereby simultaneous online access is offered alongside a facility for short-term downloads from the same collection.

Equally, although ebrary now offers the facility to purchase individual titles as well as the 'whole collection' approach, the basis of supply for all companies is usually one or the other of those two models.

However, the principal aspect that remains unchanged is the very weak position in which public librarians find themselves when looking to develop digital collections, compared to that for print collections. For one thing, bibliographic control of digital material remains almost non-existent, and although companies such as Nielsen[13] and BDS[14] are working hard to remedy this, it seems likely that it will still be some time before a position remotely similar to that enjoyed for print material is achieved. For example, the question of whether different electronic formats of the same title should have separate ISBNs is but one area where trade-wide agreement appears still to be some way off.

Nevertheless, one approach aimed primarily at academic libraries – 'e-books in SwetsWise'[15] – shows how a different solution to this question can be adopted in the digital arena, by combining a degree of bibliographic control with an ordering facility. Describing itself as 'the most comprehensive e-book procurement catalogue available', it is provided by Swets Information Services[16] and does include suppliers who are also active in the public library market such as ebrary and Ingram's MyiLibrary.[17] However, at the time of writing, a product of this type designed to serve a purely public library audience has yet to appear.

Most importantly, however, the reliance on some kind of platform for delivery of digital material to the end-user means that currently, collection development is still essentially determined by the content that is available from individual suppliers. If a specific title is required to which that supplier does not have access, then the library is simply unable to provide it to its users. For the public librarian used to the print world, and buying not only a physical item but also the freedom to use it in perpetuity (or until it falls apart or becomes out of date, at least . . .), it can be easy to forget that with digital material what is being purchased is essentially a licence to use it for as long as a platform on which it can be used exists – and nothing else.

This, clearly, is a fundamental problem in terms of collection development, but it is unfortunately further complicated by another recent advance in the digital world – the appearance of a new generation of e-book reader.

E-readers

Most members of the public – currently at least – tend to think of an 'e-book' as a device rather than as the content it contains, and the recent rapid growth in the e-book reader market following the appearance of the Kindle, Sony e-reader, and many others has had something of a double-edged outcome for public libraries. On the one hand, awareness of and demand for digital content has grown hugely, but on the other, the proprietary nature of most of these devices means that problems of incompatibility often mean that not all (and in some cases, no . . .) public library content is capable of being read by them. Amazon's development of the Kindle and its content has (to date, at least) seemingly excluded any consideration of possible public library use, and so its material is effectively unavailable for library consideration.

This is further complicated – for downloads at least – by the need for the use of Digital Rights Management (DRM) software with library content (not only to protect copyright, etc. but also to manage loan periods and other library-specific requirements). As a result, the public library digital 'collection' available for use by individual borrowers will be determined by a combination of two factors – the supplier employed by the library and the device being used by the member of the public.

Digital collection development in public libraries – is it possible?

In that light, it could be suggested that collection development is simply not feasible in any meaningful sense for public libraries looking to offer e-book services to their users. At one end of the process, unpredictable and often seemingly random publishing programmes, usually further filtered by aggregators and with no universal database to indicate the availability of material, mean that locating and obtaining a specific title can be very difficult. At the other end, even if successfully delivered, it is unlikely that the item will be in a format that can be decoded by all the different devices held by individual library users.

A recent example of this was the appearance in digital format of the Dan Brown title, *The Lost Symbol*. Much was made of the fact that this title, describing the further adventures of Harvard 'symbologist' Robert Langdon, was being made available in digital format on the same day as the hardback print version. In Essex – as in many other public libraries, no doubt – this created enough interest on the part of the public to create a pre-publication waiting list for the e-book as well as that for the print version, albeit on a somewhat smaller scale.

This was certainly a significant development, and gave some indication that the public were beginning to expect, rather than being surprised, to see e-books provided by their library service. However, in terms of collection development it created a situation which public librarians – used to having to ensure the easy availability of series and sequels for a public keen to pursue titles linked by character or plot – would find unacceptable for print material. This was that while the popularity and same-day availability of *The Lost Symbol* could certainly be seen as an important event in public library e-book provision, its predecessor *The Da Vinci Code* was not available as an e-book (to UK public libraries at least) at the time *The Lost Symbol* was published on 19 July 2009, *The Da Vinci Code* not appearing as an e-book until July 2010.

The *Lost Symbol* also illustrates some of the quirks and anomalies relating to format. Much of the popularity of *The Lost Symbol* with public library e-book users could be attributed to its availability in the rapidly developing ePub format. As such, it was compatible with the Sony e-reader and some other popular handheld devices.

A few months after the release of *The Lost Symbol*, the launch of the iPad made much of its adoption of the .ePub format for its impressive 'i-Book' facility. For public library e-book users, this looked very promising, particularly as publicity (Apple, 2010) for the device seemed to indicate that it might be compatible with public library e-books:

'And because the iBooks app uses ePub, the most popular open book format in the world, you can also use it to read ePub books you get from other sources with your computer...'

Unfortunately, this proved not to be the case as the iPad (and iPhone . . .) were not designed to work with the ePub format when used in conjunction (as public library downloads do) with DRM. A solution to this has now appeared in the form of an app developed by Bluefire Productions,[18] which resolves this particular problem for Adobe formats, at least. While clearly a welcome development, it nevertheless provides a clear illustration of how and why the rapidly changing digital environment is a source of confusion for librarian and library user alike.

So, in view of this lack of structure and the seeming impermanence of much of the world of digital provision, it would perhaps be understandable if public librarians felt somewhat helpless when asked to respond to, let alone anticipate, what appear to be perfectly reasonable demands from library users, and so to abandon any attempts at coherent collection development.

However, while it is true that many of the collection development tools available to public libraries for print material currently have no digital counterparts, and that the availability of the material itself owes more to happenstance than to design, it also seems possible to suggest ways forward that at worst might manage the limitations of existing provision and at best could provide the basis for a rational policy in future.

The way ahead?

As a starting point it is clearly necessary to accept that print and digital are different, and that it is not possible – or even desirable – to apply all the principles of collection development learned from decades of best practice with print material to e-material. At the same time, such a pragmatic approach should not be allowed to justify a straightforward abandonment of professionalism, or even common sense. In fact, it seems reasonable to argue that the constraints that currently affect the provision of digital material in public libraries make the discipline of some kind of collection development policy all the more pressing.

It will be necessary, for example, to recognize the fundamental differences in approach implied by the supply model chosen – whether the purchase of individual titles or entire collections. While the latter may seem unique to the digital world and be seen by some to be an abdication of professional responsibility, it seems little different in practice – and in philosophy – from the widely adopted use of supplier selection for print material.

Similarly, the method of delivery will also have an impact on how collection development is approached. Online access will largely obviate the need for concern about format, since this method will typically make the entire collection available to anybody with a PC, Mac, Smart phone or any web-enabled device. Conversely, it will also mean that what is provided in this way will be unavailable to users of most e-reading devices since they have tended not to have any web access at all (Kindle and a small number of others excepted . . .) and so consequently may well not be perceived to be an e-book service by many people.

On the other hand, a service based on downloads will be attractive to the increasing number of users of dedicated e-readers, attracted by their improving specifications and falling prices. It will, unfortunately, also require the development of some kind of rationale regarding choice of format; at the time of writing, the most widely accepted one appears to be ePub, and this seems likely to continue to be the case for some time. The availability of the Bluefire reader app also shows that the DRM problem can be resolved for users of some generic devices such as the iPad and iPhone, but DRM seems likely to continue to cloud the issue for librarians and users alike for the foreseeable future.

The statement by Stephen Page, Chief Executive Officer of Faber, at the UK Public Library Authority Conference in 2010 (Page, 2010) outlined four criteria which represented UK publishers' starting point for making e-books available to public libraries, the most controversial of which was that library users would have to 'come on to the library's physical premises and download an e-book at a computer terminal onto a mobile device'.

He also made it clear, however, that some publishers might not make such a stipulation.

Perhaps what these issues actually illustrate is that at least some librarians may have an unrealistic view of the e-book world, and judge it by criteria that they do not apply to that of print, particularly in terms of the longevity and popularity expected of the e-material they buy.

For example, it is perhaps understandable that concerns about future proofing and protection of investment should figure highly, particularly in light of the set-up costs of some digital services. However, although paperback books are bought in the expectation that they will achieve somewhere between 50 and 80 loans before they fall either apart or out of favour, the e-book's theoretical permanence (platforms and access permitting) may have created an unwitting impression that its purchase is a once-and-for-all activity, and that the principles of stock management – with the need to edit and withdraw items – no longer apply.

This, clearly, is not the case. While part of the attraction of the e-book is its durability, being able to be lent an infinite number of times in theory, it nevertheless needs to be recognized that this may not always be an advantage. A ten-year-old guidebook to Los Angeles needs to be withdrawn regardless of whether its format is one of print or pixels, and so the basic principles of collection development do still appear to have a place in the toolkit of the manager of the digital public library.

Conclusion

Although e-books are still a comparatively new resource for the public librarian, it does seem clear that collection development concepts can be applied effectively to them. However, the digital world is one of rapid change and continuous development, and the structure of the e-book world is different from that of the print industry. Consequently, the relative freedom that the public library enjoys in developing its print collection is not available in the digital environment. This is because of the need to accommodate a range of approaches to models of supply, platform provision, mode of delivery and choice of format – all of which impinge on the ability of the end-user to access the material.

This complexity suggests that public library managers will need to employ a much wider range of criteria than those used traditionally to inform their collection development policy. This is inevitable in light of the questions of compatibility and usability arising from the technology, but there will also be some states of affairs over which individual public libraries can have little influence.

Industry-level approaches to technological developments and problem solving obviously mean that some collection development decisions are effectively made for librarians by others – although national groups and organizations representing librarians may (and do) engage in trying to influence decisions.

However, within such constraints, it seems clear that the success of any public library e-book service aiming to meet and anticipate the demands of its users is likely to be just as dependent as its print-based cousins on a clear and rational collection development policy.

References

Apple (2010) *Using itunes to add epub files to ibooks*,
www.apple.com/itunes/itunes-news/2010/04/using-itunes-to-add-epub-files-to-ibooks.html.

Dearnley, J., McKnight, C. and Morris, A. (2004) Electronic Book Usage in Public Libraries: a study of user and staff reactions to a PDA-based collection, *Journal of Librarianship and Information Science*, **36** (4), 175–82.

McKnight, C., Dearnley, J. and Morris, A. (2008) Making ebooks Available Through Public Libraries: some user reactions, *Journal of Librarianship and Information Science*, **40** (1), 31–43.

Page, B. (2010) *PA Sets Out Restrictions on Library e-book Lending*,
www.thebookseller.com/news/pa-sets-out-restrictions-library-e-book-lending.html.

Notes

1 www.oclc.org.

2 www.overdrive.com.

3 www.ebrary.com.

4 www.gutenberg.org.

5 www.franklin.com.

6 http://gdgt.com/nuvomedia/rocket ebook.

7 www.ingramcontent.com.

8 www.bloomsbury.com.

9 www.publiclibraryonline.wordpress.com.

10 www.askews.co.uk.

11 www.dawsonbooks.co.uk.

12 www.wfhowes.co.uk.

13 www.nielsenbookdata.co.uk.

14 www.bibliographicdata.co.uk.

15 www.swetswise.com.

16 www.swets.com.

17 www.myilibrary.com.

18 www.bluefirereader.com.

7

Stewardship and curation in a digital world

Bradley Daigle

Introduction

In order to get a sense of what is at stake in the necessary stewardship and curation of collections, one can simply look at what is valued today. We often look to history to help us learn, grow and avoid repeating mistakes. How do we do this? We do this by consulting materials that have been passed down from age to age. The research process is one that builds on what has come before it. This process relies on the availability of content from all areas of life. These initially raw materials have been gathered, collected and preserved: they have been stewarded. It is largely due to this stewardship practice that they have survived till today. Granted, some element of serendipity has been involved in determining what survives across time but more importantly, there is human intervention. We create repositories and archives to properly house these materials. We describe and arrange these materials so that we know what we store. These activities can be described as stewardship and curation. All the traditional skills used to preserve content now apply equally – and perhaps one could argue to an even greater degree – to digital materials. If we are to avoid Terry Kuny's 'digital dark age' (Kuny, 1997) then we need to apply the same attention to digital materials as we do to physical ones. Therefore digital stewardship and digital curation pay homage to our efforts to preserve physical materials as well as guiding us in what we need to do for digital content.

To be successful in digital curation in the 21st century one must understand the environment in which one works. This is perhaps the most difficult information to gather and understand. Knowing what your area of influence relies upon: what are the internal and external dependencies is critical to achieving success. Therefore any strategic plan needs to be based in a form of practical reality – tied to what is actually achievable given the environment and resources at hand. As will be discussed later in more detail, it is often the responsibility of individual curators (in this sense) to paint a picture for policy makers and administrators of what is needed for the proper stewardship of library materials. Learning what the issues are and how they will affect your mission is your main goal. You must ascertain a sense of the big picture.

Most institutions and departments already have one or many of the components of a successful curation programme. Examples of these components are copyright policies, service agreements with other units in the organizations and production standards for new materials. However, it is rare that any one place has all the components. This is due to the complexity of the stewardship landscape and the fact that proper stewardship will often require more resources than any one unit can support. There are many interdependencies that need to be worked through – relationships and collaborations among partners who hold different pieces of the overall puzzle that must be considered. Knowing where you and your department, unit, library, archive, organization and institution fit into the interdependencies of stewardship is essential to supporting the longevity and success of your mission.

What you will learn in this chapter:

- Defining the terms: preservation, stewardship and persistence.
- Outlining the components of digital curation.
- We have proved that we can digitize, can we prove that we can steward?
- The importance and practice of stewardship.
- The concept of curation in a digital world.
- The difference between digital and analogue curation.
- Crafting the appropriate stewardship policy.
- Stewardship strategies: digital forensics; migration; sustaining digital scholarship.

Defining the terms: preservation, stewardship and persistence

Is there a difference between preservation and stewardship? Yes. Stewardship as a concept has been around for centuries. It relates to the management of resources. It can be interpreted as the philosophy and means by which an institution exercises ethical accountability in the use of resources. This can extend beyond just library content but within library discourse, stewardship builds the trust between libraries and users[1] (Curry n.d.). At their core, libraries have committed to making materials available and useful to users. A proper stewardship philosophy underscores this trust and manages the resources required to execute the terms of that trust as defined by the institution. Often, people consider preservation to be synonymous with stewardship but it does not necessarily mean the same thing. In other words, there is a potential disconnect between what users have historically considered to be preservation and what now is possible with stewardship. This is particularly true when the content in question is digital. To put it differently: when one is speaking about digital objects, one can say that something is 'preserved' but preservation does not imply that objects are accessible to a user. Inaccessibility could be due to elements such as format limitations and hardware/software obsolescence. So, byte by byte this object may exist complete in its integrity, that is, it has been preserved, but there may be no practical way to deliver it to a user. A good example of the disconnect between preservation and stewardship lies in the handling of physical media. Archivists can 'preserve' a diskette as a physical object but can they deliver the information it contains? Without delivering the content, what use is just preserving the physical object? Does that act of preservation meet your users' needs? The answer should be tied to your organization's stewardship philosophy. In addition to the act of physically preserving the physical object, the stewardship process is a carefully curated series of actions,[2] guided by a set of policies which can indicate to users a series of actions that can be executed on a set of digital objects. Another way to view the concept of stewardship is to consider what level of access users need. More recent academic discourse has taken up the term 'persistence' to represent the long-term need for access to the digital object. In the world of digital scholarship, it is paramount that digital objects or even aggregations of objects be identifiable as discrete materials.[3] There is a symbiotic relationship in the digital realm that exceeds that of the physical. In the latter, objects can be linked by bibliographic citation and within libraries there is confidence that those physical materials will be available for other scholars to consult. However, in the digital realm, those links are unreliable dependencies, a condition known as 'link rot'[4] (Bugeja and Dimitrova, 2010; Howard, 2010). Persistence can be considered from a technological standpoint (i.e. an image file will remain an image file and be accessible in some real way) but also from a 'bibliographic' perspective. It is no easy task to maintain the integrity of a digital object but it is an additional commitment to maintain persistence to those objects. Any librarian should carefully consider the implications of putting materials online that others will want to use, cite or repurpose in some way.[5] Part of a librarian's responsibility in proper stewardship is to consider these issues.

What is digital curation?

How does curation fit into a stewardship plan? Curation adds value to library content and places it within a larger scholarly context and technological framework. Good stewardship practice has curation as one of its cornerstones. Proper curatorial practice dictates that an organization is only stewarding content that it can manage and justify as part of its mission – materials that fit into its collecting criteria.[6] Digital curation tracks the life cycle of the digital object.[7] It covers the creation of digital objects, their proper management and ultimate preservation. In other words, digital curation forms a significant part of the stewardship process. In many ways, the most important part of digital curation is the selection and creation of digital content. This is where most organizations struggle with their overall stewardship strategy and it requires special attention.

We have proved that we can digitize, can we prove that we can steward?

By the late 1990s scanners were in use by libraries across the USA. At that time, given their cost, size and format restrictions, they did not have a major impact on digital production output. They were still seen as a technological oddity, inferior in many ways to photographic reproduction and certainly not as reliable. Also, librarians needed to learn new skills to support and manage them. Technologies such as SCSI interfaces, firewire and serial ports all had to be understood and supported to make these scanners do their magic. Only flat materials could be effectively scanned. However, over time, as computer skills became more ubiquitous and scanner design more responsive to user needs it became much easier to convert physical materials to a digital format.

By the mid 2000s, terms such as 'mass digitization' began to filter into the discourse of library professionals. Mass digitization was the marriage of production and content. Most major academic libraries were in a technological arms race to build digital library production centres to do massive collection refactoring on a scale previously unknown to users. These production sites churned out digital content at high rates. On the one hand, mass digitization seemed to serve the needs of their users but on the other hand there were also calls by librarians for a concerted approach to digital collection development.[8] This wound up being too difficult to manage from a curatorial perspective – particularly with respect to metadata. Therefore there arose an attempt to use systems such as the Open Archives Initiative (OAI) model.[9] Unfortunately several years later much of the data produced through these efforts remains localized, unrelated and not connected up to larger needs for a centralized clearing house of digitized objects. Given that a great deal of the content created by libraries could be considered rare and unique, many individual institutions are hesitant to give up their 'branding' of the materials and have them redistributed in a form that is disassociated from the original repository. An excellent example of mass digitization with unclear curatorial practice is the Google Book Project.

When the Google Book Project hit the content scene in 2005, the approach to stewarding digital content took an entirely different angle. The issues of the Google debate have been heavily discussed and disputed elsewhere[10] (Vaidhyanathan, 2010). For the purposes of this discussion, the Google Book Project is an excellent example of how mass digitization without clearly articulated goals and objectives can cause controversy, confusion and consternation among users, librarians and publishers. Google Books is an example of mass digitization that focuses on getting content up and available and less on the quality of the digital product. Users and administrators often cite the increased availability of content as a desirable goal. However, it is unlikely that any one organization can muster the same resources as Google. Even local versions of mass digitization are unsuccessful when there is no commensurate support strategy in place. In other words, the content is made available but there is no stewardship strategy for the content. It lives as an inchoate mass – often more frustrating to users than no accessibility at all. This is why an organization should be careful in creating new content when there is no digital curation and stewardship policy in place. Before one embarks on crafting such a policy, a librarian should conduct an environmental scan.

The importance and practice of stewardship

In order to avoid the realities of digitization without a clear goal in mind there should be discussions that relate to what an organization seeks to accomplish. A good place to start would be for an organization to assess the costs of its stewardship and curation strategy. Costs often come in the form of staff time and effort for both the management of legacy and new content. Costs such as equipment, warranties and training are obvious.

In addition to these there are indirect and often buried costs that relate to organizational infrastructure. For example:

- Are there adequate system administrators to manage the hardware?
- What are their current tasks?
- Do the librarians have access to tiered storage for your materials?
- Does the delivery solution have what is required by users to interact with the materials?
- Does the organization need developers to enhance the user interface, the system architecture?
- Does the institution use an 'out of the box' software package to deliver content?
- What is the state of the collection's metadata? Is it sufficient? Does it need enhancement? If so, who will undertake that work?

These are all essential questions for developing a successful stewardship strategy but are often overlooked. Avoiding the traps of absorbing hidden costs can be best achieved by determining the workload and timeframe. Librarians and others involved in planning the digital strategy should articulate goals and outcomes as granularly as possible for the organization including those who will be managing the work. This is best accomplished by matching goals to financial ability.

Within any organization, much of this cost will directly relate to the level of staff involved. Each person who will be involved should be part of this cost structure. Equipment such as scanners, computers, cameras, hard drives – any hardware or software – should be included as well. Not only should the cost of that material be included but it should also take into account the technology refresh rate (i.e. how often the equipment would need to be replaced) and warranties. Any student labour that may be involved, vendor services and contracts should all be part of the equation. The more your organization can account for all interdependencies in the digitization process, the better its overall strategy will map to your organization's mission.

The concept of curation in a digital world

Curation is a vexed proposition in today's digital world. In fact, like our physical collections, the need to have properly curated collections is more relevant than ever. Think about how libraries have functioned in the past: libraries, archives, repositories of content (at least the good ones) all had carefully crafted collection development policies, mission statements and a solid sense of who their main constituents were. For example, academic libraries understood that their mission often was to directly support the teaching and research of their students and faculty. There were external users and researchers, but their primary goal was to develop curated collections that reflected the research areas of their faculty. This is also true for public libraries. Collections and services that are offered by public libraries should always reflect the direct needs of their users. Depending on the size of the library, these services could be as local as the library's immediate neighbourhood. If curation is done properly then it will align with the users' needs and the role of the library will be obvious. However, if there is little or no intentionality behind the collections, it is difficult to justify the resources required to house these collections.

The difference between digital and analogue curation

Digital stewardship embodies many of the same core principles involved in the curation of physical collections. As mentioned earlier this can mean elements such as the selection of content, intellectual and technical analyses of content, determination of copyright and intellectual property issues, and access issues. Digital curation becomes more complex with regard to the scope of materials and their access. Volume of materials is also a major issue. In a physical world there could be a collection with millions of items in it, but that is unusual. In the born-digital world, this is much more the norm. Also, there is the need to assign the appropriate levels of access to individual items within those millions of objects. Some of this can certainly be done programmatically but much of it will have to be conducted by a human process of selection and identification. This is just the beginning. Properly curating a digital collection is a highly complex task that no one individual can do alone. There are differences among the collection types as well[11] (Cunningham, 2007). It is highly unlikely that a single person can undertake the selection, description, processing, technical assessment, IP verification, ingesting, etc. into a managed environment. It is more likely that it will consist of a team working with finely tuned workflows. Therefore, in order to ascertain what is involved in your organization's stewardship practice, one must have a policy (or set of policies) for guidance.

One cannot stress enough the critical role of metadata in the stewardship world. Without properly described objects, then both stewards and users are overwhelmed quickly by content. It is only through the appropriate description of materials that curation can take place. There can be no added value to content if users cannot discover and interact with it. Therefore, a pivotal part of any stewardship strategy involves metadata creation. Frequently, this work is done in another unit besides the one that is stewarding the digital objects – this is why collaboration among units is so important in the stewardship process. This applies to all collections that are being stewarded.

Crafting the appropriate stewardship policy

How does one provide for a successful digital stewardship practice? In general, good practice comes from clear institutional policy. This policy should be undertaken as a co-operative agreement among the participants involved in the workflows that provide for digital stewardship. The policy should contain the overall mission of the organization with respect to digital materials as well as indicators as to how the mission will be accomplished. The following section highlights some basic questions to guide creation of a successful digital stewardship policy. This list is not meant to be exhaustive but rather suggests some of the high-level areas of consideration. Depending on your organization, some areas might not apply, but each is a good step toward creating a digital stewardship strategy.

1   Determine the scope of your organization's policy. In other words, who are your major constituents? Does your organization support faculty research? Teaching? Community development? Corporate archives? If the mission is to manage corporate archives, then you will not necessarily have to worry about teaching needs or the community interacting with the materials. If your organization is an academic library, you will be concerned with the faculty's need for collections that relate to their teaching and research. Undergraduates will also be heavy users of your content and rely on its availability for their classes. Public libraries have a combination of research, teaching and general community access. Most likely your organization has a sense of what its mission is, though it may not be formally articulated. If you are charged with creating a stewardship policy then talk to administrators at all levels of your organization to determine the core mission.

2   Integrate your stewardship work with your organization's collection development policies. If your organization has a mission, then it is likely that collecting principles are tied to it. For example, if a library supports a business school, then the library's main collecting area is well defined – business topics. Similarly, a public library might collect mainly local materials combined with other general collection content. It is critical that your organization determines its collecting goals and strengths first, in order to then have a successful stewardship philosophy. Inevitably, your organization will need to prioritize some materials over others. This is even true of special library collections. As a result of designating priorities, resource decisions need to be made. Assessing the state of your organization's collection development strategy will allow you to extrapolate its tenets and apply them to digital collections: they should match each other.

3   Establish provenance. Where does your organization get its digital materials? Is it primarily through transforming its own physical collections? Is it exclusively the output of your organization? Does your library have a combination of owned and licensed content? Is there purchased content? Documenting the disposition of content will help guide treatment of the materials. In other words, your organization needs a strategy for each type of content. Ownership will relate directly to what level of stewardship your organization can provide for the materials. In mixed environments of owned, licensed and purchased content, it will be a challenge to establish consensus as to how the materials need to be managed. That is why each type of content should have its own management strategy.[12] You will need to know exactly what actions can be executed on which materials.

4   Develop a shared understanding. A memorandum of understanding (MOU) will be needed for materials that are given to a repository or organization, especially if the organization wants to include the collection in its managed environment. With vendors and purchased content this is often in the form of a contract, agreement, or EULA (End User Licence Agreement). Vendors often provide MOU templates filled with legalese, which is often only given a cursory glance by end-users. It can often be easier starting with a template document and modifying it on a case-by-

case basis. A formal MOU between your organization and a group or individual is often based on a generic structure but then is customized to accommodate the specific situation. These MOUs should contain all the basic agreed upon principles that will establish a shared understanding of what the content is, how it can be used (e.g. redistribution rights), what level of access can be granted and other details such as service level agreements (SLA).[13]

5 Determine the appropriate level of service and the service owners. A proper stewardship policy should be able to map specific services to levels of operation. This is essentially what an SLA does. For example, if your organization employs an integrated library system (ILS) then it is likely that that is the most heavily used access point for your content. As such, it should garner the highest level of service. This could mean that the hardware and software delivering content might have a support plan to guarantee 'up time' of 24 hours a day, 7 days a week, 365 days a year (24x7x365). Other, less critical services might only require a 9 to 5 weekday-only model (9x5x5). This will depend on both the available infrastructure (staff, resources) as well as the demand on content. Your critical content, your high, medium, low priority content should all map to a specific level of service with the service owners clearly identified. Who gets the call at 3 a.m. on a Sunday to address problems with the service? The appropriate owner must be able to solve the problem – system administrators, software developers, user services, for example. The creation of a workable digital stewardship policy relies heavily on the existing infrastructure. Therefore, all those involved in creating policy need to have a thorough knowledge of infrastructure capacity. These services may also be tied to production-related activities. If you create your own content – high-resolution images, PDFs, XML text – consistency is the key. Multiple formats make for a more complex and more expensive stewardship practice. If your organization uses a vendor to create or transform your data, then this work will still need to be quality checked and verified by local staff. Any content that is either created locally or by a vendor needs appropriate quality assurance, otherwise you may be confronted with a mass of useless materials floating around the internet.

Stewardship strategies: digital forensics

Your organization's stewardship strategy may involve different approaches to curatorial practices. These are as varied as your group's production options. Depending on your curation strategy some options need to be considered for the stewardship of digital materials. Digital forensics is an example of one approach that adopts a highly granular view of digital stewardship. This approach seeks to capture as much data as possible from physical media (diskettes, CDs, hard drives, etc.) as well as third party hosting solutions (Google Docs, Flickr, Facebook, etc.). After collecting this data, the goal then is to recombine the whole of an individual's digital expression in as many forms as it has been manifest.[14] Take for example, the work of the Maryland Institute for Technology in the Humanities (MITH), Emory University, and the British Library. These organizations take digital forensics seriously and have been pushing new frontiers in the stewardship of digital materials through forensics. They often collect old computer hardware and software in order to represent the materials as they were in their original environment. Emory and the British Library have examples of collections that are curated from a deeply forensic perspective. At Emory, the Salman Rushdie collection features several computers owned by Rushdie. All the machines are running the operating systems and software that Rushdie used.[15] The British Library was one of the first organizations to recognize the role that forensic specialists could play in the archival world. The Digital Lives Project exemplifies issues that surround personal digital archives in the 21st century and is worth careful examination.[16] The primary goal of such an approach is to manage the content through the historical computer environments that originally delivered it. This is a very complex and difficult approach to take. Most organizations will opt for a blended strategy that migrates the content from version to version or format to format.

Stewardship strategies: migration

Forensic approaches examine the bits and bytes of collections and adopt a very atomistic approach to their curation. However, there are other collection arrangement and description approaches that focus largely on the aggregate approach. Just like in the analogue world, the digital world can have collections that are described at the item level or collection level. For example, when retrieving information from the physical media (e.g. a hard drive), a repository might keep a logical or forensic disk image of the materials because their stewardship strategy is one of migration, not emulation. In other words, rather than create an actual or emulation environment that ran the original software, some kind of transformation needs to take place. To put it differently, an original hard drive might have documents written in the original 1980s' WordStar application. However, the repository has no means to deliver WordStar files to an end-user so these files are transformed into PDFs – perhaps. That is an example where the choice could be made to keep the original WordStar files as part of the original capture from the hard drive but then a copy is also made for transformation and delivery. That is the blended nature of this approach: the original content is preserved at some level but a transformed version is what is used for the access copy. The description of the object is the same but the delivery strategy differs.

Stewardship strategies: sustaining digital scholarship

Unlike many personal archives, which are the sum of many different files, there is also the concept of digital scholarship. Digital scholarship has many forms but can be loosely defined as a digital project where the content, tools and methodologies of creation are all equally important and must be preserved as accurately as possible. This becomes very challenging when the software and environment in which the materials were created become integral to their preservation.[17] There can be many different levels of preservation, depending on your organization's aspirations and realities with regard to staff, resources and technology. The University of Virginia has identified five general different areas to which we map each project.[18]

There is a significant difference between the handling of materials that are already digitized and those that are in production to be converted from analogue to digital. However, a good rule of practice is to streamline the workflows. This is not always possible but streamlining should be a goal. One way this can be achieved is to standardize certain formats for stewardship. However, this may not be possible when dealing with very old materials. What then? Solid curation practice anticipates the digital stewardship of all materials. Therefore your organization must have a strategy for content that does not meet its current standards for digital materials. For example, what about the case of a website that only contains JPEG images and no archival masters exist? Does a library decide not to collect the material for stewarding or do staff try to find the originals again and redigitize? These are tough questions and will undoubtedly be undertaken on a case-by-case basis. In other cases, updating a format type (e.g. software versions) is more straightforward. That said, do not underestimate the resources involved in such an undertaking. This type of refactoring work needs to be part of the cost analysis in your stewardship model. If an organization adopts a refactoring (or migration) strategy then the reality is that this task will be iterative and ongoing.

Controlling and being intentional about the types of content your area creates is critical to long-term plans of curating these materials. It is more difficult to sustain content if your organization is managing multiple formats within a given service. For example, if a unit has to maintain similar materials (e.g. images) that are in variant formats, stewardship becomes much more difficult because of the format expertise and required training. One approach is to develop exemplars for each file type. Exemplars can often fall under the best practices of creating archival master files, delivery masters and derivative delivery files. Using this strategy, your organization can more easily manage its content by only curating the archival files and recreating delivery files as needed or as the technology changes. So if your organization contains a production service that creates digital images, it may want to decide that TIFF is standard archival format and JP2 is the delivery master with thumbnail JPEGs for metadata and quick reference. This provides a fully functional suite of image services that can be used to manage digital images for as long as needed.

Finally, a good stewardship policy has access and delivery issues firmly in mind when mapping out strategies. I have mentioned how an organization must understand its audience with respect to curation and stewardship activities. But how do users fit into those activities? What do your organization's users want to do with the content? Edit it? Download it? Enhance it? Save it to their account? These are just some examples of functionalities that may need to be built into any system your organization uses. User interaction with content will largely depend on your organization's systems architecture. For example, can users only find individual manuscripts by searching through the online finding aids or are those objects discoverable as discrete items?

One overarching issue related to any stewarded materials is intellectual property (IP). This can often be confused with copyright but they are not quite the same[19] (Hirtle, Hudson and Kenyon, 2009; King, 2008). Copyright also varies whether or not an object has been published. Therefore, it is very important that both the stewards and the curators of content understand what the implications can be for making materials available online and what their options are if this content needs to fall under a stewardship policy. Bringing in legal counsel when sorting out intellectual property issues is prudent. However, it is ultimately the organization's responsibility to understand how IP issues fit in with a stewardship. Having a delivery architecture that can be sensitive to the many layers of rights is fundamental to having a functional plan for stewarding content. These rights policies often are masked in discussions of metadata and should be added to the caveats mentioned above. It would also be advisable that a digital object management system allows for the easy editing of the rights metadata. That way much of the work updating the policies on digital objects can be accomplished through software programmatic scripts. Copyright and IP issues are a significant challenge to stewardship but are not insurmountable. It is for issues such as these that a stewardship policy is critical to making your content available to users in an appropriate manner.

Conclusion

The major key to success in both the curation and stewardship of any organization's content is understanding what the goals are for making this content available. Selecting, producing, managing and preserving content becomes more straightforward when there is clarity around why this work is being done. To make this possible, collaboration plays a major role. Unless you work within a very small organization, there will be handoffs to and from other units. Raising as many issues related to the stewardship of the content before users rely on it may seem like a lot of work, but it will be work that saves you much, much more down the line. Here are some final questions to consider, the answers to which should help decide where your organization needs to put effort:

• Does your organization have a stewardship policy?
• Who are the major stakeholders in these stewardship activities: selection, production, management, intellectual property, and preservation? Does each of these areas know where the other activities fit in to theirs?
• Does your organization have published standards to follow for the digitization of materials?
• What is your organization's preservation strategy? Is it emulation, migration, forensic? Does it even have one?
• What are the major components of a stewardship strategy that your organization can take on? What might it have to outsource?
• Does each service your organization offers to its constituents have an 'owner'? Can this owner articulate the real costs of that service?

Further reading

Allard, S., Mack, T. R. and Feltner-Reichert, M. (2005) The Librarian's Role in Institutional Repositories: a content analysis of the literature, *Reference Services Review*, **33** (3), 325–36.

ARL Digital Repository Issues Task Force (2009) *The Research Library's Role in Digital Repository Services: final report of the ARL Digital Repository Issues Task Force*, Washington, DC: Association of Research Libraries, www.arl.org/bm~doc/repository-services-report.pdf.

Dale, R. L (2007) Digital Curators: who, what, and how: a perspective from OCLC Programs & Research. Paper presented at DigCCurr2007: An International Symposium on Digital Curation, Chapel Hill, North Carolina, www.ils.unc.edu/digccurr2007/slides/dale_slides_3-3.pdf.

Farb, S. (2006) Libraries, Licensing and the Challenge of Stewardship, *First Monday*, **11** (7), http://firstmonday.org/htbin/cgiwrap/bin/ojs/index.php/fm/article/view/1364.

Hilse, H.-W., and Kothe, J. (2006) *Implementing Persistent Identifiers: overview of concepts, guidelines and recommendations*, Consortium of European Research Libraries, http://nbn-resolving.de/urn:nbn:de:gbv:7-isbn-90-6984-508-3-8.

Kirschenbaum, M. (2008) *Mechanisms: new media and the forensic imagination*, MIT Press.

Read, M. (2008) Libraries and Repositories, *New Review of Academic Librarianship*, **14** (1/2), 71–8.

Tibbo, H. R. (2003) On the Nature and Importance of Archiving in the Digital Age, *Advances in Computers*, **57**, 2–69.

Vardigan, M. and Whiteman, C. (2007) OAIS Meets ICPSR: applying the OAIS Reference Model to the Social Science Archive Context, *Archival Science*, **7**, 73–87.

Walters, T. O. (2007) Reinventing the Library – how repositories are causing librarians to rethink their professional roles, *portal: Libraries and the Academy*, **7** (2), 213–25, http://smartech.gatech.edu/handle/1853/14421.

Watterworth, M. (2009) Planting Seeds for a Successful Institutional Repository: role of the archivist as manager, designer, and policymaker, *Journal of Archival Organization*, **7** (1/2), 24–32.

References

Bugeja, M. and Dimitrova, D. V. (2010) *Vanishing Act: the erosion of online footnotes and implications for scholarship in the digital age*, Litwin Books, LLC.

Cunningham, A. (2007) *Digital Curation/Digital Archiving: a view from the National Archives of Australia*. Paper presented at DigCCurr2007: An International Symposium on Digital Curation. Chapel Hill, North Carolina, http://ils.unc.edu/digccurr2007/papers/cunningham_paper_7.pdf.

Curry, D. (n.d.) *Digital Stewardship Now (blog)*, http://digitalstewardshipnow.wordpress.com.

Hirtle, P., Hudson, E. and Kenyon, A. T. (2009) *Copyright and Cultural Institutions: guidelines for U.S. libraries, archives, and museums*, free download: http://ecommons.cornell.edu/handle/1813/14142.

Howard, J. (2010) Publishers Find Ways to Fight 'Link Rot' in Electronic Texts, *The Chronicle of Higher Education* (05 November), A14–15.

King, E. (2008) British Library Digitization: access and copyright, *World Library and Information*

Congress: 74th IFLA General Conference and Council, August 2008,
http://archive.ifla.org/IV/ifla74/papers/139-King-en.pdf.

Kuny, T. (1997) *A Digital Dark Ages? Challenges in the preservation of electronic information,* 63rd IFLA
Council and General Conference, http://archive.ifla.org/IV/ifla63/63kuny1.pdf.

Vaidhyanathan, S. (2010) *The Googlization of Everything: how one company is disrupting culture, commerce,
and community – and why we should worry,* www.googlizationofeverything.com/.

Notes

1 David Curry's blog, *Digital Stewardship Now* (http://digitalstewardshipnow.wordpress.com/)
offers a multi-disciplinary perspective on stewardship: 'we see convergence phenomena
across libraries, archives, museum and heritage institutions of all types as signaling an
important evolutionary period as new types of collaborative projects, new business models,
and new organizational forms are explored.' See also Farb's article listed under Further
Reading, which discusses the mixed success of a cultural heritage organization's adoption of
a true stewardship role.

2 These actions can take the form of physical preservation, metadata description, documenting
of work done on both the physical and digital object, copyright and intellectual property
clearance, identifying owners of the content, and the services it requires for use.

3 This is particularly true when one considers the need for proper citation. Consider this: if
one has built a work of digital scholarship – a website, exhibit, a representation of complex
relationships among digital objects, etc., one must also provide the means to refer to
persistent digital objects outside of the creator's sphere of control. If those objects are
transient, then the scholarship that is based upon them may lose its integrity and the quality
of scholarly discourse suffers.

4 Link rot, or as Bugeja and Dimitrova call it, 'footnote flight' has been the subject of recent
debate in the publishing industry. Jennifer Howard has written about this in her column, 'Hot
Type' in the *Chronicle of Higher Education.*

5 One major component that is outside the scope of this article relates to the relationship of
the economic sustainability of stewardship. There has been some excellent work in this area
as of late. In the UK there is the Life Cycle Information for E-Literature (LIFE) project
(www.life.ac.uk/) as well as the Blue Ribbon Task Force on Sustainable Digital Preservation
and Access (http://brtf.sdsc.edu).

6 These collecting criteria would be assembled in a collection development policy – hopefully
one that covers both analogue and digital content.

7 This is perhaps most famously captured by the Digital Curation Centre's digital curation
graphic that has been extensively repurposed and reused:
(www.dcc.ac.uk/sites/default/files/documents/publications/DCCLifecycle.pdf).

8 There was some concern by librarians that there was a significant amount of duplication of
digitized materials that was squandering their limited resources. Therefore, it was hoped that
a union database of digitized materials would alleviate some of that duplication. In the early
2000s, in the USA, the Digital Library Federation attempted to create a single lookup for
materials that had been digitized: the Aquifer Project. DLF's Aquifer Project is no longer

active. There is some information related to their work on an archived version of the DLF website (www.diglib.org/aquifer/).

9 For more information on the OAI system see: Reference Model for an Open Archival Information System. Washington, DC: Consultative Committee for Space Data Systems, 2002. Figure F-1: Composite of Functional Entities. http://public.ccsds.org/publications/archive/650x0b1.pdf. To see an example of how Aquifer attempted to use OAI to accomplish this see the Aquifer blog post: http://dlfaquifer.blogspot.com/2007_12_01_archive.html.

10 See for example Siva Vaidhyanathan's *The Googlization of Everything: How One Company is Disrupting Culture, Commerce, and Community — And Why We Should Worry* www.googlizationofeverything.com/.

11 Adrian Cunningham from the National Archives of Australia made the point in 2007 that digital curation is not the same as collection management. Cunningham argues that the curation of digital records should be considered a distinct curatorial activity – once that merits a different name: digital archiving.

12 At the University of Virginia Library, for example, we have broken out our content into two main arenas: library-managed and scholar-managed. Content from the former category is material that we are directly responsible for in terms of access, preservation and stewardship. The latter we may index and deliver but we are not responsible for either the content or its management.

13 MOUs can be for internal as well as external use. Often, the stewardship of complex collections that draw upon resources beyond your unit or department but still within the organization requires a charter or MOU.

14 There are many ethical issues to be considered in this process, particularly if the donor is no longer living. Natasha Mauthner and Odette Parry provide a helpful overview of ethical issues related to digital data and exposing that content to others (http://eresearch-ethics.org/position/ethical-issues-in-digital-data-archiving-and-sharing/).

15 See www.emory.edu/home/academics/libraries/salman-rushdie.html.

16 See www.bl.uk/digital-lives/.

17 The University of Virginia undertook a prominent example of this effort with the *Valley of the Shadow Project*. This stewardship project took over a year to be successfully completed and can be read about on their website: (http://www2.lib.virginia.edu/digitalcuration/services/ValleySDS.html).

18 See http://www2.lib.virginia.edu/digitalcuration/services/SDS_Intro_final.html for an in-depth discussion of what levels of preservation could mean for an academic library.

19 These terms are often used interchangeably. However, copyright is only one form of intellectual property. Other forms of IP can be trademarks, patents, and designs. This is not an exhaustive list but there are excellent sources available for clarification. See the World Intellectual Property Organization (www.wipo.int/about-ip/en/) and for copyright issues related to digitization, Peter Hirtle, Emily Hudson, and Andrew Kenyon's excellent resource *Copyright and Cultural Institutions: guidelines for U.S. libraries, archives, and museums* (free download: http://ecommons.cornell.edu/handle/1813/14142). Also see Ed King's British Library

Digitization: access and copyright, *World Library and Information Congress: 74th IFLA General Conference and Council*, August 2008, (http://archive.ifla.org/IV/ifla74/papers/139-King-en.pdf) for a helpful overview of the issues.

Part 3

Trends in library supply

8
Managing suppliers for collection development: the UK higher education perspective

David Ball

Introduction

Publishing has traditionally been regarded as a profession for gentlemen. This is an outmoded term to be sure, but it conveys the impression of a trade that was not overly concerned about profit, of practitioners focused on some higher ideal. Librarians have also traditionally exhibited this trait of not focusing on money, perhaps by emulation, perhaps by an innate commitment to collaboration and the ideal of learning. This is epitomized in the title of the library journal devoted to the commercial nexus linking libraries, publishers and intermediaries, *Against the Grain*,[1] which implies that its subject matter is somehow at odds with traditional professional concerns.

In contrast to the USA, such distaste may have been fostered by the long existence of retail price maintenance for books in many European countries, such as Austria, France, Germany, Greece, Holland, Italy, Portugal and Spain. In Germany, for instance, publishers are legally required by the Buchpreisbindungsgesetz to set the price, including tax, at which books are sold to the end-user. The price remains fixed for a minimum of 18 months, or until a new edition is published.[2]

The UK form of retail price maintenance, the Net Book Agreement (NBA), enabled publishers to fix the prices at which books could be sold. Booksellers were not allowed to give discounts, except a fixed 10% discount under the so-called Library Licence. Libraries received the fixed discount on condition that they made their stock available to the public. This condition, obviously fulfilled by public libraries, was generally not considered too onerous by university librarians: virtually all allowed walk-in access to stock. The notable exception was the poet Philip Larkin, who as Librarian at the University of Hull from 1955–85, would not allow students of the local teacher-training institution access to the university library, and hence forfeited the 10% discount (Hinton, 1987, 45), an example of the triumph of principle over economics.

The early 1990s saw the discounting of book prices by some of the larger bookselling chains, by the mid-1990s publishers were withdrawing support and in 1997 the NBA was ruled illegal. This opened the way for the three-for-two offers and the heavy discounting by supermarkets and Amazon that are such a feature of the book trade today. The demise of the NBA also prompted academic and public libraries to seek better terms from their suppliers: booksellers were now expected to compete not only on quality of service but also, and perhaps more importantly for library and university managers, on price. The book budgets of probably all university libraries were easily big enough to fall within the purview of the European Union's procurement directives for public bodies .

Given the requirements of the directives, the application of the procurement discipline of the purchasing profession, whether through individual institutions or the university purchasing consortia, became more necessary. This of course is another instance of the trend, as the environment changes, for librarians to import and learn from the expertise of other professions: a current example is the widespread adoption of project management techniques, long used in the IT and other industries.[3]

This chapter will follow the adoption of this new procurement discipline by academic libraries since the demise of the NBA. It will first examine the standard procurement cycle, with particular reference to libraries and book supply.[4] It then discusses library purchasing consortia and their contribution to managing and developing the library marketplace for books, identifying three phases of operation. It closes with some reflections on the future prospects of collection development.

The procurement cycle

The standard procurement cycle comprises, briefly, the following five elements: identifying the need, preparing the specification, finding the supplier, awarding the contract, and measuring and monitoring performance. Following and understanding this cycle is fundamental to taking control of relationships with suppliers and of the marketplace (more detail on this process is given by Ball (2005a)).

Identifying the need

The first step is to determine precisely what is required and on what basis it should be procured – bought, leased, hired, shared . . . With hard-copy information, the emphasis is on buying and servicing the physical product. With electronic information, libraries are generally buying a service not a product: the emphasis is on access and the terms that govern it. This is a fundamental difference. With hard copy, libraries are limited only by the law (for instance of copyright); they may buy, sell, lend, do anything with the information. With electronic information, libraries are restricted by the terms of the licences, which generally limit the uses and users of the information.

It should be noted that in much procurement for libraries, the users are not consulted directly about their needs: the budget-holders, librarians, act as proxies. This may lead to a concentration on the technical issues that affect the library, such as processing of books or electronic data interchange (EDI), rather than on those that directly affect the user, such as the functionality of e-book offerings.

Preparing the specification

Once the need has been identified, it has to be expressed in a specification. This specification is fundamental to any procurement: it informs potential suppliers of what is required, how, when and to what standards. If the specification is wrong, there is no chance of satisfying adequately the procurement needs. It should contain enough information and detail to ensure that both suppliers and purchasers are addressing the same requirement, and that suppliers can cost fully the products or services required. However, except for technical compatibility, it should not be so overly specific, for instance in detailing procedures, that it prevents negotiation or discourages suppliers from proposing innovative solutions. Suppliers know their own business better than librarians do; over-specifying stifles creativity and the development of partnership, and hence decreases the potential benefits of any procurement.

It is important that the specification should also promote open and fair competition. It should not discriminate, explicitly or implicitly, against particular suppliers or products. For instance, it may be superficially attractive to prefer local suppliers. However, a relatively distant supplier that can meet the requirements (such as next-day delivery, response times) may in fact offer a higher quality service or a better price than the local supplier. A supplier should be judged on performance against the specification, not on the purchaser's preconceptions of how the goods or service should be supplied. This approach opens up competition, fostering lower prices and higher quality.

While each procurement is individual in nature, expressing an individual requirement, specifications should wherever possible adopt national or international standards or de facto standards (such as MARC). In the longer term, the adoption of standards leads to reductions in the costs of both goods and services. Suppliers are geared towards offering, for instance, shelf-ready books, with standard MARC records, Library of Congress (LC) subject headings, Dewey Decimal Classification (DDC) class numbers and standard processing. They lose economics of scale and simplicity by having to classify to local schemes or to provide (as happened in one procurement) a particular shade of duck-egg blue spine labels.

Cost is obviously an important element of any procurement. The specification should as far as possible address whole-life costs: for instance when buying or leasing equipment, costs of consumables, call-outs and maintenance should be taken into account, as well as the purchase or lease price.

The specification also provides the yardstick for evaluating any tenders received, so should be capable of being turned into measurable criteria. Obviously, this is easier for some procurements than for others. The discounts offered by booksellers on a basket of books can be compared relatively easily one with another. However, concepts such as quality of service or the user-friendliness of a system are far more difficult to quantify. This should be borne in mind when drawing up any specification: how will one score suppliers against each other when evaluating their responses?

Finding the supplier

The tender

Often the marketplace is approached through a tender process. In the UK, this process is governed by the European Union's procurement directives (underlying practice in other countries will generally be similar; pointers can be found through the national associations affiliated to the International Federation of Purchasing and Supply Management.[5] Issuing the tender document is the first step in a process leading to a contract between purchaser and suppliers. The involvement of procurement professionals from the start of the process is essential. A key element is the specification of requirements just discussed; this will in many cases be supplemented by a statement of the service levels required, for example, for supply times or customer care and any performance indicators.

The document also specifies the information required from the potential suppliers. This should include audited accounts, quality assurance accreditations, membership of professional organizations, qualifications and experience of key staff, evidence of commitment to staff development (ISO 9000, Investors in People, policies, etc.), number of staff employed in key areas and a list of major accounts. A selection from the last can be contacted for references on the performance of the supplier against key indicators.

A further important element required from potential suppliers is the price schedule. Several pricing models might be applied to library procurements:

- **Fixed price** – This is the most obvious model and the easiest to evaluate. It is used for one-off purchases or commissions, such as consultancy.
- **Discount from list price** – Hard-copy books and serials tend to be bought under this model, with intermediaries – booksellers and serials agents – offering a discount from the cover price. While ostensibly simple, some care has to be taken when evaluating suppliers under this model to check that they are quoting the same price; different approaches to exchange rates, for instance, can lead to distortions. Evaluation becomes even more complex when suppliers offer discounts that vary with the level of discount they themselves receive.
- **Cost-plus** – In the past, booksellers have tended to offer a single discount across the board. There is some risk for them in this model, since the discounts they receive from publishers or wholesalers vary: if customers order unexpectedly large numbers of titles attracting low or no discount, the bookseller will lose money. Cost-plus eliminates this risk: the supplier charges the price paid for the items and adds a fixed charge for the work carried out. This model has attractions for both sides: the supplier has a guaranteed return; the purchaser knows that the best price is achieved. However, it can be difficult to audit and manage, and, with perhaps only one exception, has generally not been offered by library suppliers.
- **Management fee** – Increasingly, library management systems suppliers are offering a facilities management service, where they not only supply the system but also manage it. This model is generally used in such cases.

Evaluating the suppliers

Generally, there are four elements to be evaluated: the financial health of the supplier, the price quoted, quality and the ability of the suppliers to meet the specification. Typically, a number of resources are used in the evaluation: published information and analyses (particularly financial), the returned tender documents, visits to suppliers' premises, customer references and meetings to clarify the information provided.

First, especially for contracts that are large or last for a number of years or are critical for carrying on the library's business, one will want to evaluate the financial viability of the potential suppliers. The companies' audited accounts give information on turnover, profits and growth and performance trends. Organizations such as Dunn & Bradstreet provide overviews of the financial health of a company, compared with any industry standards. Financial health is a pass-fail requirement. If there are justifiable doubts about the viability of a company, it should be rejected unless there are very good reasons to the contrary. No library will want to appoint a supplier that does not have the financial standing to invest in product development or may cease trading within the life of the contract.

It may also be inadvisable to award a large contract if it would form a significant proportion of a supplier's business: how will the supplier cope with the suddenly increased volume? It may be argued that the above tends to eliminate the small or new supplier, increasing the consolidation of the market. This is certainly a danger to be addressed in any tender, particularly in marketplaces that are shrinking: it is not in the purchaser's interest to decrease competition.

Second, one will of course want to evaluate the price quoted, bearing in mind the different cost models discussed above and the need to evaluate the cost over the whole life of the contract.

Third, one will evaluate quality. This can be the most difficult area: quality is not easy to quantify, involving judgement rather than facts such as cost; moreover, one may well be in the position of judging the likely performance of a supplier with which one has had no dealings. There are some relatively concrete indicators, particularly accreditation under quality schemes such as ISO 9000 or Investors in People and membership of professional organizations. One may also take account of the qualifications and experience of key staff, and of staff development policies and programmes. Much information can also be gained from formal visits to suppliers' premises. These should be as structured as possible, with the team of evaluators having a checklist of quality measures under investigation. References from existing customers are also valuable. However, it is advisable to choose from a list of major clients, for instance all those spending over a certain amount with the supplier, rather than from a list of referees. The latter will be chosen by the supplier to give a favourable report; the former can be picked according to the purchaser's interests. One should also ask the reference sites chosen specific structured questions about performance and quality, such as supply times, rate of errors and customer care.

Finally, one may wish to evaluate the ability of the supplier to meet the specification.

This applies particularly in procurements that are complex, for instance of a library management system, or seek to develop new services, such as shelf-ready books or supplier selection. Suppliers may not provide initially all of the functionality or services required; one will therefore need to judge how close they are to being able to meet the requirements.

Apart from the pass/fail requirement of financial health, the above elements of cost, quality and ability to meet the specification will differ in importance, depending on the situation of the purchaser and the type of procurement; one will therefore wish to recognize these differences by weighting the three elements accordingly (a fully worked example of how one can apply weighting to complex decision making is given by Ball (2005a)). In many cases, such as a contract for the supply of books, cost will be most important, and one might assign weightings of 40:30:30 respectively to the three elements. In other cases, for instance the procurement of a library management system, ability to meet the specification might be equally important; one might therefore apply weightings of 40:20:40.

Awarding the contract

The deal is concluded. The obligations of the supplier and buyer, based on the specification, are written into a contract. The contract will normally be supplemented by service level agreements and performance measures.

Measuring and monitoring suppliers' performance

The procurement cycle is far from over after the contract has been awarded. Contract management, the process of ensuring that specification, service level agreements and performance measures are met over the period of the contract (which may be five years or more), is essential if suppliers are to be managed satisfactorily. This is generally achieved through quarterly or six-monthly contract review meetings with individual suppliers, who are expected to provide management information on the performance measures, drawn from the specification and detailed in the agreement. For a book contract these might include discounts achieved, time taken to supply books and to resolve queries, number of books supplied in error.

Conclusion

The above illustrates the procurement cycle. Fundamental to this cycle and its successful management is the specification of requirements: it is the basis both of selecting the best supplier(s) and of ensuring their performance throughout the life of the contract. It is crucial to produce a specification that reflects the purchaser's requirements accurately and fully, and in a form that can be quantified as far as possible. Writing the specification is not an easy process, but the time and effort expended at the start of the procurement cycle pay dividends throughout.

Managing suppliers and the marketplace: library purchasing consortia in the UK

Turning from some of the techniques of procurement, a number of strategies have been adopted to manage suppliers and the market in which they operate. This section examines approaches to the procurement of hard-copy resources through traditional library purchasing consortia, perhaps the most useful tool for carrying out procurements.

Aggregation of purchasing power brings many advantages over and above leverage on price. New services, for instance the truly shelf-ready – catalogued, classified and processed – book, have been negotiated through the strength of consortia. Quality of service is monitored closely and enhanced through continuing management of contracts based on tight specifications of service; pooled knowledge of suppliers' performance against these specifications lends force to this process. There are considerable savings in terms of the time needed by individual libraries to manage complex European procurement procedures and the resulting contracts.

Consortia can be powerful entities, particularly when they take a holistic view uniting both print and electronic procurement: publishers produce and deal in both media; libraries integrate print and electronic forms in their service to users; they should integrate the procurement of them too. Consortia are the only library organizations that have a chance of affecting the marketplace; individual libraries certainly do not.

In some countries, such as the USA, where individual libraries have large book budgets and the ability to negotiate good discounts, and some European countries, where retail price maintenance applies to books, library consortia have concentrated on automation and resource sharing. These countries have seen as a natural progression the concentration of consortia on the collaborative procurement of electronic resources rather than hard copy (Nfila and Darko-Ampem, 2002). However, other countries, such as Australia, share the UK experience of hard-copy procurement (Baudinette, 2004).

Collaboration between consortia

The situation in library procurement for UK higher education is complex. There are seven regional purchasing consortia, covering together the whole of the UK, and with the majority of higher education libraries in active membership. Some of these, such as the Southern Universities Purchasing Consortium (SUPC)[6] have grown from consortia that handle procurement across the whole range of university activity. Others, such as North East and Yorkshire Academic Libraries (NEYAL),[7] have grown from library collaboration, but have links to a wider university consortium. The value of procurement through their contracts is estimated at £100m *per annum*. All the regional consortia, together with the Research Council libraries and the British Library, form Procurement for Libraries.

Procurement for Libraries aims to be a forum for the exchange of experience between consortia, to offer a unified voice to the higher education sector, suppliers and other bodies, and to enhance procurement practice across the sector through staff development activities. It is also a forum where consortia can determine the appropriate level for any procurement, regional or national. The then Joint Procurement Policy and Strategy Group for HE, a body bringing together the general university purchasing consortia, established a protocol requiring a business case to be made evaluating the advantages and disadvantages of the national and the regional approach. Following this protocol, library consortia have generally adopted the regional approach for the supply of hard-copy resources: there are so few suppliers, particularly serials agents, that to award a national contract to only one or two might put the others out of business. Since 2009, however, there has been a new strategy: under the Procurement for Libraries umbrella all the English purchasing consortia have undertaken a very successful joint tender for the supply of books and other materials.

Individual consortia may also be members of the International Coalition of Library Consortia (ICOLC).[8]

The individual consortium

While size can be important for the individual consortium, in aggregating demand and providing libraries with a strong voice in negotiations with suppliers, it also brings problems. A UK higher education consortium may have more than 50 members, ranging from the small very specialist performing arts institution, through the medium-sized research-oriented university, to the teaching-oriented university with large numbers of undergraduates.

Each of these types of institution will have a very different focus – extensive serials holdings or large quantities of textbooks for instance – and require very different specialist resources. The large geographically defined consortium will need robust mechanisms for consulting its members and ensuring that their diverse requirements are reflected in any procurements. Generally, this is achieved by plenary meetings, held once or twice a year, which decide strategy and working groups with representatives from the different types of library, which undertake the detailed work of the procurement cycle. These working groups have the advantage of enabling a number of people to be involved and build up expertise in the procurement process, an example of the new skills increasingly required by the library and information profession.

Given the diversity of the geographically defined consortia and their sometimes unwieldy numbers and spread, it may be argued that specialist consortia, representing only one type of library or a particular subject, could be more effective and indeed obtain better prices for their members. However, it is possible to instigate joint specialist procurements by the regional consortia, through the mechanism of such groups as Procurement for Libraries discussed above. It is also possible to segment procurements by an individual large consortium in order to develop specialist services.

Traditional procurement of hard copy

One can identify three phases in the operation of library purchasing consortia in procuring books.

The first phase began in 1996 during the demise of the NBA, and unsurprisingly, given the prevailing restrictive terms of the Library Licence, concentrated on price. Booksellers are intermediaries. Publishers set the price at which they believe a book should retail and offer a discount from that price to the booksellers that supply the end customer. This discount varies depending on the terms the bookseller can negotiate and the number of copies likely to be sold. Generally, the bigger booksellers and the more popular titles attract the highest discounts. Only the booksellers and publishers know the discount models and terms. However, discounts of 30–40% for the more popular academic titles are reportedly not uncommon.

The discounts that the library purchasing consortia can obtain from booksellers are therefore limited by a number of factors: the discount obtained by the bookseller, the efficiency of the bookseller in keeping costs down and the profit margin required by the bookseller. The NBA discount of 10% under the Library Licence was obviously not at all generous and may have contributed to inefficiency and complacency within the trade. When the library purchasing consortia turned their attention to books in the mid-1990s, across-the-board discounts as high as 23% of the list price were obtained. This level of discount represented a saving of over 14% on the old NBA terms and was ostensibly good news for library budgets. However, it proved unsustainable; some suppliers had apparently underestimated the proportion of low- or no-discount titles bought by academic libraries and experienced some financial difficulties.

The second phase saw some correction in the level of discount offered, and focused on costs and quality of service. Ordering, receipting, cataloguing, classifying and processing a book is a costly and routine process, and one that notoriously resulted in backlogs of new stock in libraries, which caused discontent among users. Booksellers, through economies of scale, were able to offer a fully shelf-ready service at a much lower cost than libraries were able to achieve: books would arrive catalogued, classified and processed, ready to go direct to the shelf on arrival. This is a classic case of successful outsourcing: routine processes, characterized by peaks and troughs of demand, can be carried out much more cheaply by specialist agencies. Libraries were, however, required to standardize their requirements, and suppliers to invest in equipment and staff, something that only the discipline and volume of business provided by the library purchasing consortia could achieve.

One instance of improved quality of service achieved is the decrease in supply times. Typically in 2002–3 the average time taken to supply a book, from order to receipt, was over 38 calendar days; 5% of orders were received within 14 days; 66% of books were received within 31 days. By 2009–10 the average supply time was down to 22 days, with over 25% of orders received within 14 days and nearly 90% received within 31 days. This improvement resulted from library purchasing consortia a) including supply times in their specifications; b) being able to get an accurate picture of supply times by averaging them across a large number of libraries, hence discounting local variations; and c) in contract review meetings monitoring performance closely against a service-level agreement.

The elimination of backlogs within libraries through the shelf-ready service, coupled with the much shorter supply times achieved, represents a huge improvement in quality of service to the end-user in terms of prompt availability of new stock.

This second phase also saw an attempt by the SUPC to introduce a service relatively new to the UK – the so-called slip or approval plan (the term 'slip plan' is preferable: 'on approval' implies that the items can be returned if not approved). Under this arrangement libraries would outsource at least some collection development decisions to the book supplier. Typically, the library would define as closely as possible their collection development policies, and record with the supplier parameters such as the subject areas, languages and intellectual level (e.g. undergraduate or research) for purchase. The bookseller would then supply either an electronic record of books proposed to be bought or, in its fullest form, the books themselves without this intermediate stage.

Such slip or approval plans are quite common in the USA, and do decrease the work inherent in book selection by individual libraries, for instance obviating the need to monitor publishers' catalogues or search booksellers' databases and place orders. However, there has thus far been little take-up in the UK, probably because of cultural and educational differences, the amount of work necessary to define a library's requirements in sufficient detail and the generally smaller book budgets enjoyed in the UK (supplier selection in public libraries is dealt with elsewhere in this volume).

The third phase saw a widening of the scope of procurements to other materials. The first of these was e-books, in a groundbreaking agreement negotiated by the SUPC with two major suppliers. The emphasis of this agreement was on the purchase of collections, as well as on procurement of single titles. Such collections provided libraries with a critical mass of over 40,000 e-book titles. These collections, searchable at the level of individual words in the texts, were used by many students as databases, just as electronic journals are. E-books quickly became established as a medium both familiar and useful for students, with modern functionality such as bookmarking and immediate easy availability.

There is an interesting lesson here for collection development. These large collections of e-books, with good searching functionality, were heavily used by students at all levels: Bournemouth University's experience showed annual totals of over 60,000 user sessions, viewing 826,000 pages from 13,000 individual titles. However, the collections did not in large measure contain the recommended reading that librarians would generally have bought. Ease of access and use and availability in quantity, rather than selection by library or academic staff, seem to be the determining factors for our users, a fact that should not be surprising in this era of the internet.

E-book technology gives a very accurate picture of usage, and has enabled the introduction of so-called 'patron selection' or 'patron-driven acquisition' (PDA). Suppliers of e-books are now offering libraries the opportunity to make available a fund to be spent on new e-book titles as they become popular with library users. PDA is becoming increasingly popular: a recent survey of 250 libraries in the USA showed that '32 have PDA programs deployed; 42 planned to have a program deployed within the next year; and an additional 90 plan to deploy a program within the next three years' (Lenares, 2010). Librarians are able to impose some restrictions – for instance specifying subjects or ranges of titles; otherwise selection is taken out of the hands of librarians and entrusted to users (see Crowley and Spencer (2011) for other examples of patron selection). As PDA matures, it will be interesting to compare the usage of titles selected by users with the usage of titles selected by librarians or academics.

A further development in this third phase was collaboration on a national level by the regional library purchasing consortia. This scale made it viable to include in the procurement materials generally bought in, relatively small quantities even by the largest consortia; examples are out-of-print books and audio-visual materials.

Procurement of serials

Thus far we have concentrated on the procurement of books. The procurement of hard-copy serials is in some ways less interesting. As with books, library purchasing consortia have dealt with intermediaries, the serials agents. But this is a business of high volumes and very low margins, now perhaps only 6–7% (in contrast to the 30–40% discount on books): there is not the scope for obtaining discounts. Rather the focus is on keeping surcharges down; serials agents have seen their margins eroded as spending on the high-value high-discount scientific, technical and medical (STM) journals has been channelled either through other intermediaries, such as JISC Collections in the UK, or directly to the publishers themselves.

The procurement of e-journals, dealt with elsewhere in this volume, is even more challenging. The pattern varies from country to country. Some, such as in the UK with JISC Collections,[9] and in Greece with the Hellenic Academic Libraries LINK (HEAL-Link),[10] take a national approach. Others take a sub-national approach, for example, the Consorci de Biblioteques Universitaries de Catalunya (CBUC),[11] in Spain. The USA, given its size and complexity, takes a regional approach, but has produced some so-called 'mega-consortia' such as OhioLINK.[12] Guzzy (2010) has an interesting analysis of US consortia, as does Carbone (2007) for the European experience. Organizations such as JISC Collections in the UK and the large regional consortia in the USA have negotiated directly with publishers and obtained large amounts of e-content for prices based on print subscriptions (the so-called Big Deals). These have been welcomed by many: they have delivered large amounts of content for our users. However, there are dissenting voices, for example Ball (2005b), who argues that too much power has been ceded to the major publishers. Very large proportions of library budgets, especially in the big research libraries, are committed to a small number of publishers, such as Elsevier and Wiley Blackwell, in Big Deals. These agreements typically included punitive no-cancellation clauses. This, combined with the length and the all-or-nothing nature of such agreements, severely limits libraries' freedom to make or alter purchasing decisions. The result has been severe reductions in spending on monographs and a squeeze on publishers outside the Big Deals.

Further complications arise from the restrictions on use and users enshrined in the licences, discussed above, and the potential cost and difficulty of maintaining access to back-sets after a subscription is cancelled.

The end of collection development?

This chapter in a sense has been retrospective. It has concentrated on the supply of hard-copy books, a market set to decline in importance as book budgets are squeezed and e-books become available in larger quantities. However, the techniques of procurement, particularly specifying needs and monitoring and managing contracts, will remain fundamental.

Turning to the future, the concept of collection development is under threat. With the Big Deals power has shifted considerably in the publishers' favour, and freedom to make collection development decisions has been curtailed. If the trend towards national deals and block payments continues, these decisions will be relinquished even more. This can be seen for example in the Scottish Higher Education Digital Library (SHEDL),[13] which has been evaluated by the Research Information Network (2010). As far as procurement is concerned, the Big Deals have simply exposed a malfunction in the market: all publishers are monopolists, sole suppliers of monograph or journal content. Competition, so central to the procurement process, is severely limited, applying essentially only to intermediaries such as booksellers.

A notable response to the power of the publishers' monopoly is the open access movement, which aims to make scholarly literature freely available to all. One route is through open access publishing, where typically the author, or their institution or research funder, pays the cost of peer review and publishing. The content is then freely available without the need for subscription to the journal. The journals themselves may be completely open access or hybrid, publishing a mixture of subscription-based and open-access content. The other route is the deposit of pre- or post-prints of traditionally published materials in the author's institutional repository (IR) or in a subject repository such as arXiv,[14] which covers physics, mathematics and related disciplines.

The open access movement is still in its infancy, with many obstacles and vested interests to overcome. However, it exemplifies a trend to access to information unmediated by libraries. The internet is the prime example of this; Google's massive digitization programme is another; patron selection of e-books yet another. As this trend intensifies, traditional collection development will decline in importance.

In the disintermediated world the librarian's role is changing. It will in my view become increasingly focused not on externally produced resources, but on creating, developing and maintaining repositories of materials, whether learning objects, research data-sets or research outputs such as papers, produced in house in their own institution. Traditionally, librarians have sought through the art of collection development to obtain the outputs of the world's scholars and make them available to the scholars of their own institution – an impossible task. However, our role is now being reversed: it will be to collect the outputs of our own institution's scholars and make them freely available to the world, as outlined as long ago as 1996 by Ball and Spice (1996). This task is capable of achievement and attains the aim of universal availability of scholarship to scholars. However, it is not collection development as it has been practised down the years in the print world; that art, it can be argued, will no longer be needed in the era of disintermediation.

Conclusion

This chapter has discussed the procurement cycle as applied to libraries. The key lessons are:

- The importance of support from the procurement profession
- The continuing need for librarians to develop new skills
- The need to manage suppliers throughout the life of a contract
- The remarkable success of library purchasing consortia in driving down prices, decreasing costs through shelf-ready services and improving quality of service in terms, for instance of supply times
- The need to manage the marketplace, for instance in broadening the scope of procurement to new formats such as e-books.

Issues for you to consider:

- The effects on the marketplace and on library budgets of Big Deals
- The advisability of pursuing national deals with monopoly suppliers
- The demise of collection development in the disintermediated world
- Transferring decision making to the end-user
- The changing role of the librarian, from collector of everything in the world of scholarship to collector and publisher of the product of one's own institution.

References

Ball, D. (2005a) *Managing Suppliers and Partners for the Academic Library*, Facet Publishing.

Ball, D. (2005b) Signing Away our Freedom: the implications of electronic resource licences, *The Acquisitions Librarian*, **18** (35–6), 7–20.

Ball, D. and Spice, C. (1996) The Big Flame: a model for a universal full-text electronic library of research. In *Libraries and Associations in the Transient World: New technologies and new forms of co-operation: conference proceedings: Third International Conference 'Crimea 96'* [The Organizing Committee].

Baudinette, K. (2004) Purchasing Books Collaboratively: the Academic and Research Libraries Acquisitions Consortium: Paper presented at ALIA Acquisitions SA Seminar 'New ways of purchasing, publishing and printing' October 29, 2004, Adelaide, http://hdl.handle.net/2328/3328.

Carbone, P. (2007) Consortium Negotiations with Publishers – Past and Future, *Liber Quarterly*, **17** (1–40), 98–106.

Crowley, E. and Spencer, C. (2011) Library Resources: procurement, innovation and exploitation in a digital world. In Dale, P., Beard, J. and Holland, M. (eds), *University Libraries and Digital Learning Environments*, Ashgate.

Guzzy, J. (2010) *U.S. Academic Library Consortia: a review, library papers and presentations*, Paper 8, available from http://scholarspace.jccc.edu/sabbatical-projects/2/.

Hinton, B. (1987) Librarians as Unacknowledged Legislators, *New Library World*, **88** (3), 44–7.

Lenares, D. (2010, April 30) *Patron Driven Acquisition: librarian survey.* Message posted to www.libraries.wright.edu/noshelfrequired/?p=932

Nfila, R. B and Darko-Ampem, K. (2002) Developments in Academic Library Consortia from the 1960s Through to 2000: a review of the literature, *Library Management*, **23** (4/5), 203–12.

Office of Government Commerce (2008) *EU Procurement Guidance: introduction to the EU Procurement Rules*, http://webarchive.nationalarchives.gov.uk/20110601212617/http://www.ogc.gov.uk/index.asp.

Office of Government Commerce (2008) *An Introduction to Public Procurement*, http://webarchive.nationalarchives.gov.uk/20110601212617/http://www.ogc.gov.uk/index.asp.

Research Information Network (2010) *One Year On: Evaluating the Initial Impact of the Scottish Higher Education Digital Library (SHEDL)*, www.rin.ac.uk/our-work/using-and-accessing-information-resources/evaluating-impact-shedl.

Notes

1 www.against-the-grain.com.
2 http://de.wikipedia.org/wiki/Buchpreisbindung
3 Information on the purchasing profession in the UK and internationally is given by the Chartered Institute of Purchasing and Supply (CIPS) at www.cips.org/en-gb.
4 A more general approach is provided by the CIPS purchasing and supply management model at www.cips.org/en-gb/resources/purchasingsupplymanagementmodel.
5 www.ifpmm.org/.
6 http://supc.procureweb.ac.uk.
7 http://neyal.procureweb.ac.uk/public/home.htm.
8 For more information and a list of member consortia see www.library.yale.edu/consortia. Its focus is mainly on electronic resources.
9 www.jisc-collections.ac.uk.
10 www.heal-link.gr/journals/en/.
11 www.cbuc.es.
12 www.ohiolink.edu.
13 http://scurl.ac.uk/WG/SHEDL/index.html.
14 http://arxiv.org.

9

Outsourcing in public libraries: placing collection management in the hands of a stranger?

Diana Edmonds

Introduction

This chapter examines how outsourcing has become embedded in stock management in public libraries in the UK. It considers the implications of EU procurement requirements and discusses the outsourcing of library services to companies such as Instant Library. Looking to the future, it explores how shared services can offer economic benefits to local authorities.

Outsourcing – whatever is it?

As a well trained librarian, when faced with a question, I consult a reliable reference source. So, when considering outsourcing, I started by looking up the definition in a dictionary – and then in another . . .

The *Oxford Dictionary of English* (2010) defines outsourcing as 'obtaining goods or a service by contract from an outside supplier'.

Outsourcing is a practice which is now widespread both in private companies and in national and local government organizations. It has become attractive, the *Dictionary of Economics* (2009) suggests, because the products and services procured externally are often better than those provided in-house – and that they are better because of the specialist skills and expertise available from external suppliers. Outsourced products and services can also be cheaper as the outsourcing organization can benefit from economies of scale or scope – and so costs are reduced.

Outsourcing allows organizations flexibility: it is easier and faster to reduce the value of a contract than reduce the size of an in-house workforce. The *Dictionary of Economics* (2009) comments that it may also be easier to enforce contracts with outside suppliers than deal with a unionized internal workforce.

The *Dictionary of Business and Management* (2009) discusses which activities might be outsourced: activities which are regarded as non-core to the organization's activities are often the first areas to be contracted out. Functions such as finance, IT, legal and personnel services, are often the first areas to be considered. Outsourcing non-core functions enables the organization to focus more effectively on their core activities. To do what you do best and outsource the rest is a popular adage!

For private sector organizations, the strategy of outsourcing is often part of an overall approach to gain competitive advantage and drive down costs by restructuring, eliminating bureaucracy and re-engineering business processes.

The practice of outsourcing is routine in the private sector but, in the 21st century, is also becoming popular with local authorities which have found themselves increasingly financially challenged. The concept of 'commissioning' services is becoming more common amongst local authorities and they are now increasingly commissioning or procuring a range of services which were previously undertaken by in-house employees. The outsourcing agency commissioned to undertake these activities may be a private sector company but is just as likely to be another local authority or a 'third sector' or voluntary body.

But surely not for libraries?

Public libraries in England and Wales are provided by local authorities: the statutory requirement for this provision is enshrined in the 1964 Public Libraries and Museums Act which obliges local authorities to provide a 'comprehensive and efficient' public library service. The idea of outsourcing the operation of a public library service is alien to many within the profession of librarianship – and when first suggested was greeted with horror by many librarians.

The initiation of outsourcing in local government came with the Local Government Planning and Land Act in 1980 which obliged local authorities to undertake a competitive tendering process for certain categories of building work and maintenance. Compulsory competitive tendering required local authorities to undergo key elements of the contracting process to test the efficiency and cost-effectiveness of their current in-house providers. These competitive tendering requirements were extended in 1988 to other services such as street cleaning and school meals, driven by the need to address public criticism of local authority performance, and a belief that opening up services to competition would result in improvements in efficiency and, hence, value for money.

In 1988 the Government also began to turn its attention to the financing of the public library service and published a green paper which sought to elicit views on the extension of competitive tendering and contracting out into the arena of the public library service. The debate did not reach a speedy conclusion – and it was not until four years later, in 1992, that Peter Brooke, the then Secretary of State for National Heritage, stated that it was felt that Compulsory Competitive Tendering (CCT) was not necessarily the best way forward for public libraries. He announced, however, that five pilot projects would be established to test the feasibility of contracting out of all or parts of the library service. The five pilots were:

1 The development of a detailed client/contractor specification for the library service in Kent;

2 Management by contract of the whole library service, operating through business units, of two libraries in the London Borough of Brent;

3 The franchising of library services in Hertfordshire;
4 The contracting out of cultural services in libraries in Hereford and Worcester;
5 The establishment of whole service trusts in Dorset.

In 1994, to follow through on this issue of outsourcing of public libraries, the Department of National Heritage (DNH) commissioned KPMG and Capital Planning Information (CPI) to investigate the extent to which the provision of public library services could be contracted out. The results were published in the following year and included reports from the pilot projects as an appendix.

The KPMG study (KPMG/CPI, 1995) concluded that it is technically feasible to contract out all or parts of the library service, but that the prospect of significant reduction in cost of service is limited, while the cost of the outsourcing process could be substantial. The report produced on its completion stated that there was, at the time, no natural market for the provision of the service because the skills and experience required to deliver library services were simply not readily available in the outside marketplace. Although it might be feasible to apply contracting out to the library sector, there remained concerns about establishing outputs and performance measures and limited evidence as to the benefit of the process.

The principal conclusions reached by the consultants were that:

- There is a strong case for library service provision to remain essentially within the public sector;
- Management techniques and processes which can demonstrate that value for money is being obtained should continue to be developed and applied;
- There is a need to address issues of contracting out alongside the outcome of the Public Library Review which was considering the future funding of the service, and how public/private sector partnerships can be achieved;
- Although there is no natural marketplace for the range of current activities, there is a market for some elements of the service and this market should be explored.

The appendix to the KPMG report described the pilots which had been undertaken to assess the potential for outsourcing elements of the service – or indeed an entire public library service. One of the pilots had involved a tender for the management of two libraries within the London Borough of Brent. The library service had effectively been divided into six contracts, most of which included the provision of the two libraries, with additional elements of management responsibility for the entire service included in some of the work packages. The contracts were formally offered via a tendering process and, although external companies applied, the contract was awarded to the in-house team (Tyerman, 1994; Grimwood-Jones, 1996). The opinion of the majority of the profession at the time is effectively summarized by Walker's review of the exercise (Walker, 1994) which concluded that Brent's experiment would ultimately prove to be 'disabling' of the public library service and 'should not be extended'.

But don't touch the collection . . .

Although the outsourcing of the entire public library service was rejected in the 1995 KPMG report, the report concluded that there was potential for outsourcing some elements of the service. Public libraries are part of the local authority structure and when local authorities have outsourced functions such as maintenance, cleaning and security, the libraries have been maintained, cleaned and protected by external companies. These developments had not been viewed as particularly contentious by librarians, mainly because they were not directly responsible for the decision to outsource, and because maintenance, cleaning and security are not viewed as core to their professional activity.

What was considered contentious, however, was the outsourcing of any element of collection management. The collection was seen as the heart of the library – and the management of the collection as a core function of librarianship. The purchase of books for public libraries was traditionally managed by the Chief Librarian or the Stock Editor and the relationship with the bookseller was preciously guarded. There was little need for discussion about price because the price of books was fixed under the Net Book Agreement (NBA), initially established in 1900, which ensured that publishers could set the price of the works which they published. Booksellers were allowed to offer a discount of 10% to libraries on condition that public access to material was allowed.

Because the discount rate was standard, the selection of a bookseller was traditionally based on other aspects of the service which they provided. Stock was often selected at a showroom, and so the range of stock held by the supplier was a key factor. Staff enjoyed their visits to the showrooms because they gave an opportunity to see and handle books rather than selecting simply from a description of the contents and reviews – and, besides, a showroom visit also gave an opportunity for a day out of the library! This was, however, an expensive use of staff time, and so the book suppliers provided approvals collections which circulated from library authority to library authority and were used as the basis for selection. Again, the quality of the approvals collection was a significant issue for discussion with the bookseller.

Speed of supply was – and is – a key issue in the selection of a library supplier: how quickly was an item delivered to the Bibliographic Services department? One question which was rarely asked, however, was how long the item remained in 'Bib Services' before being available to the customer. Shelf-ready items could not be provided because virtually all libraries catalogued and classified the items they purchased in-house. So, although books arrived with some processing already undertaken by the supplier, most libraries undertook additional work on all items supplied.

The processing of stock is, in fact, a classic area for outsourcing. Although the selection of stock and the provision of an appropriate collection for library users is core to the business of librarianship, processing stock is not – and it can be undertaken more cost effectively by others. Libraries found that it was cheaper for library suppliers to process library stock than undertaking this routine work in-house. So library suppliers provided book covers, fixed spine labels to the exterior of the book, glued date labels to the inside of the book and stamped ownership marks on specified pages within the book. Branch librarians often disagreed as to the best place for the ownership stamp – or the prettiest colour for a label, and so the book suppliers were faced with a plethora of instructions for each authority. The fact that an external organization was undertaking these tasks highlighted the inconsistency of approach both across library services and within library services, with different branch libraries adopting a rainbow approach to the application of date labels, using a variety of colours applied in a variety of locations. Libraries gradually realized that these idiosyncrasies made the cost of processing more expensive but added nothing to the quality of customer experience (Capital Planning Information, 1996) and considerable work was undertaken to develop a standard approach.

Over the years, the relationship with the library supplier has become more formally managed via procurement processes. Procurement specialists were rarely involved in the relationship between bookseller and librarian while there was little price differentiation between the suppliers. The price of books was governed by the NBA which had allowed publishers to set the pricing for the works which they published. Libraries were allowed a standard discount of 10% for allowing public access to material purchased. In the 1990s, however, a small number of larger booksellers began to offer larger discounts and eventually, in 1997, the NBA was abolished. Its demise opened the floodgates for the discounting of book prices and has resulted in the three for two – and even the two for one offer we so often see now in the larger bookshops and supermarkets. More significantly for those managing public libraries, it meant that the procurement specialists in local authorities became involved with the procurement of other library materials such as music and video as well as books. This involvement was initially resented by many professional librarians who felt that the collection was their prerogative and theirs alone. The procurement specialists were conversely scathing about what they clearly regarded as a 'cosy' relationship between librarian and bookseller.

The involvement of the procurement specialists resulted in a much more formal specification of requirements than was ever reached over lunch between librarian and bookseller. Many of the contracts now being placed relating to the stock fund are of a value that qualifies for European tendering, although in practice the suppliers of UK public library materials still tend to be located in the UK.

So, in the 21st century, significant elements of collection management for public libraries are outsourced to library suppliers. Despite the reticence of many in the library profession, the work previously undertaken by large teams of bibliographic services staff who selected, procured, catalogued, classified and processed books and other materials for public libraries, has been outsourced to library suppliers. Library suppliers routinely provide the bibliographic record with the book, uploading the record directly into the library's catalogue. They undertake all processing of the item, applying RFID (radio-frequency identification) tags as well as ownership and date stamps. Items are delivered, sometimes direct to the individual library, 'ready for shelf'. Invoices are then provided electronically to the purchasing library service. And increasingly, library suppliers are selecting the stock for libraries, moving directly into collection management which has traditionally been core to the discipline of the librarian.

Stock procurement in the 21st century
Invitation to Tender

The process of procuring stock for public libraries in the UK is now governed by a formal process which is initiated by the issue of an Invitation to Tender (ITT) for the provision of stock and for the associated services which are required from the supplier. Because some suppliers still specialize in specific areas of stock, typically material for children, the ITT may reflect those specializations and cover, say, Children's Stock, Adults' Stock or Audiovisual material. The provision of e-books and other e-resources is usually procured in separate exercises: the provision of e-books via public libraries is a relatively new service and the purchase is often made directly from the small number of suppliers currently active in this marketplace.

The ITT issued by the authority will contain a number of sections. It will initially provide information about the library authority and the value of the contract. It is necessary for the supplier to have details relating to the library authority in order to understand whether they can provide an appropriate service: these details will include the location of the library authority and whether delivery is required to a central location or to a number of individual libraries. They will include information on the library management system which is used and whether RFID tags are required. They will note requirements for EDI and whether the library service wishes to order and track the orders which have been placed online as well as receiving invoices online.

Information on the value of the contract is also included. The approximate spend and the proportion of the spend which is to be allocated to hardback and paperback fiction and nonfiction items is important information for the supplier in assessing the level of discount which would be appropriate: clearly the larger the spend, potentially, the larger the discount. The balance of stock is also important: the ratio of fiction to non-fiction and paperback to hardback will also inform the supplier's calculations relating to the costing of the proposal.

The Specification of Requirements

The ITT includes a formal Specification of Requirements which covers a variety of elements. Each element within the specification requires a response from the supplier and allows the supplier to offer innovative solutions to the client's requirements.

Speed of supply is a particularly important element and so the specification will request details of supply times. Supply times will be required in relation to particular types of title, including those ordered pre-publication and various categories of published items, including newly published and in print titles, requests and urgent orders and stock ordered from a showroom.

The client will also wish to be reassured that there is a good breadth of material available. Public libraries, like retail booksellers, need to market their collections effectively and will wish to select a supplier who can provide an exciting and attractive range of stock. Selection tools are also important for the library staff. Most selection is now undertaken via the supplier's website – and the quality of the website can impact significantly on the ease and speed of ordering material. The supplier's website needs to be easy to navigate and have the ability to provide instant information on price and availability.

The outsourcing of stock selection to suppliers is becoming increasingly common with stock being provided according to parameters agreed with the library service. Selection at the supplier's location may be undertaken either by professional librarians or by other suitably trained staff, or may simply rely on automated selection processes to provide the range of stock required by the customer. Supplier selection normally involves the individual library setting a budget threshold. This budget will then be allocated across the various subject categories, depending on the pricing of material in particular areas of stock. When the selection is made, the chosen books will be placed in a 'shopping basket' for review by the library staff. This process can be omitted if librarians become confident that they can rely on the process. One of the key benefits of supplier-led selection is the release of staff time for other activities. Customers can change their requirements as and when they require; supplier selection can be introduced for one area of stock and gradually expanded to take more categories of material.

The performance, or rather the impact, of the service can be measured statistically by monitoring the number of issues of areas of stock. Normally, customers are not represented formally in the selection process: it is the librarians who decide on a supplier, rather than library users. However, in this process their views on the effectiveness of this outsourced supply process can be directly measured. Both the publishing trade and library customer needs are changing exceptionally quickly and we understand our customers need to reflect these changes in the stock that is purchased. Supplier selection can reflect any changes quickly and efficiently to ensure precious funds are directed exactly where they are required for maximum impact and to provide value for money.

The evaluation process

The evaluation of responses to the ITT normally follows a weighted model: details of the weightings will normally be provided to those wishing to tender to ensure that the supplier clearly understands the priorities of the service. Some of the evaluation will relate to the supplier, with the financial stability of the company being a key factor. Some of the evaluation will relate to the technical requirements specified within the tender document, while undoubtedly price and the level of discount will be the killer issue. We have moved so far from the 10% standard discount levels of the 1990s, controlled in regimented fashion by the NBA, and public libraries will now expect discounts in the region of 30-40% on list price, depending on the category of stock. For a public library service with a rapidly declining revenue budget, the level of discount makes a significant difference to the number of books available to its customers and is therefore a significant factor in the selection of a supplier.

Working together to procure – and to outsource

Because of the complexity of procurement processes, libraries are increasingly joining together in consortia to purchase books and the associated services which suppliers now provide. The London Libraries Consortium is particularly interesting in that all members share a catalogue and use the same Library Management System (LMS) which is provided on a facilities-managed basis by the LMS vendor. In an era in which fewer and fewer public library services have their own in-house IT teams, this is another area which is ripe for outsourcing to external suppliers.

Outsourcing collection management

The 1995 Report stated that there was no market for the outsourcing of public library services, although elements of the service could be outsourced. In less than 20 years, we have moved to a situation in which collection management is routinely outsourced. Suppliers now routinely select stock; process items supplied and provide catalogue records directly into the library's catalogue. But the librarian retains control, monitoring the performance of the stock selection process both in terms of delivery and in terms of customer reaction: issue figures provide an excellent method of monitoring the outcome of the selection process. For most librarians, this type of outsourcing is a success. Indeed, as pressure grows on public library funding and we see libraries across the country under threat of closure, this type of outsourcing is a financial necessity.

Outsourcing the lot!

If this element of outsourcing public library services can work, what about the rest? While the public sector was trialling and rejecting the outsourcing route for library services in the 1990s, the private sector simply got on with it. The private sector saw the library and information service as another function which could be outsourced if a financial saving or an improved service could be delivered.

A number of 'special' library services were outsourced at that time to Instant Library Ltd, a company which had been established with the aim of operating outsourced library services. The company aimed 'to do whatever an in-house library service can do' and in addition to providing a range of technical activities, such as procurement, cataloguing and automation, also offered to outsource entire library and information services. Instant Library was particularly successful in the oil industry, and by 1994, when the pilot exercise to outsource public library services in the London Borough of Brent was being so soundly rejected, was operating library and information services for fuel companies such as Elf, Total and British Gas. Other major corporate clients included London Underground Limited whose large Engineering Information Service was outsourced to Instant Library and 3M who outsourced the management of its UK-based services to the company. Clients even included the TUC (Trades Union Congress) whose library service was contracted out to Instant Library for a while. By the beginning of the 21st century, Instant Library was also moving into contracts in the public sector. The first was a contract to operate a school library in Northamptonshire, which provided services both for the school and for the local community. The second, in 2001, was the management of the public library service in the London Borough of Haringey. Haringey's Library Service had recently been inspected by the Audit Commission and had been awarded 'no stars' in a star rating system which normally awarded between one and four stars, and was felt to have 'no prospect of improvement'. Instant Library's task was to turn around the service and this was achieved with dramatic increases in the number of visitors to libraries in the Borough and the number of issues of library stock. Instant Library managed the Council's Library, Museum and Archives Services until 2005, when the company's Managing Director became a council employee and took over the in-house role of Head of Service (MLA, 2010).

Another significant example of outsourcing a total service occurred in 1998, when the London Borough of Hounslow identified an alternative vehicle for delivering library services and for a number of other 'leisure services' and established a trust. Placing these local authority services in a trust has financial advantages since business rates, National Non-Domestic Rates (NNDR), can be reclaimed and released to provide additional funds for the service. The trust model has since been followed in a number of locations, including Wigan and Luton, and has the advantage of offering financial benefits and also liberating an entrepreneurial approach to the management of the service. The establishment of the trust does not normally cause concern, either within the profession or amongst the customer base, because the development appears to be a natural extension of the provision of the service by the local authority. Indeed, with the pressure on public library services, it has the perceived benefit of safeguarding funds for the service, by virtue of the Service Level Agreement (SLA) with the local authority and the associated funding agreement.

A departure from this process occurred in 2008, when John Laing Integrated Services was contracted to manage a number of public services on behalf of the London Borough of Hounslow,[1] services which had previously been managed by the trust. The services include libraries, a museum, historic buildings, a theatre, arts workshops, parks, allotments, cemeteries and an urban farm. John Laing Integrated Services established the Hounslow Community Trust, a not-for-profit company, to employ the staff and manage the services. This was a significant development because it signalled the extension into library services of the activities of large companies interested in outsourcing a wide variety of functions, rather than simply focusing on the specific and relatively small area of public libraries.

In the new world of commissioning local authority services, a number of local authorities are reviewing the option of outsourcing the public library service which they are still, under the 1964 Act, obliged to provide. In 2010, Slough outsourced its small public library provision to be managed by Essex, a considerably larger service. This shared service model is likely to occur elsewhere, indeed three London Boroughs, Hammersmith and Fulham, Kensington and Chelsea and Westminster, which are currently considering the provision of a single service across the three boroughs.

There is now clearly a market for the provision of outsourced library services and a marketplace of potential suppliers, ranging from commercial companies to local authorities, with trusts and social enterprise agencies also expressing interest.

Just as the market for the supply of library materials has developed over the years the market for the provision of the total package of public library services will also develop. Local authorities themselves are simply instructed in the legislation to provide a comprehensive and efficient service. In order to assist the development of public libraries it is to be hoped that local authorities will issue more detailed specifications, requiring the contractor to expand the use of public libraries, and rewarding good performance.

What of the future?

Faced with closing library services which are clearly valued by the public, local authority managers are now looking closely at operating costs and trying to do the same for less. We are now seeing the increased use of technology and a concomitant reduction in staff numbers; the use of volunteers instead of paid staff; shared services for both back and front office and the outsourcing of public libraries.

Since public libraries were established in the UK, their core function has been to provide books for loan and for reference. Although many additional services have been added to the menu of provision, the collection has remained at the heart of the library and collection management has remained a key professional skill.

In a world in which the public library is outsourced, will there still be a role for the collection manager? We should, perhaps, ask:

- Is the collection still at the heart of library services?
- Should a library service which chooses to outsource specify requirements in relation to the provision and management of collections?
- Do library suppliers have an increased role to offer in this area?
- What do the customers think of it all?

References

Capital Planning Information (1996) *The Value to Libraries of Special Services Provided by Library Suppliers: developing a costing model* (British National Bibliography Research Fund Report), CPI.

Dictionary of Business and Management (2009) Law, J. (ed.), Oxford University Press.

Dictionary of Economics (2009) Black, J., Hashimzade, N. and Myles, G. (eds), Oxford University Press.

Grimwood-Jones, D. (1996) Contracting Out in the Public Sector – issues and implications, *Library Management*, **17** (1), 11–17.

KPMG/CPI (1995) *DNH Study: contracting out in public libraries*, KPMG and Capital Planning Information Ltd.

MLA (2010) *The Opportunity of Devolved Governance for Museums, Libraries and Archives*, Museums, Libraries and Archives Council.

Oxford Dictionary of English (2010) Stevenson, A. (ed.), Oxford University Press.

Tyerman, K. (1994) Love Me Tender, *Library Association Record*, December, 668–9.

Walker, G. (1994) *Enabling or Disabling? The voluntary contract tendering of Brent Council's library service*, The Author, London.

Note

1   www.laing.com/index.php?item=467&menu=i_sector_leisure.

10
Open access

David Brown

Introduction

The scholarly publishing industry has witnessed considerable pressures to change during the past decade – for it to adapt to the many external developments which make dissemination of education and scholarship more relevant in an age in which authors and researchers are coming to terms with the potentials offered by the internet, by new forms of social collaboration and by new needs for information in different formats, amongst others.

One such change is in the business models which are becoming more relevant as external developments find traction within scholarship. One of the key drivers for change is that many of the external pressures are geared around 'openness'. The open source initiatives within the Information and Communications Technology (ICT) industry at large are influencing the needs and requirements of academics and researchers – there is a growing support for openness, transparency, interactivity and free access within and between the constituents or traditional stakeholders of the scholarly information industry. These are new and are at odds with some of the traditions governing scholarly communication in the past.

Open source initiatives have manifest themselves in the rise of so-called 'open access' (OA). This latter is not a single or even unified movement. There are a number of routes being considered for open access, as explored later in this chapter, and it is a reflection of the novelty of this development that the various routes are not always operating in harmony.

The net effect, nevertheless, is that a growing portion of scholarly, formally published literature is appearing as open access. Instead of librarians having to pay to access the results of research work, the 'toll-based' access system (TA), some 20% of the formal published literature, is now available for free to the library (OA). This has the potential to change the acquisitions budget of libraries considerably. It also has the potential to change the functions performed within the library to support and accommodate open access.

Knowledge workers

Why is open access so important? It faces up to the need to reach beyond the research library's clientele, into the professional, small and medium enterprise (SME) and 'amateur scientist' communities which have hitherto been denied access because of the prevailing toll-based subscription system. These communities have been largely excluded from the research results generated behind academic garden walls. Though they could have by-passed the high subscription costs for journals in gaining access to research results through a pay-per-view (PPV) option offered by publishers, the charges for PPV were also very high. They have therefore been locked out of the scholarly information system by commercial reasons even though the occasional article might be highly relevant to their professional needs or personal interests.

The open access movement has the potential for embracing these communities within the new scholarly information system. It could extend the outreach of article delivery which potentially would be beneficial to the publishing industry (if they could come up with appropriate business models) and certainly to society at large. If the sum of those articles from the many individuals who might only want very occasional access is aggregated then a substantial new business opportunity is created. This relates to the Long Tail principle in which Anderson (2006) argued that the digital revolution was unleashing a huge latent demand for information which the traditional print paradigm was unable to meet. No longer would end-users be constrained by physical warehousing and distribution systems: electronic storage and internet developments would now enable those individuals at the periphery of the scholarly sector to become active participants. In many instances the additional new demand from the 'tail' (the non-core sector of demand from professional sectors) could exceed the existing core academic and corporate R&D (research and development) markets.

Very little research work has been done on how extensive the reach for open access publications could be. Nevertheless, there are anecdotal indications that the internet has broadened the potential market for scholarly publications beyond the traditional confines of the research library and its institution. Depending on how large this is will determine whether open access results in a significant change in the business models for scholarly publishing and a change in library operations to cope with its challenges and opportunities.

Budgetary constraints

Separate from the issue of extending outreach into new market sectors, open access also addresses a key problem facing the traditional outlets for scholarly publications. Research libraries have been battling against a so-called 'serials crisis' whereby the typical budget for collections has fallen behind the sheer growth of article numbers and, in particular, the costs of buying all the articles its patrons need. Open access business models make little or no demands on the library's acquisitions budgets, enabling it to focus its funds in supporting other services. As such, 'open access' has gained considerable support from within the library profession worldwide.

Open access

Open access currently consists of three main routes – grey, green and gold. The three 'g's are supported by agreements or understandings which took place at conferences and meetings held at three geographical centres some ten years ago – in Budapest, Berlin and Bethesda (the three 'B's). However, such simplicity is not reflected in the details underpinning open access within scholarly communication. Each of the three routes to open access will be analysed within this chapter.

Grey open access

There are threads going back several decades within the traditional scholarly publishing system which set the scene for what has become a 'grey' open access movement.

early draft on author's website

For many decades it has been a feature of scholarly publishing that – in return for the work put into the research and subsequent writing up of the results for publication – an author was entitled to a number of physical, printed reprints of the published article. The numbers of reprints supplied to authors varied according to the policy of the publisher, but some 30 copies were typical. In addition the author could also purchase additional quantities from the publisher. These were used by the author to send to colleagues, peers, friends and family. They were an informal exchange of such reprints, all free, all open and through the mail. But it was peripheral to the mainstream toll-based publishing system.

Along came the internet and the web, bringing with them electronic publishing capabilities. No longer was it necessary to send reprints by snail mail – downloading copies from file servers either at the publisher's site or from the author's own web address became possible. It was faster and more convenient. Instead of potential users requesting a printed reprint from authors, they could now collect the electronic version from the author's website. The leading researchers in any given field – the invisible college – usually had their own website which would include their achievements as well as their publications in full text.

Here is the problem. The final version of the article – the so-called article of record – technically belongs to the publisher if the author had given up his or her copyrights by having their work published by the publisher. The author has in the past willingly given up many of the intellectual property rights associated with the article in order to get the publication into the scholarly system. There has been little alternative but for the author to give up these rights in order to gain international recognition, more research funding and in some cases tenure. However, this means that the author would be contravening the publisher's copyright if they allowed anyone to access and download the final (or stage 3) article. But grey open access does not specify that the final version be the one which authors would make available on their personal website. They could equally include an earlier version – before final mark-up and pagination is undertaken as in stages 1 or 2 of the manuscript preparation – on their own site without contravening copyright.

This grey open access is not always accurate or citeable. But as an indicator of the broad research results it is often useful – and is available for free.

However, the real difficulty with such an informal system is that there is a wide global scattering of researchers in any one area. Reprint exchange and its online version – grey open access – remains very decentralized. Skipping between various author websites to pick up their latest (stage 2 and earlier) articles was time consuming and not always comprehensive. It was only in 1991 that Dr Paul Ginsparg, then at the Los Alamos National Laboratory (LANL) in the USA, provided a centralized facility whereby physicists – high energy physicists in particular – could deposit their research findings in a central facility and a new feature of open access began. This ushered in the era of green open access.

Green open access

Green open access has become synonymous with deposition in a dedicated digital repository. Initially the repository was a subject-based one – such as the arXiv[1] database of physics material which emerged from Dr Ginsparg's early efforts. During the past two decades there has been a spread of such subject-focused central facilities covering most areas of physics, mathematics, computers and IT and some aspects of economics. They have the same mission – to enable easy, unencumbered access to the latest results of a researcher. It combines all the grey websites of researchers in a given subject area. It also includes manuscripts from authors who do not have their own website. Subject repositories are a potentially powerful new way of disseminating research results.

Leading on from Professor Stevan Harnad's 'subversive proposal' (Harnad, 1994) an additional twist to the green open access movement came in the form of institutional repositories (IRs). Though not adopted with alacrity, IRs have become the focus of much interest by policy makers and librarians in recent years. The aim was that each institution would have its own resource – the institutional repository – into which all the authors from the institution would voluntarily deposit the latest research results. The institution – in many cases through the library – would manage the inflow of material into the repository to ensure that it met quality and bibliographic standards. The material would be sourced from all research areas undertaken within the institution – they would not be confined to any one subject area alone, nor just a single format as any relevant digital files could be included. They would also adopt accepted international standards to allow the deposited articles to be freely accessible to anyone throughout the world by means of adopting standards such as Open Access Publications – Protocol for Metadata Harvesting (OAP-PMH). The key was to ensure that the metadata was applied to the article – a bibliographic process which was close to the professionalism of the librarian – so that specialized open access search engines such as OAIster[2] could find relevant works across the global network of IRs.

That was the theory. Many supporters of the green open access movement used this process as a stick with which to beat the scholarly publishing industry. Many felt that the exorbitant profit levels achieved by commercial organizations such as Elsevier, Wiley, Springer, etc. in recent years was counter to the welfare of science and that commercial publishers in particular were parasites on the body politic of scientific endeavour. Any means whereby their functions could be trimmed would be supported. Not all green open access advocates were so belligerent, and Professor Harnad, who is seen as the leading proponent of the green open access movement, has been at great pains to claim that traditional scholarly publishing and IRs containing pre-published manuscripts could co-exist. This is not how many publishers, and also many researchers see it. They see it as a destructive force and one which, if adopted to a significant extent, would undermine the established and heavily supported scholarly publishing edifice. In particular it would destroy the refereeing infrastructure on which quality is imposed on publishing output. The lack of control and authority would allow noise to creep into the system which would be counterproductive to the research effort.

The International Association of STM Publishers (2011) has stated that their commitment is to the wide dissemination of and unrestricted access to content they publish, on the understanding that the services that publishers provide is paid for in some way. It adds that journal publishing agreements have traditionally addressed issues about scholarly use and re-use by authors of their own work. This includes questions about compliance with research funder policies. According to the April 2011 STM announcement, conflating author rights issues and institutional content licences add greater complexity and possible legal uncertainty to such licences without benefiting authors. Instead, the statement encourages ongoing dialogue, objective research and assessment on the impact of IRs.

One ongoing research study on the impact of green open access on subscription-based journal publishing is Publishing and the Ecology of European Research (PEER)[3]. This is a European Commission co-funded project which is comparing the usage of seven IRs in several European countries with the subscription records of journal publishers. This study has been long in the preparation and the work is due for completion in mid 2012. It may give an evidence-based indication of the impact of green open access on traditional commercial journal publishing activities. There have been earlier works in this area, such as by Beckett and Inger (2007) which used multivariant analysis to separate out issues which would dictate whether open access was preferred or not, but none of these studies have been definitive over whether green open access will destroy journal publishing.

In the meantime, authors at those centres with IRs have not been persuaded that it is in their best interests to deposit their articles into the local IR. Various other studies (Rowlands, Nicholas and Huntington, 2004; Swan and Brown, 2005) have indicated that this reluctance is based on their concerns at being caught in the crossfire over copyright interpretations and the worry that the traditional publishing system could be compromised without anything robust and acceptable being available in its place.

In the face of this resistance to voluntarily deposit articles in the local IR, a number of important funding agencies and institutions have mandated that researchers be required to make such deposits. The intention is to enhance the visibility of the institution by demonstrating to the world the output and value of the local research effort. Whilst in administrative terms such mandates would appear to be valuable, the issue is whether authors and researchers accept how their work is made available – whether they prefer alternative routes in meeting their needs.

In fact, despite the increasing number of such mandates, again there is no universal commitment towards the green open access movement by authors. Nor are there strong indications that end-users and researchers are seeking out such green collections as a primary information resource. Green open access represents a slow and gradual adoption of the overall principles of open access.

Gold open access

Just over a decade ago, a new business model for scholarly publishing was introduced by the entrepreneur and pioneer Vitek Tracz. Backed by funds from the sale of his previous publishing business to Elsevier he then proceeded to establish something which challenged the commercial heart of the traditional commercial scholarly journal publishing operation. He launched a company called BioMed Central[4] (BMC) which gave the opportunity to researchers to have their final, stage 3, article disseminated to everyone irrespective of their affiliation. It was a challenge to the toll-based journal publishing system which required libraries to pay an annual subscription fee in advance of receiving an estimated number of articles within a journals package. Subscription-based publishing was creating a huge problem for librarians at the time as the annual subscription fees for a fixed number of journals was growing at rates far greater than their library acquisitions budget. It was made worse, as several large publishers were offering an attractive option to the sum of journals selectively subscribed to by each publisher by creating so-called 'Big Deals'. The larger number of titles thereby acquired, including their previous holdings, gave the appearance that they were getting more bite for their bucks. It reinforced the libraries' commitment to buying serials, increasingly at the expense of other materials and services which the library could offer. The 'serials crisis' emerged.

With that as background, Tracz established a company which had its key operational feature in the free and open distribution of all refereed articles which went through his company's system. He recognized that the prime beneficiary of the traditional scholarly journal publishing system was the author. If the author achieved global visibility and respect for the quality of their research, as summarized in the published article, they would be in a better position to gain additional research funding, tenure, and image recognition generally. As such the author should pay for the publication charges and not the reader. BioMed Central was set up with a stable of quality biomedical journals, each of which carried an Article Processing Charge (APC) which the author, or their funding agency, was expected to pay. In those cases where there was financial hardship the author charge could be waived. This is the gold route to open access.

Other organizations also adopted a similar system. The US-based Public Library of Science[5] (PLoS), which had its roots in the concerns about the way scholarly publishing was being controlled by commercial publishers, also established a programme of quality biomedical titles. In this case the corn seed funding came largely from the Gordon Moore Foundation. A third example has been Hindawi,[6] a Cairo-based publishing house which has transferred its commercial business model from a subscription to gold open access. In this case the low editorial costs as a result of being based in Egypt made this a viable proposition.

The concern by the rest of the publishing industry is that a total switch from a toll-based/subscription model to open access would mean that their profitability would drop dramatically. Much of the commercial advantage in the traditional scholarly publishing system is in the redundancy of much/most of the articles published and sold under subscription or licence. Having a guaranteed income before any costs for the year are incurred is a great system (for the publishers). To give this up in favour of having to charge every author to have their article published – and if it fails to pass the refereeing stage the costs would still be incurred by the publisher, not the rejected author – is much more speculative and unattractive.

Hybrid

Nevertheless, and under pressure from the growing band of devotees for the open access cause, several large journal publishers have adopted a halfway house approach in adapting themselves to the new business models. Led by Oxford University Press and Springer S&BM, they gave room in their established subscription-based journals for gold open access articles. The editorial process for both types of articles is the same – the difference is that the open access articles would be financed by author payments and be available for free, whereas the traditional toll-based articles would be subject to the authentication and authorization procedures which was the traditional way.

This raises problems for those agencies which supply individual articles under document delivery. For delivery or articles online, document delivery agencies are required to charge the traditional operational fee (£8.25 from the British Library Document Supply) plus the royalty rate applicable for that journal title. However, when gold open access (author paid) articles are included in a subscription title document, delivery agencies have no way of disentangling those articles which are gold (and therefore would bear no royalty charge) from those articles which have gone through the normal licensed paid route. As such it is conceivable that articles which should be delivered free from royalty charge would in fact bear the rate applicable for the host journal – giving publishers a double income for the same article. Whether a particular author finds that such double charging has occurred and wishes to take out a class action is something which is open to speculation. In the meantime, the situation could be resolved if publishers were scrupulous in attaching appropriate metadata describing whether an article is a gold open access article or a toll-based article, and making this metadata widely available, particularly to intermediaries such as document delivery agencies. This would reduce any potential double charging. It puts the onus on the publisher to make such distinctions – only they are aware of what is for free and what is not.

Data sets

The discussion thus far has been focused on journal articles. These are, after all, the main source for information about relevant research studies being undertaken elsewhere. However, in the internet age there is an emerging demand for other forms of 'publication'.

In the traditional publishing system it was often necessary to find a home for the supplementary or support data which were relevant to a particular research study. Such supplementary material, if it could be accommodated in a printed format without upsetting the balance and style of the journal issue, would be included or made available separately from the publisher or author. But the procedure was neither clear nor well used. However, there has been something of a perfect storm as computer technology has enabled vast amounts of support data to be created, as the internet has allowed easy transfer of large amounts of digital information, as Big Science has emerged which has focused on the collection of data rather than providing written reports, and as international collaboration has grown creating global 'collaboratories' which have the need to switch large amounts of research data quickly and easily between centres.

In many subjects and topics, the primary output of the research is no longer the refereed article – whether open access or not. It is the supporting data which can be manipulated and used as appropriate for local circumstances. It is no longer ideal to rely on written reports by one author for one particular set of circumstances – a more locally relevant approach is required.

As mentioned at the beginning of this chapter, the initial stimulus for the open access movement in scholarly publishing was in the open source initiatives in ICT generally. This has resulted in a large catalogue of freely available software which can be used to manipulate data. The tools are free – and so is the raw research data in most instances.

The publishers have by-and-large ruled themselves out of participating in the data curation challenge. They see that no viable business model will enable them to cover the costs of quality assessment of the data set. They are happy to see data sets available as part of open access. Therefore the management and control of the supporting data sets for research in an open access environment is a challenge yet to be met. The international library community has stepped up to this challenge and established a collaborative group which allocates digital object identifiers (DOIs) to data sets which are sent to the member libraries in a DataCite[7] collaboration. DataCite was initially developed by Hannover Technical University but through the sponsorship of the International Council of Scientific and Technical Information (ICSTI) has a global network of organizations which allocate DOIs to locally produced data sets. It is suspected that this is just the tip of the iceberg and that there are many thousands of small-scale data sets being created in support of the world's R&D which remain as bibliographic orphans.

In addition, how are the thousands of small, medium and large data sets to be accessed? Is this a role for publishers or the library community or other intermediaries? Data sets and other supplementary material represent a broad new frontier which faces the open access movement.

Summary and recommendations

For open access to succeed as the dominant means of scholarly information dissemination there has to be some powerful reason to convince authors and users/researchers to change their habits and support open access over toll-based publishing mechanisms.

There have been recent studies which have looked at open access from the perspective of economics to establish whether there are grounds to assume that open access delivers beneficial returns to society as a whole in comparison with the established, traditional system. A leading researcher in this area has been John Houghton, Professor and Director of the Information Technologies and the Information Economy Programme, Centre for Strategic Economic Studies,[8] Victoria University, Melbourne. He initially produced a macro-level model which showed that open access is in fact a preferable system in that its cost/benefit is far greater than toll-based publishing. Following on from that study he looked at several European countries, including the UK, to show that at the national as well as the overall level, open access was a better option (Houghton and Sheehan, 2006). Publishers, understandably, viewed the assumptions made and the results of Houghton's work with scepticism.

More recently the Cambridge Economics Policy Associates (CEPA) has completed a study (2008) for a group of UK funders led by the Research Information Network[9] (RIN) which addressed the dynamics of the scholarly communication in journals with a five-year time frame. They identified five main business models which could be the alternatives. Green open access, gold open access, transactional-based publishing (pay per view), national licensing and deferred open access were all looked at and modelled in the course of this research. Grey open access is not a business model, more a social network, and as such was not included in CEPA's assessment.

CEPA's view was that authors should be encouraged to make use of the green open access route through local IRs as the costs of establishing this infrastructure have in many cases already been incurred. However, it should be borne in mind that this strategy bears some risks in that the existing scholarly publishing system overall could be undermined. CEPA also recommended that policy makers support a transition to gold open access as long as the APCs charged by publishers remain below £1,995, and that the hybrid gold open access journals do not result in excessive additional costs being charged to higher education institutions.

So the jury is still out as far as deciding which of the business models is the most appropriate for UK and global scholarly publishing. The next five years should see greater clarity as more experiments are undertaken and the resistances by authors and users are whittled down through greater exposure to the benefits arising from open access publishing.

Issues to be addressed

1 What incentives can be given to attract local authors to deposit their articles in the institutional green archive?

2 How significant will be the use of individual researchers' websites as a medium for scholarly intercourse (grey open access)?

3 How can non-bibliographic information (supplementary information such as data sets, software programmes, videoclips, etc.) be brought more effectively into a structured open access public domain?

4 What price ranges would be realistic and acceptable for authors to pay to have their articles posted in gold open access journals?

5 How can the gold (author-pays) articles be distinguished from traditional toll-based articles in hybrid journals? What role do librarians have in this?

6 Are some disciplines and subject areas more likely to accept open access publication than others, and if so, which and why?

7 Should users (as opposed to authors) be incentivized to make use of open access in IRs over subject-based repositories?

Further reading

Gentil-Beccot, A., Salvatore M. and Brooks, T. C., (2009) *Citing and Reading Behaviours in High-Energy Physics: how a community stopped worrying about journals and learned to love repositories*, http://openaccess.eprints.org/index.php?/archives/607-guid.html.

Guédon, J.-C. (2004) The 'Green' and 'old' roads to Open Access: the case for mixing and matching, *Serials Review*, **30** (4), 315–28.

Houghton, J. et al. (2009) *Economic Implications of Alternative Scholarly Publishing Models: exploring the costs and benefits*. A report to the Joint Information Services Committee (JISC), Victoria University and Loughborough University, www.jisc.ac.uk/media/documents/publications/rpteconomicoapublishing.pdf.

LISU and SQW Consulting (2008) *Open Access to Research Outputs: final report to RCUK*, www.sqw.co.uk/file_download/171.

Pinfield, S. (2005) A Mandate to Self Archive? The role of open access institutional repositories, *Serials*, **18** (1), 30–4.

Publishing Research Consortium (PRC) (2009) *Journal Authors' Rights: perception and reality*, Summary Paper 5, Sally Morris (Morris Associates), www.publishingresearch.net/documents/JournalAuthorsRights.pdf.

Swan, A. (2008) *Key Concerns Within the Scholarly Communication Process: report to the JISC Scholarly Communications Group*, Key Perspectives Ltd, www.keyperspectives.co.uk/openaccessarchive/reports.html.

UK Select Committee of Enquiry on Scientific Publications (2004) *Scientific Publications: free for all?*, Tenth Report of Session 2003–04 House of Commons Science and Technology Committee, www.publications.parliament.uk/pa/cm200304/cmselect/cmsctech/399/399.pdf.

Universities UK (2007) *Policy Briefing. Publishing research results: the challenges of open access*, Universities UK.

References

Anderson, C. (2006) *The Long Tail: how endless choice is creating unlimited demand*, Random House Business Books.

Beckett, C. and Inger, S. (2007) *Self Archiving and Journal Subscriptions: coexistence or competition? An international survey of librarians' preferences*, Scholarly Information Strategies Ltd: Publishing Research Consortium (PRC), www.publishingresearch.net/documents/Self-archiving_report.pdf.

Cambridge Economic Policy Associates (2008) *Activities, Costs and Funding Flows in the Scholarly Communications System*. Commissioned by the Research Information Network (RIN) in association with PRC, SCONUL and RLUK, www.rin.ac.uk/system/files/attachments/Activites-costs-flows-report.pdf.

Harnad, S. (1994) *Publicly Retrievable FTP Archives for Esoteric Science and Scholarship: a subversive proposal*. Paper presented at the Network Services Conference, London 28–30 November, 1994.

Houghton, J. and Sheehan, P. (2006) *The Economic Impact of Enhanced Access to Research Findings*, Centre for Strategic Economic Studies, www.cfses.com/documents/wp23.pdf.

International Association of STM Publishers (2011) *STM Statement on Negotiating Rights for Institutional Repository Postings and Author Rights, April 2001*, www.stm-assoc.org/2011_04_19_STM_statement_on_licensing_and_authors_rights.pdf.

Rowlands, I., Nicholas, D., Huntington, P. (2004) Scholarly Communication in the Digital Environment: what do authors want? *Learned Publishing*, **17** (4), 261–73.

Swan, A. and Brown S. (2005) *Open Access Self-archiving: an author study*, Key Perspectives Ltd, http://eprints.ecs.soton.ac.uk/10999/.

Notes

1. www.arxiv.org.
2. www.oaister.org.
3. www.peerproject.eu/.
4. www.biomedcentral.com.
5. www.plos.org.
6. www.hindawi.com.
7. www.datacite.org.
8. www.cfses.com.
9. www.rin.ac.uk.

11

Collection development and institutional repositories

Josh Brown

Introduction

An Institutional Repository (IR) is an online, digital archive, set up and hosted by an institution to house research publications and other materials written by its staff. IRs have increased in number extremely rapidly in the early years of the 21st century, and it is rare that a research institution does not have one in one form or another.

The collections held in IRs tend to be a mix of open access versions of published work and simple catalogue records. These records are usually created using Dublin Core, a metadata schema originally developed to describe websites, for items which for a variety of reasons are not available. IRs are overwhelmingly based in libraries and are often managed by professional librarians. However, they need to liaise with the full spectrum of staff in a research institution, from academics and administrators to technical developers. Outside the institution they also need to liaise with a varied group of stakeholders, ranging from other members of the repository community to publishers. This variety of contact and roles makes managing a repository collection an extremely interesting and varied professional activity, while also offering value to the wider information profession:

> The development of repositories, especially institutional repositories (IR), could represent the opportunity for the library profession to deploy its skills and professionalism in an increasingly important area. As IRs become more valuable, the status and standing of librarians, and other information specialists, will become better recognized and appreciated. But this will not happen while IRs remain a repository only for research outputs. They need to form the core information repository for an HEI for all the information it wishes to make available; crucially, this must include, where appropriate, research data and educational resources.
> (Read, 2008, 72)

One of the key factors to consider in developing a digital collection using an IR is that they are a relatively new and heterogeneous phenomenon and have, in a short space of time, achieved considerable diversity in aims, structures and implementation. They have evolved rapidly into an international community of practice, alongside the open access movement; but there is no single model, as yet, of best practice in handling many aspects of IR collections. This is chiefly because, although IRs are often almost entirely concerned with research publications, the needs of research institutions vary considerably, as do research environments from country to country. This ecology has shaped a pragmatic outlook on collection development amongst IR managers, and debate and questioning are the hallmarks of the field.

There is no doubt that IRs represent an opportunity for information professionals to extend their field of practice and develop new relationships with varied communities across the academic sector, from principal investigators to national funding bodies. The drive is towards building new services on the established and emerging repository infrastructure, but without sufficient, quality assured content, these services and opportunities are doomed. This places pressure on repository managers to expand the content in their repository and for the collection to be seen to be growing. However, IR content cannot be acquired in the same way as other digital content, such as electronic journal articles or e-books, which can be licensed from vendors. This is a system that largely evolved from the traditional purchasing model for libraries. IR content, on the other hand, is usually provided voluntarily by the research community within an institution, adding an extra task to already busy working lives.

It has also been noted that IRs can contain a wide range of digital materials, each of which imposes a different set of priorities and constraints upon the IR collection manager. Content housed in IRs can range from 'published articles, conference papers and posters, book chapters, preprints, technical reports, working papers, presentations, data sets, websites, dissertations, theses, and other student work, digitized material from library holdings, administrative records, curricular materials, audio, video, and other materials' (Shreeves and Cragin, 2008, 90–1).

Aschenbrenner et al. (2010) observe that more types of material and more services built on networks of repositories mean that more of the benefits of repositories are felt away from the institution, for example, going to the users of search aggregators or other services which exploit the data held in IRs. These users may be anywhere in the world. This means that IR managers must make the network speak back to the repository to monitor and demonstrate the impact of its collection. In this context, Web 2.0 phenomena such as trackbacks (which enable producers of online media to monitor references and links to their work) can be seen as a new form of citation and impact measure. This marks a departure from traditional collection monitoring where usage is relatively easy to measure and requirements can be fed into the library from the community of users. In the absence of clear, direct personal benefit, it can sometimes be difficult to persuade researchers to make the effort to deposit their research outputs in the IR. Thus, there are a set of challenges to building a strong and comprehensive IR collection that do not necessarily apply in other areas of librarianship.

These challenges are further complicated by the range of strategic priorities that an IR may be called on to serve, from research evaluation to open access to new forms of publication, all of which have implications for the management and development of the collection.

In light of this, this chapter begins by exploring the diversity of repository practices and approaches that have emerged over the last decade, and demonstrates the challenges for collection development raised by their differing priorities. The main part of this chapter focuses on the practical realities of advocacy, and the ways that tools and services that are available to aid deposit and to make use of IR content can support this work. In conclusion, emphasis falls on the centrality of good collection development practice to the success of the IR, and its contribution to its home institution.

Institutional repositories: the practical implications of diversity

Repositories have evolved rapidly in the early years of the 21st century. Early digital archives tended to be subject based, such as the high energy physics repository, arXiv,[1] based at Cornell University, or tied to specific content types, such as the electronic thesis and dissertation repository at Virginia Tech.[2] Brown (2010, 117) identifies five distinct types of repository:

- Institutional: repositories established by a particular university or other research institution to house outputs from its staff
- Departmental: repositories serving a specific department or laboratory
- Subject: established to collect material from a particular discipline
- National: for the use of scholars working in a particular country
- Topic-based: such as a newspaper, or an e-theses archive.

Of these, the largest and most visible individual repositories are subject repositories, fed by an international community of scholars, but the most numerous by far are institutional repositories. National bodies such as the Joint Information Systems Committee (JISC) in the UK, the National Institute of Informatics (NII) in Japan and the Australian National Data Service (ANDS) have funded and provided services to numerous IR development projects. These projects have overwhelmingly focused on building repository infrastructure, supporting developments in metadata standards and so on, but have not been geared towards expanding the content available via repositories, and as a result, many (though by no means all) IRs languish, under-populated and consequently underused.

In part, this is due to the fact that IRs emerged in parallel to the open access movement, as a part of the strategy of 'green' (author self-archiving) OA (Ferreira et al., 2008) and this approach has not proved universally popular amongst OA advocates, let alone amongst scholars (see, for example, Harnad (2005) and Guédon (2004)). In addressing content development in IRs, it is important to note that as well as functioning as a potential component in an OA world, they face separate challenges and function as part of other infrastructures.

Practical challenges in building IR collections

Numerous approaches can be suggested for individual repository managers to increase the volume and range of materials held in their IR, but there is no 'one size fits all' advice that can be offered. There are simply too many variables to be factored in to repository advocacy for this to be possible. As noted above, the repository field is chiefly distinguished by the range of approaches that have been adopted, implemented or argued for. This means that repositories, and IRs in particular, are fabulously flexible and diverse constructs but it also means that it can be difficult to apply successful collection-building initiatives from other institutions, since they may very well not be directly applicable to one's own professional circumstances.

Take differing national approaches as a case in point. In the USA the overwhelming focus of repository development has been directed at OA, which means that collections are driven by the need for full text. In the UK, many IRs have been called on to serve as a publications database for their institution, which has meant that they contain a large proportion of metadata-only records. These are often used to populate researchers' institutional web pages and for research evaluation reporting, but it does mean that the standard arguments used in OA advocacy are diluted and the usefulness of the collection is limited outside its institutional context. However, it also means that more researchers are likely to interact with the IR, through activities such as uploading records and using services built on the IR, and this helps to give the manager some idea of how much potential content is missing from the IR.

Shared solutions

Many institutions have chosen to join repository consortia, which pose particular challenges for collection development. There are a variety of different possible models for repository consortia, but perhaps the most significant challenge from a collection development perspective comes with shared repositories, defined as those 'in which a group of institutions, generally without individual pre-existing repositories, come together to develop a single instance of a repository to house content from all participating institutions' (Brown, 2009b, 3).

Shared repositories, such as Washington Research Libraries Consortium's ALADIN Research Commons[3] in the USA or the White Rose consortium's White Rose Research Online[4] in the UK create a larger repository collection, since the pool of available content is extended across multiple institutions, but the centralized nature of their staffing creates distance from the communities they serve, which poses a barrier to the kind of direct advocacy and relationship building which has tended to underpin IR advocacy (Brown, 2009b, 7).

Other practical issues which may directly affect the ease of building up content levels in an IR include the hosting of the repository, the constraints imposed by repository software itself and the balance of disciplines within the IR's community of researchers.

There are a variety of possible means of building a repository infrastructure beyond participation in a consortium. The two most common are locally managed implementations of one of the main software platforms and commercially hosted, often proprietary systems. A locally managed instance of, say, Eprints or DSpace has the benefits of responsiveness and clear ownership on the part of the institution, but can be a drain on staff time that could otherwise be devoted to content acquisition and advocacy. Staffing is the major consideration in outsourcing to a ready-made publishing platform and server space (Foster, Bankier and Wiley 2008, 3) but having fewer staff working on the repository within the institution can reduce the visibility of the IR, which rather hampers advocacy work from the outset.

The effects of different disciplines

When selecting a software platform, whether local, shared or commercially hosted, it is crucial to assess the likely range of formats and content types that the IR is going to be called upon to house. A medical school will produce an overwhelming majority of journal articles, most of which will be simple, text-based PDF files. An arts-based institution will be an entirely different prospect, with complex digital objects, records of various events, performances, installations and so on and often composite records, linked to images, video, sound and websites. In the former case, a fairly standard repository software installation will serve the needs of a growing collection admirably. In the latter case, such a set-up would rapidly prove a damaging constraint on the capacity of the IR to represent the output of the institution, and a specially adapted software should be deployed, such as that developed by the KULTUR project in the UK, which customized the popular Eprints platform to make it more arts-friendly.[5]

The disciplinary base in an IR's home institution can have a significant impact on more than the likely range of content types to be housed in the IR. Rates of deposit in IRs have historically been consistently lower in the arts and humanities than in the science, technology, and medical disciplines (Heath, Jubb and Robey, 2008). If the physics and astronomy communities represent extremes at the top of the statistical range for repository deposit, largely thanks to arXiv which many researchers actually prefer to journals (Gentil-Beccot, Mele and Brooks, 2010), then the humanities represent the outliers at the bottom of the statistical range.

Heath, Jubb and Robey (2008) claim that this situation is slowly changing, but print remains the dominant medium for the humanities and is likely to for some years to come, although such projects as the Europeana digital library[6] and the Transcribe Bentham initiative,[7] as well as commercial resources such as Early English Books Online, are steadily increasing the value of digital content to researchers in this area. The possibilities offered by embedded media, hyperlinks and similar technologies to humanities publishers are serving to fuel more enthusiasm for digital publication in these disciplines. This means that there will be more born-digital content available to populate IRs in the near future, although the case for OA still needs to be made to researchers in these disciplines.

What makes collection development in institutional repositories unique?

It has been observed that 'many of the management issues that repository managers are facing are novel' (Zuccala, Oppenheim and Dhiensa, 2008) including approaches to collection development. There are many ways that IR collection development can be said to be unique. Chief amongst these is the relationship with researchers as suppliers of content rather than consumers, which brings a whole set of skill requirements around advocacy and liaison. Genoni notes that in terms of collection management practice in IRs as opposed to other areas of library activity 'there is one area of practice that will be altered substantially, that of acquisitions. Whether dealing with print or digitally formatted material, libraries have previously identified wanted items, and then dealt with a publisher or supplier in order to acquire the item by paying for permanent retention or licensed access.' Instead, 'with institutional repositories, the producers (authors) of material are requested to provide digital copies without financial compensation' (Genoni, 2004, 304).

While this content is ostensibly free, it must be extracted from the information service's user base, either as a matter of institutional policy or as a matter of voluntary action. If an IR manager is lucky enough to work within the tiny proportion of research institutions around the world which have adopted an institutional OA mandate, then perhaps the biggest challenge will be handling the sheer volume of content pouring into the repository. This kind of success brings significant workloads, in assuring metadata quality and accuracy or in checking full-text materials for copyright infringement for instance, but these are, perhaps sadly, minority concerns. For most IR managers, the difficulty lies in populating the repository. Swan and Carr found that 'over 60 percent of repository managers reported that recruiting content to their repository has been possible but not easy: one-third said they have found it difficult or very difficult' (Swan and Carr, 2008, 32) and so it is this difficult aspect of collection development which will occupy much of this section.

As already discussed, the purpose of IR collections can vary between nations, disciplines and institutions, but at their core, 'digital repositories are strategic instruments to develop coherent and co-ordinated approaches to the capture, identification, storage and retrieval of intellectual assets such as data sets, course material and research papers' (Ayris, 2009, 66). In order to serve this strategic role, IR managers must develop a nuanced approach to the context of their collection. The institution will often be seeking the kind of strategic gain described by Ayris, but 'repositories are very flexible entities, and different stakeholders have different views of their uses – until there is a better perceived "fit", the performance of self-deposit will remain low' (Ayris, 2009, 69–70).

In order for repository managers to achieve this 'fit' with the goals and ambitions of their various research communities, they must become very 'active, not passive, collectors of content' (Salo, 2008, 119). The collection must be made to serve the needs of as many separate constituencies of users as possible.

Simple steps to collection growth
Easy deposit
Amongst the first steps to be taken by repository mangers in adopting such an approach is ensuring that deposit is as easy as possible. Kim (2010) analysed cross disciplinary self-archiving practices among researchers, and identified the most significant barriers to depositing items as:

- concerns about copyright
- the extra time and effort involved in deposit
- perceived technical challenges in preparing and uploading files to the repository.

These are all practical concerns, and attending to these issues by providing mediated services for copyright checking, upload and document conversion (from, say, Microsoft Word .docx format to PDF(a)) IR managers can create an environment in which those with a weaker commitment to deposit are not effectively excluded.

Practical tools such as the Simple Web-service Offering Repository Deposit (SWORD) protocol[8] (based on 'Atom', which is used for creating and updating web resources) can be used to create opportunities for straightforward repository deposit from within authoring software, to create customized deposit interfaces or to offer useful services such as simultaneous deposit to multiple locations. Such tools and services can integrate the repository with virtual learning environments (VLE) or even with social media sites like Facebook (Lewis, et al., 2009, 412). Such tools can go a long way towards encouraging those less willing to deposit, and also towards sustaining deposit levels amongst the more enthusiastic.

If practical barriers have been lowered as far as possible, the advocacy and outreach that builds a strong IR collection can be tailored to differing audiences, different classes of content and institutional priorities much more coherently. In this sense, it can be beneficial to consider the content housed in an IR as not one collection, but several, and to review the purpose and intended audience of each.

E-theses
One of the major trends at present in the UK is towards electronic theses. A survey undertaken by University College London found that 81% of UK higher degree awarding institutions either already accept submission and archiving of electronic versions of theses, or have plans to within five years (Brown, Sadler and Moyle, 2010). These institutions collectively award more than 99% of UK doctoral qualifications, which means that theses will make up a valuable part of an IR's content.

Traditionally, the bound, print versions of theses have been underused. In comparison, theses that are made available electronically are much more heavily used, and often make up one of the most-downloaded content types in a repository (Brown and Sadler, 2010). This is without taking into account the impact of the UK's national E-Theses Online Service (EThOS),[9] which offers an aggregation and digitization service and provides the largest single source of UK doctoral theses. Increasingly, this service harvests from IRs, meaning that depositing a thesis in an IR is a fast way to raise one's visibility and reach as an early-career researcher. As well as being a major boon to literature reviewing researchers and other postgraduates who can gain access to the latest research findings, it also serves as a steady supply of large, high-quality materials for the IR, ensuring the collection has both currency and relevance.

However, while these benefits are real, they do come at a cost for the collection manager. Careful attention must be paid to third-party copyright content within theses, which may have been included under the copyright exception allowed for material for examination, but will no longer be covered by this once the thesis is freely available online. Other issues, such as the concern that the IR may in effect scoop an author's formal publication of their findings can be addressed by the measured use of embargoes (delays on the release of the full text of a thesis). The EThOS toolkit provides guidance on best practice in addressing such issues.[10]

This means that, in order to realize the benefits of a strong and comprehensive e-theses collection, the IR manager must accept a certain amount of drain on staffing resources, and some attention to careful risk management. The use of embargoes as a cure-all for risks with e-theses also limits the utility of the e-thesis collection to all the possible user communities, within and outside the institution.

Capitalizing on research infrastructure and services

As noted above, IRs form a part of a wider research information infrastructure. Genoni noted in 2004 that 'negotiations regarding content suitable for inclusion in institutional repositories will require librarians to become more familiar with the full life cycle of scholarly research, communication and publishing' (Genoni, 2004, 8). It is revealing of the pace of change in IRs that this requirement is in large part now a reality. Repositories now interact with each other, with publishers' databases and citation indexes, with research offices, with research funders and with research activity across the institution. IRs have become a key component of the Current Research Information System (CRIS) architectures being adopted in increasing numbers of HEIs (Jeffery and Asserson, 2008; Sheppard, 2010).

This interaction can impose strain on collection management policies. It can result in a dilution of the full-text content in IRs by an influx of metadata-only records, raising the spectre of the IR becoming, in effect, a catalogue more than a repository. IR managers, for the most part, have to be pragmatic about these concerns. By participating in local and national infrastructures, for the strategic management of research, ensuring institutional compliance with the OA mandates adopted by most major research funders or for research evaluation and statutory reporting, IRs have been positioned as vital tools for the successful management of a research institution. This has meant that funding and, most importantly, staffing for development and administration have been easier to obtain and the medium-term future for most IRs promises to be relatively secure. These are not trivial benefits for any repository.

The question for the IR manager seeking to extend the comprehensiveness of their collection, then, is how to capitalize on these developments. Two strategies have emerged, both of which offer valuable chances to increase the content of an IR, and which are made possible by exploiting the very circumstances which have threatened the balance of the IR collection. The first is to take advantage of the extra research information made available to the IR manager by increased integration with campus and other research systems. The second is to use the enhanced research infrastructure to provide new services and opportunities to researchers, encouraging them to engage much more actively with the IR and to actively build up the range and volume of content that it contains.

Rumsey (2010, 175) has demonstrated the benefits of using the extra information made available to an IR by its links to other campus systems. This information can be used to generate metadata automatically in deposit processes, further lowering the practical barriers to deposit. It can also be used to provide details of researchers' publication records, which can then be used for targeted approaches to individual researchers. Royster (2009) notes that often, such approaches are most effective when directed to senior researchers with lengthier CVs. Junior researchers, who would seem to have the most to gain from an expanded online presence for their work can be the most agnostic about IR deposit (although it is likely that this will change as more researchers begin their careers by depositing their thesis in an IR, a move that, it is to be hoped, will inculcate the idea of self-archiving). This also offers an opportunity to check if the publications list is complete.

The increasing prevalence of relatively complete publications lists also enables more accurate analysis of which departments or research teams are showing a greater commitment to full-text archiving. This can be used in approaches to department heads (indicating that the level of full-text available from their department is above or below the institutional norm can be a very effective advocacy strategy) and can also be used to ensure that advocacy is properly targeted. It is all too easy to focus on the departments that are most visible, which tend to be the ones that are already engaging with the IR.

The second strategy, building services on the IR, can take two forms. One is to increase the range of content housed in the repository, which can enhance the number of possible uses the IR has for researchers and teachers. Housing learning objects or reading material in the IR, enabled by the same kind of campus-wide integration with, for instance, VLEs, that improves deposit rates can be a valuable service for researchers. By storing primary research data, especially those which take the form of text transcripts or audiovisual media, the repository can function as a 'keep safe', preserving and securing crucial data sources and linking them to ensuing publications.

The second group of services tends to focus on supporting researchers in the administration and recording of their work. Automatically populating web pages, ensuring compliance with funder mandates by linking research grants to publications and performing onward deposit to funder-sanctioned subject repositories are all extremely important services to busy researchers. This also builds a community around the IR, for whom regular engagement with its services is a natural part of their working life. The value of this cannot be overstated when it comes to advocacy work.

New possibilities for scholarly communication

An IR stands at a unique juncture in the scholarly communication process, and as Foster, Bankier and Wiley observe, 'digital repositories really do create information possibilities' (Foster, Bankier and Wiley 2008, 9). This also provides opportunities for the enterprising IR manager to develop new content and strong bonds to the research community. IRs are central to green OA strategy, which has clear implications for the nature of research and publication, not least of which is a substantial increase in the range of resources available to individual researchers. They are also seen as a means of creating new publishing opportunities for scholars.

These possibilities have engendered considerable debate across the entire scholarly communication spectrum, from 'librarians who need parameters on which to base collection development strategies to policy makers who weigh the benefits of Open Access, and from scientific publishers developing business models and platforms to scientists as users of scientific information' (Gentil-Beccot, Mele and Brooks 2010, 346). The point at which all these groups converge most fruitfully is the emergence of 'overlay' journals, or campus-based publications which use a repository as the basis for their archive and dissemination activities (Brown, 2009a).

Frantsvåg (2010) has noted that scholarly publishing forms a classic 'long tail'. Nearly one-third of journals are published by 27 publishers, while 83.7% of academic publishers only publish one journal, which accounts for another third of the journals currently available to scholars. By using an IR as the basis for a small-scale publishing endeavour, and joining this 'long tail', small research communities can communicate in a cost-effective and highly efficient way. Software, notably the Public Knowledge Project's Open Journal System,[11] has been developed that enables the repository to handle journal submissions, peer review notifications and version control. This is beyond doubt a major service to be able to offer to a community of researchers, and has been memorably described as a 'win-win-win-win' for publishers, repositories, authors and readers (Hendler, 2007, 3).

Collection development nonetheless

Having explored some of the challenges and opportunities that make collection development in IRs so unique, it is worth noting that collection development remains a key part of what links repository management to the library 'mainstream'. Salo outlines the damage that can be done by an IR which is sparsely filled with unstructured, poorly recorded content of variable quality (Salo, 2008, 106). Good collection development practice is the key to avoiding this fate. Neubauer notes that libraries are central to successful IRs 'because they know better than anyone else how to handle metadata' (Neubauer, 2008, 121) but there are far more important factors at work in the centrality of librarians to the IR.

Whilst it must be acknowledged that a digital repository is a distinct endeavour from a digital library, it has been observed that 'repository managers are focused on how to develop their repositories and are intent on encouraging individuals to deposit, but over time they will have to focus more on understanding long-term user needs' (Zuccala, Oppenheim and Dhiensa, 2008). This focus on the requirements of the various constituencies of users of IR content extends to the setting of priorities for the IR. Genoni (2004, 305) notes that 'Libraries have extensive experience in talking to user groups about their information needs as a part of the selection of material for inclusion in print and digital collections. This will be a crucial step in the selection of content for institutional repositories'. He also lists the evaluation of the performance of the collection, decisions relating to access (be it to e-theses, correct versioning of publications and the maintenance of so-called 'dark archives' of institutional records and works in progress) and the management of conservation and preservation as 'classic' collection development skills which underpin IR management.

> In applying these core skills, IR managers can create a truly comprehensive and useful collection for their IR. If this can be achieved, then the repository serves both as 'a library and a showcase. It is a library in that it holds the collection. It is a showcase because the online open access display and availability of the collection may serve to impress and connect, for example, with alumni of the institution or the colleagues of researchers. Moreover, such an institutional repository could have an important function in regional development. It allows firms, public bodies and civil society organizations to immediately understand what kind of expertise is locally available' (Romary and Armbruster, 2010, 48).

A well managed IR collection can also build on the benefits of global networks in a way that is seldom available to more 'conventional' digital libraries. As the volume of research outputs, of all kinds, housed in repositories grows and is made accessible worldwide thanks to the de facto indexing services provided by Google (amongst others) then 'the repository will become the competitive tool for maximizing research visibility, status, and reputation of an institution.... The locus for promotion of the institution, therefore, moves from institutional and departmental web pages and other marketing channels to a new place— its digital collections of real outputs and resources' (Swan and Carr, 2008, 33).

Conclusion

This chapter has explored some of the features of IRs that make collection development in these fast-evolving digital archives unique. These features are diverse and often challenging, merging cultural considerations (such as academic disciplines and the politics of OA) with practical issues (modern workloads and research reporting obligations) and technological innovations. The key to meeting these challenges successfully is to use as wide a range of solutions as possible.

It can be said that there are two main user groups for IR content: home researchers and researchers. Researchers within the repository's home institution are the primary target of the collection development effort, and need simple processes and clear benefits to encourage them to make the effort to deposit their work in the IR. Researchers the world over access, read and cite the collection, and monitoring this usage is central to demonstrating the value of an IR. It also requires the IR manager to keep a careful watch on evolving services and standards which seek to exploit IR collections. Ensuring that your IR has a broad collection and that its content is shared as widely as possible is the best way of supporting both groups of researchers and other repositories.

Issues to consider

- What are the features that distinguish an IR from other kinds of repository (subject, national, etc.)?
- If content isn't in the IR, where is it being stored?
- Who are the most influential depositors of material into the IR? Why do they use it? Can you make them 'champions' for the IR?
- Consider the most significant difficulties different groups of researchers might face in depositing their work into the IR. Do they vary by discipline? Age? Career focus?
- What is the value of the IR to senior managers in your institution? Can you prove that the IR is delivering what they want it to?

References

Aschenbrenner, A., Blanke, T., Kuster, M. W. and Pempe, W. (2010) Towards an Open Repository Environment, *Journal of Digital Information*, **11** (1).

Ayris, P. (2009) New Wine in Old Bottles: current developments in digital delivery and dissemination, *European Review*, **17** (1), 53–71.

Brown, D. J. (2010) Repositories and Journals: are they in conflict? A literature review of relevant literature, *Aslib Proceedings: New Information Perspectives*, **62** (2), 112–43.

Brown, J. (2009a) *An Introduction to Overlay Journals*, University College London.

Brown, J. (2009b) *Comparing Consortial Repositories: a model-driven analysis*, University College London.

Brown, J. and Sadler, K. (2010) *Vision, Impact, Success: mandating electronic theses. Case studies of e-theses mandates in practice in the UK Higher Education sector*, University College London.

Brown, J., Sadler, K. and Moyle, M. (2010) *Influencing the Deposit of Electronic Theses in UK HE: report on a sector-wide survey into thesis deposit and open access*, University College London.

Ferreira, M., Rodrigues, E., Baptista, A. A. and Saraiva, R. (2008) Carrots and Sticks: some ideas on how to create a successful institutional repository, *D-Lib Magazine*, **14** (1–2).

Foster, C., Bankier, J.-G. and Wiley, G. (2008) *Institutional Repositories: strategies for the present and future*. Paper given as a part of the Strategy Session, NASIG 23rd Annual Conference, June 6, 2008.

Frantsvåg, J. E. (2010) The Size Distribution of Open Access Publishers: a problem for open access? *First Monday*, **15** (12), 6 December 2010.

Genoni, P. (2004) Content in Institutional Repositories: a collection management issue, *Library Management*, **25** (6–7), 300–6.

Gentil-Beccot, A., Mele, S. and Brooks, T. C. (2010) Citing and Reading Behaviours in High-energy Physics, *Scientometrics*, **84**, 345–55.

Guédon, J.-C. (2004) The 'Green' and 'Gold' Roads to Open Access: the case for mixing and matching, *Serials Review*, **30** (4), 315–28.

Harnad, S. (2005) Fast-Forward on the Green Road to Open Access: the case against mixing up green and gold, *Ariadne*, 43.

Heath, M., Jubb, M. and Robey, D. (2008) E-Publication and Open Access in the Arts and Humanities in the UK, *Ariadne*, 54.

Hendler, J. (2007) Reinventing Academic Publishing: part 2, *IEEE Intelligent Systems*, November/December 2007, 2–3.

Jeffery, K. and Asserson, A. (2008) Institutional Repositories and Current Research Information Systems, *New Review of Information Networking*, **14** (2), 71–83.

Kim, J. (2010) Faculty Self-archiving: motivations and barriers, *Journal of the American Society for Information Science and Technology*, **61** (9), 1909–22.

Lewis, S., Hayes, L., Newton-Wade, V., Corfield, A., Davis, R., Donohue, T. and Wilson, S. (2009) If SWORD is the Answer, What is the Question?: Use of the simple web-service offering repository deposit protocol, *Program: electronic library and information systems*, **43** (4), 407–18.

Neubauer, W. (2008) About the Future of Libraries, *Information Services & Use*, **28**, 121–2.

Read, M. (2008) Libraries and Repositories, *New Review of Academic Librarianship*, **14** (1), 71–8.

Romary, L. and Armbruster, C. (2010) Beyond Institutional Repositories, *International Journal of Digital Library Systems*, **1** (1), 44–61.

Royster, P. (2009) *Institutional Repositories*. Paper given at: American Library Association Annual Convention, Chicago, Illinois, July 12, 2009.

Rumsey, S. (2010) A Case Analysis of Registering Research Activity for Institutional Benefit, *International Journal of Information Management*, **30**, 174–9.

Salo, D. (2008) Innkeeper at the Roach Motel, *Library Trends*, **57** (2), 98–123.

Sheppard, N. (2010) Learning How to Play Nicely: repositories and CRIS, *Ariadne*, 64.

Shreeves, S. L. and Cragin, M. H. (2008) Introduction: institutional repositories: current state and future, *Library Trends*, **57** (2), 89–97.

Swan, A. and Carr, L. (2008) Institutions, Their Repositories and the Web, *Serials Review*, **34**, 31–5.

Zuccala, A., Oppenheim, C. and Dhiensa, R. (2008) Managing and Evaluating Digital Repositories, *Information Research*, **13** (1) paper 333.

Notes

1 www.arxiv.org.
2 http://scholar.lib.vt.edu/theses.
3 http://aladinrc.wrlc.org/.
4 http://eprints.whiterose.ac.uk/.
5 http://kultur.eprints.org/about.htm.
6 www.europeana.eu/portal/.
7 www.ucl.ac.uk/transcribe-bentham/.

8 http://swordapp.org/.
9 http://ethos.bl.uk/.
10 http://ethostoolkit.cranfield.ac.uk.
11 http://pkp.sfu.ca/?q=ojs.

Part 4
Making and keeping your collection effective

12
Collection development policies for the digital age

Wendy Shaw

Introduction

Collection Management embraces a range of different activities, including selection and acquisition, collection evaluation, collection review, preservation and promotional aspects. To support these essential collection management processes, there needs to be a viable and pragmatic written Collection Development Policy (CDP). An informal, verbal agreement is insufficient if you are going to have a commitment to systematic collection building or development.

This chapter will define *what* a CDP is and describe the individual components and overall structure that make up a written CDP. The role of a CDP will be discussed and guidance offered on how to devise and implement a CDP. Extracts from existing CDPs are offered as working examples to illustrate points and for you to explore in more detail.

A CDP: what is it, and why do I need it?

Let us begin this discussion by asking the question: What is a CDP? A CDP is a formal policy document or statement which maintains a commitment to systematic collection building and development. Johnson states that 'libraries without collection development policies are like businesses without business plans. Without a plan, an owner and his employees lack a clear understanding of what the business is doing now and what it will do in the future, and potential investors have little information about the business's prospects' (Johnson, 2009, 72).

The emphasis here is on the importance of the document and its multi faceted use. You may also hear of the document being referred to as the selection, acquisitions or stock policy; the terms are often used interchangeably in the professional literature. Even when a stock policy already exists and is in use, however, a CDP goes further.

Evans and Saponaro describe a CDP as a 'framework within which individuals can exercise judgement' (2005, 52). The CDP document or statement will form a comprehensive and detailed written 'contract' between users and the library and plays an essential part in collection management, as will be explored in this chapter. The CDP is used as an advocate for the library in terms of public relations with users (to inform), for administration purposes (to build reputations) and for justification for funding bodies (to enable communication between external users and internal staff). A CDP helps demonstrate the accountability of the library in times of financial uncertainty.

The CDP therefore has multiple purposes, including:

- aiding decision-making processes for administration and organization
- operational effectiveness and efficiency
- accountability for actions
- setting standards for selection and weeding process
- continuity, co-operation and facilitates co-ordination
- consistency of approach
- acting as a tool for in-house staff training
- communication (informs and minimizes personal bias)
- promotion and marketing
- assisting in allocating funds and demonstrating how the budget is spent within the collection
- acting as a tool for managing stakeholder expectations.

A CDP will serve the wider community and keep it informed of the library's intentions both in the short and longer term. The document defines relationships with other libraries and assists in resource sharing. It will clarify objectives; support the library's mission, goals and aspirations; define the scope, type and level of resources; highlight collection strengths and identify priorities for the selection, acquisitions and evaluation of resources. The CDP can be used as a guide for those staff involved in collection management decisions; as a public relations tool for your library; and as an insurance policy in case of collection-related challenges. A written policy also provides a basis for continuity and consistency for the institution.

How to devise and implement a written CDP

You should aim to describe the scope, strengths and limitations of what is in existence in the collection now (both in print and electronic) and provide guidelines for the development into the future.

Smyth (1999, 29) notes that the key to creating a workable policy lies in preparing one that is specific enough to be useful without being cumbersome; is honest and realistic in respect of monetary and other resources; lays out a practical guide for allotting those resources and is easily updated. Futas (1995, 5) describes the devising and implementation process as: planning to plan; collecting information for decision making; the document; from document to policy and document approval.

Simplified, there are three stages to the formulation of a CDP for your library. These are preparation, data gathering and the writing up of the document.

Stage One: Preparation

The formulation of a CDP from scratch is a major task that will require consultation with staff and possibly the wider community. As a CDP is an official document, you will need to start by preparing the ground. Begin by informing the library board or similar entity of your intention to prepare a policy. It is helpful to have sought guidance from staff in a similar position in another library, and to seek out advice online or from the literature about preparing a CDP.

The National Library of Australia offers a useful reference document on their website[1] entitled 'Guidelines for the preparation of a collection development policy', which has been devised to assist libraries who are about to formulate or revise a CDP. You may like to consult this document for your own particular use.

Before consultation with other staff, you will need to establish a realistic time-frame for the whole process (this may be as long as 12 or even 24 months); who is to be involved and what will be included in the document. A project leader should be identified to oversee the process for continuity to clarify the participants' roles and responsibilities and ensure smooth and efficient communication. The team of participants will decide upon the content of the CDP and a final deadline for completion of the CDP. An insight into the key elements of a CDP will be advantageous at this stage. The document will need to be reviewed and evaluated to determine its effectiveness. Co-operative agreements should be scrutinized as new developments may arise in digital collections which could co-exist in print form.

Stage Two: Data gathering

The second stage involves collecting relevant documents and data to inform the process. The information required will consist of community data; strategic planning documentation; collection assessment data; existing policy statements and written procedures documentation.

Stage Three: Writing the policy document

The third stage, writing or updating the CDP, should be undertaken with care, as once formulated, it is an official document. In the words of Futas (1995, 12), the document should be a 'living, breathing entity that is always thought of, always lived with, always tinkered with, and never quite finished'. The CDP must address evolving issues around strategic plans, library priorities, budget allocation, training and communication with other departments.

Once the document reaches the final draft stage, you will need to seek approval from relevant stakeholders and accommodate any modifications before publication. Your library board or governing body may suggest the need for different versions: a full version for the library staff and an abridged version for users. The issue of style will be a consideration for potential users. Be prepared – a document of this nature may well expose library staff and management to external criticism.

The standard CDP document

The CDP has historical roots, and you may be wondering about its origins. In 1996 the

American Library Association (ALA) published the second edition of their *Guide for Written Collection Development Policy Statements*, 'to offer generic advice, collection levels, and language codes that are applicable or adaptable to libraries of all sizes and types' (American Library Association, 1996, vii). The American model developed in the 1980s and has become internationally accepted and can be adapted to meet the cultural, social and professional needs of an individual country. Johnson (2009, 73) points out that 'policy statements are not general, idealistic, theoretical, or vague, but they are not so detailed and ponderous that they become unusable'.

The basic components of a CDP are outlined here as a guide. Please note that there is no single prescription for the length and content of a CDP; one size does not fit all. The average CDP contains ten pages although those of deposit or large academic libraries may be longer.

The basic components of a CDP

This structure is based on the ALA model and comprises the following sections:

1 Introduction
2 Purpose of the CDP
3 Mission statement
4 Clientèle
5 Content
6 Special collections
7 Collection depth
8 Evaluation
9 Co-operation
10 Intellectual freedom
11 Review

1   Introduction

The introduction is a summary of the basic principles which apply to the CDP and acts as a policy framework, as in the example below, from Birkbeck College, University of London.[2] The CDP will not be an isolated policy in the library and its relationship with other policy documents must be made explicit. These might include membership, preservation, IT, networking or e-learning policies.

> This document provides an overview of how the Library's electronic, print, and audiovisual collections are managed and developed. It seeks to make transparent the criteria for decisions on selection and withdrawal of library resources.
>
> Aligning the resources available through the Library with the academic activities of the College requires a close working partnership between the Faculties, Schools, and the Library. The document outlines the respective responsibilities of academic staff and Subject Librarians in this partnership. (Birkbeck College)

2 Purpose of the CDP

You need to establish the purpose and use of the CDP as shown here in this example from The Pasadena Public Library.[3]

> The collection development policy is intended to provide guidance, within budgetary and space limitations, for the selection and evaluation of materials which anticipate and meet the needs of the Pasadena community. It directly relates the collection to the library's mission statement, and defines the scope and standards of the various collections. (Pasadena Public Library)

3 Mission statement and a statement of the goals of the collection

Decisions about the range of materials to be collected or accessed will be made in the mission statement. A written policy, such as the following example from Harvard Law School,[4] sets goals for the collection, and these will reflect the library's mission.

> The primary mission of the Harvard Law School Library is to support the research and curricular needs of its current faculty and students. The Library also supports the greater Harvard community and, to a lesser extent, the community of scholars and researchers around the world who are interested in subjects of or related to the law. (Harvard Law School)

Within the goals of the collection consideration may also need to be given to supporting computer or media literacy.

4 The clientèle to be served

The clientèle will vary depending upon the type of library (for example, academic, public, schools, special library) that it serves. Clientèle may include students, faculty, staff and members of the local community, including remote users (for example, distance learners). The policy should be clear about who the users are, as in this example from Glasgow:[5]

> The Glasgow Digital Library exists for the benefit of Glasgow people and institutions.

5 Collection content

General criteria will guide the selection of resources, depending on the library's mission and goals. At Canterbury Christchurch University, for example, the criteria reflect the institution's commitment to teaching and research:[6]

> The following factors are taken into account when selecting material for purchase or use under licence:

- relevance, immediate or potential, to teaching, learning or research
- anticipated levels of use
- appropriateness of the level of the material
- currency of content
- price
- availability of funding.

In the case of electronic resources: all of the above but also ease of use, web based access and the existence of appropriate licensing and archiving arrangements. (Canterbury Christchurch University, para. 2.4.4)

Subject statements may be used to include an overview of the collection. Such statements might include a brief history of the collection, where appropriate, the location of subject collections in multi-campus libraries. The University of Cambridge, a UK legal deposit library, makes its collecting responsibility clear:[7]

The University Library, by virtue of the legal deposit privilege, acquires almost every book published in the UK or Ireland, irrespective of its academic level or its intended readership and as such, its legal deposit collections form part of the National Published Archive. (University of Cambridge, para. 2.2)

Separate subject policies may also be defined, as at University College London[7] and New York University Libraries.[8]

The CDP will provide details on other key aspects, such as language and translations:

Languages
For subject areas that are central to the Museum's purpose, works are collected in all European languages, the criterion being the usefulness and value of the text and images. Subsequent translations into English are acquired for the more important works when there is considered to be no English equivalent, or when the translation includes important new matter. A few works are acquired in Chinese and Japanese at the behest of curators in the Asian Department; these are catalogued by non-V&A contract staff when there is no expertise within the NAL. Works in other oriental languages are very rarely acquired. (Victoria and Albert Museum, London, para. 9)[10]

The policy on gifts and donations must be made clear, as in this example from Campbell County Public Library:[11]

Donated materials
Donated material is accepted with the understanding that only those items which meet the criteria for material selection will be added to the collection. Donations are final and become the property of the Campbell County Public Library. The Library

> reserves the right to dispose of items that are in poor condition, out-of-date or not needed for other reasons, in the manner it deems most appropriate. Most materials the Library is unable to use are given to the Friends of the Campbell County Public Library for sale or disposal. (Campbell County Public Library, 24)

Likewise, the policy on multiple copies, particularly for academic institutions is important, although the increasing acquisition of e-books is changing this.

> The number of copies bought of any title will depend on anticipated demand, the number of students to whom the title is being recommended, and the cost. Paperbacks will be the preferred format on grounds of lower cost, unless the anticipated use and shelf life suggest that a hardback edition would be more cost-effective. The purchase of 10 copies of a single item is a general maximum, with a formula of one copy per 20 students used as a general guideline. The shortening of loan periods can assist with availability. Loan period information relating to each library can be found on the Lending Services Pages. (Aberystwyth University, para. 1.4)[12]

Some institutions also make a point of explaining their policy on expensive purchases:

> When budgetary restrictions are necessary, the Library will use available funds to provide resources to meet the most immediate instructional needs and to maintain its course-related research function and its basic collection strength. Purchase of expensive items and specialized material may be deferred or eliminated at such times. The Library may request written justification from requestors for expensive items and those requiring an ongoing commitment of funds. (Montclair State University)[13]

The collection content section may also set out the responsibilities for staff engaged in collection management, which helps individuals to understand their role and place in their staff structure. It will be necessary to consider the organization, staffing and liaison with users. In respect of collection overview, any significant management training would need to be included alongside the e-resources library. As an example, Columbia University include a sizeable section in their CDP which covers four areas: materials selection, liaison, fund management and preservation responsibilities.[14] Below is a more concise example, from Oxford Brookes University:[15]

> **Responsibility for selection**
> - Library subject staff have the primary responsibility for the selection of material in the subject areas allocated to them.
> - Selection is carried out in liaison with academic staff; with reference to reading lists and newly published material; and on the basis of knowledge of existing stock.

> • Areas of general interest not the responsibility of any subject staff are overseen by the Deputy Librarian – Academic Services, the Head of Learning Resources – Harcourt Hill and Wheatley, and the Librarian: Site Services – Wheatley. (Oxford Brookes University)

In the *Collection Content* section, the library will also state its policy towards particular formats, whether they are to be included or excluded and, if so, for what reasons. Monterey Public Library[16] have a *specific collections and formats section* in their CDP which describes each collection area and states the collection level goal. Under their *materials for adults*, for example, print is separated from non-print and each section is broken down further into sub-categories:

> **2. Non-print**
> a. Adult DVDs and video-cassettes
>   This collection consists of a mix of educational and entertainment programs in DVD and/or VHS format . . . The collection is intended for home use and not curriculum support. Most titles are purchased in DVD format. VHS video cassettes may be selected based on anticipated use, demand, availability and cost.
> b. Educational [General interest level]
>   The educational DVD/video collection consists of material designed to meet the general informational, educational, and recreational needs of the community. Special emphasis is placed on subjects that can best be conveyed visually, rather than by the printed word. Materials for learning languages, including English as a Second Language (ESL) are located in the Language Instruction Collection (X.A.3) (Monterey Public Library, p. 13)

The University of Bradford's library CDP[17] illustrates the priority of content over form:

> Material will be acquired on the basis of information content rather than format type and decisions on whether to acquire print or electronic versions will be made as appropriate . . . the format offering the widest access at a reasonable price and acceptable terms and conditions of use, will be preferred. (University of Bradford, para. 3)

Libraries may choose to develop a separate policy for e-resources rather than integrating this into the general policy. The University of Akron University Libraries[18] in Ohio, has produced a CDP for e-books, highlighting its reasons for adopting such an approach:

> In order to meet their primary mission of supporting the teaching and research needs of students and faculty through their collections and services, The University of Akron University Libraries are committed to utilizing technology to enhance educational quality and access to information. The following guidelines address

> issues that are unique to the Libraries' acquisition of the format of eBooks and eBook collections, since electronic publications are often treated differently from printed publications by publishers and vendors. Because technology and information access changes so rapidly it is expected that these guidelines will be under continuing review by the Libraries' Collection Management Department. (University of Akron)

From a CDP perspective, however, e-books still present a challenge to many libraries. The University of Texas has access to over 20,000 e-books which have received steady usage over a two-year period. UT comment that 'it has been a challenge to incorporate e-books into existing routines . . . if they are to be of value, they need to achieve . . . ubiquity, utility, distribution, and stability. And if they do, and titles remain forever available and for sale, the role libraries have traditionally played in society could change significantly' (Dillon, n.d.).

6   Special Collections

A CDP may include a section specifying guidelines for the management, storage and acquisition of Special Collection material or refer to a separate policy. IFLA's CDP guidelines[19] (2001) offer advice on describing special material:

> Statements should be made of special subject or format collections that represent unique materials and for which special guidelines apply, and which formats are excluded.
>
> The scope of coverage should be described (languages collected or excluded; geographical areas covered and/or specific areas excluded; chronological periods covered by the collection in terms of intellectual content and in terms of publication dates and specific periods excluded).
>
> Subjects should be described in terms of the library's classification scheme and subject descriptors (p3).

Special Collections will typically hold historical material and unique or rare research material, as the University of Sussex Library's CDP[20] illustrates:

> **Special Collections**
> The Special Collections support research within the University and the wider scholarly community. Material is collected irrespective of format, and the collections include manuscripts, archives, printed books, photographs, audiovisual and electronic resources, architect's models and artworks. The material in Special Collections must be used under supervision in the Reading Room and cannot be borrowed . . . Rare books, including all books published before 1801, are in Special Collections, as are books and journals that relate to archival collections, and some modern books and journals that together form collections of particular research interest. A number of fragile or vulnerable items classed as 'Invigilated Reading' are also held in Special Collections. (University of Sussex Library, 6)

7 Collection depth

You may choose to indicate the relative depth and strength of your collection. This enables your collection to be compared to others and facilitates co-operation and access. Conspectus, devised by librarians in the former Research Libraries Group (RLG) in the US, became a recognized and widely used collection assessment tool during the 1980s. It has since been incorporated into web-based tools such as WorldCat Collection Analysis.[21] Conspectus is a generic tool for indicating the completeness of collections and because it uses standardized codes, it can be used in all types of libraries. The original depth indicators were as follows:

0 = Out of scope > the library does not intentionally collect in this area
1 = Minimal > collections that support minimal enquiries at a basic level
2 = Basic information > collections that serve to introduce and define a subject and indicate the varieties of information available elsewhere
3 = Study or instructional support > collections that provide information about a subject in a systematic way
4 = Research > includes major works for doctoral and research study
5 = Comprehensive > includes significant works, aims for exhaustiveness.

These codes can be extended and delineated more finely, and can be adapted to serve the needs of the individual institution or authority. An example of how the conspectus approach works in professional practice can be located by looking at Columbia University Library's policy.[22]

8 Evaluation

Collection evaluation is a vital tool to determine whether a collection is fulfilling the purpose and objectives stated for it in the CDP. It seeks to assess to what extent the collection is relevant to users. You may employ usage or user-centred methods or collection-centred methods to evaluate your collection. Librarians must decide which method is most suitable and bear in mind the implications of a collection-evaluation policy on staff resources.

Different terms are used in different types of libraries to describe the process of officially removing materials from the collection and destroying the associated records as a result of systematic weeding. You may read about terms such as: withdrawal, discarding, relegation, de-selecting and disposal. Research and academic libraries may discard print versions in favour of electronic resources to save space. The example below is from the Claude Moore Health Sciences Library, University of Virginia:[23]

Collection Evaluation
Collection evaluation is a continual process that the Library adheres to in order to maintain quality, manageable collections. Collection maintenance, assessment and weeding are all integral parts of the process known as Collection Evaluation. Shown

below are a representation of the first two elements used in this process, which are folded into the normal workflow and evaluation process. See the section on weeding for the Library's process and weeding schedule.

Collection Maintenance concerns damaged and lost items as outlined in the table below.

Damaged/Deteriorating Items

Damaged/Deteriorating items are reported by circulation or other library staff or patrons using the collection. These items are turned over to the Collection Development Librarian who evaluates whether to retain/replace the item or withdraw/reorder the item. If the item is not severely damaged and the Library chooses to retain it, a determination will be made whether the item can be fixed internally or needs to be sent to the bindery.

Lost Items

Lost items are reported by circulation to the Collection Development Librarian. A determination is then made whether the item should be replaced or the record deleted. (Claude Moore Health Sciences Library, University of Virginia)

On weeding and discarding, the policy will reflect practice and make it clear to stakeholders what that practice is, as in the example from Omaha Public Library:[24]

Weeding

The professional staff will systematically weed worn, dated, or damaged library materials as an integral part of the selection process. The process helps maintain the quality of the library collections and is not intended to sanction removal of library materials based upon any controversy surrounding the material. Staff, during this process, should consider the selection principles stated in this Policy. Weeded materials are disposed of according to the contract the Library and the City have with the Friends of the Omaha Public Library. (Omaha Public Library, section D)

Preservation is concerned with the act of preserving or protection of an item or items in the collection. In recent decades, the term 'preservation' has come to be regarded as an integral component of collection management. All libraries need to have a written preservation policy document to set out what the library is going to preserve, for how long these materials will be preserved and how these materials will be preserved. These decisions are related to other collection management decisions, such as acquisition.

9 Co-operative and consortia agreements

Involvement in a consortium is one approach a library may consider for selection and acquisition, particularly in the age of financial constraints. It is vital that you make sure that if your library is part of a co-operative or consortial agreement, that the needs of your local area are not lost to those of the wider group. Trust and communication will be essential to reach an appropriate agreement to meet the needs of all concerned. In the case of co-operative or consortia agreements, you might wish to state that libraries link together in consortium for the purchase of subscriptions to e-resources and a clear statement on the selection of e-resources is needed. The Florida Atlantic University Libraries website[25] states:

> The Libraries cooperate in the purchase or leasing of library materials with State University Libraries and other library cooperative arrangements when possible . . . in an age of developing information technologies, resource sharing activities are reviewed on a continuing basis. (Florida Atlantic University Libraries, section v)

10 Intellectual freedom, censorship and complaints issues

The issues of intellectual freedom, censorship and complaints should be built into the policy. Usually a CDP cites any national statements on those issues, complemented by more specific, institutional statement and policy censorship issues. The general principles set forth in the ALA Library Bill of Rights[26] form an indispensable framework for building collections, services and policies that serve the entire academic community and may also include a complaints policy and procedure, for example.

In respect of intellectual freedom and censorship, statements on internet access and filtering software will need to be included for a school or public library setting. Many libraries adopt the ALA Library Bill of Rights regarding intellectual freedom since the introduction of computer terminals and access to the internet. A statement on intellectual freedom and censorship is essential in the context of e-materials statements on filtering and new dimensions such as copyright issues. Libraries have a basic responsibility for the development and maintenance of intellectual freedom.

11 Review

If the CDP is to remain relevant, it will need constant revision so that it continues to reflect accurately the changing needs of the library and its clientèle. Complete revisions are most likely to take place every three years; partial revision of certain sections, for example, those related to e-resources, may be necessary in the interim. Policy evaluation is essential to demonstrate the effectiveness of the document, both in terms of results and its value as a working tool. An illustration is a short paragraph taken from the Pasadena Public library website:[27]

> As the community changes, the library will need to reassess and adapt its collections to reflect new and differing areas of interest and concern. The collection development policy will be periodically evaluated and revised as necessary to provide guidance for implementing changes in the collection. (Pasadena Public Library)

The Campbell County Public library in the USA maintains, reviews and revises all library policies annually, and electronic links are provided to Circulation, Investment, Personnel and the Collection Development Policies, for example. The library staff use these policies, established procedures and professional judgement in selecting, classifying and deselecting items in the collection.[28]

Publishing the policy on the web

Libraries should publish their strategic plans and management structures online for transparency and clarification and this should include a CDP. Straw suggests that libraries have the opportunity to 'disseminate information about their collections to a much wider audience and to create the chance of real collaboration' (Straw, 2003, 85).

By publishing a web version, users from the local community, library suppliers and other external bodies and institutions to name but a few, can obtain an overview of the collection from the comfort of their own environment which may meet their information-seeking needs and resolve any queries at a point in time that suits them. An electronic response form could be set up on the website to allow instant electronic communication with users. It is essential that contact details, with a named staff member, are included in the document for two-way communication.

What does the future hold for a CDP in the digital landscape?

The CDP is an extension of the mission, goals and purpose of the library and should be conceived as a strategic institutional policy. A good CDP will be an effective working tool that will provide clarity, consistency and continuity.

The introduction of digital resources into collections has raised a multiplicity of issues, such as access via changing technology, access vs ownership, complex licensing contracts and agreements about archiving. The e-resources dimension requires the library to continually re-think the collection's strengths and future direction to accommodate the needs of the user community. In the words of Chadwell (2009, 76):

> It is also going to be imperative that we keep our users' developmental, education and entertainment needs in mind – more than we ever did in the print realm. If libraries and collection managers wish to compete with other user-focused services, we need to enlist our users regularly in collection building and collection management activities that once were mediated by library staff.

Now consider these five questions and reflect on your own workplace.

- Does your CDP facilitate communication and resource sharing between libraries?
- Is your CDP used as an influential and strategic management tool in your institution?
- Does your CDP forge a link to other institutional policies?
- Is your CDP an information tool for working with the local community?

- Are you effectively addressing the developing developmental, educational and entertainment needs of your users in the library in the CDP?

Further CDP resources

Aberystwyth University (n.d.) *Information Services Collection Management Policy*, www.aber.ac.uk/en/is/collections/policy.

American Library Association (1996) *Guide for Written Collection Policy Statements*, American Library Association.

American Library Association, *Library Bill of Rights*, www.ala.org/ala/issuesadvocacy/intfreedom/librarybill/index.cfm.

Cambridge University Library, *Collection Development Policy*, www.lib.cam.ac.uk/CDP2008_9.pdf.

Campbell County Public Library, *Library Policies*, www.cc-pl.org/index.php/About-Us/library-policies.html.

Canterbury Christchurch University, *Stock Collection and Management Policy*, www.canterbury.ac.uk/library/library-policies/stock-collection-and-management-policy.doc.

Columbia University, *Collection Development Policy Statements*, www.columbia.edu/cu/lweb/services/colldev/materials-selector-responsibilities.html.

Florida Atlantic University Libraries, *Collection Development Policy*, www.library.fau.edu/policies/cd_fau.html.

Glasgow Digital Library, *Collection Development and Management Policy*, http://gdl.cdlr.strath.ac.uk/documents/gdlcollectionpolicy.htm.

International Federation of Library Associations and Institutions, Section on Acquisition and Collection Development (IFLA/SACD) (2001), *Guidelines for a Collection Development Policy Using the Conspectus Model*, http://ifla.queenslibrary.org/VII/s14/nd1/gcdp-e.pdf.

Library of Congress, *Collections Overviews*, www.loc.gov/acq/devpol/colloverviews.

Monterey Public Library, *Collection development Policy*, www.monterey.org/Portals/2/PDFs/Policies/Policy%20401%20Collection%20Development.PDF.

National Library of Australia, Australian Libraries Gateway, *Guidelines for the preparation of a collection development policy*, www.nla.gov.au/libraries/resource/acliscdp.html.

OCLC, *Introduction to WorldCat Collection Analysis*, www.oclc.org/collectionanalysis/default.htm.

Pasadena Public Library, *Collection Development Policy*, ww2.cityofpasadena.net/library/collection.asp#.

Texas A&M University-Corpus Christi Mary and Jeff Bell Library, *Electronic Resources Collection Development Policy*, http://rattler.tamucc.edu/policy/ERCollDevPolicy_8_Dec_2006.pdf.

University of Akron, *Collection Development Policy: eBooks and eBook Collections*, www3.uakron.edu/ul/policies/cdp-ebooks.html.

University of Bradford, Learner Support Services, *The Library Collection Development Policy*, www.bradford.ac.uk/library/documents/library_collection_development_policy.pdf.

References

American Library Association (1996) *Guide for Written Collection Policy Statements*, American Library Association.

Chadwell, F. A. (2009) What's Next for Collection Management and Managers? User-centered collection management, *Collection Management*, **34** (2), 69–78.

Dillon, D. (n.d.) *A Two Year Journey with E-books: the University of Texas experience*, www.lib.utexas.edu/admin/cird/policies/subjects/principles.html.

Evans, G. E. and Saponaro, M. Z. (2005) *Developing Library and Information Centre Collections*, 5th edn, Libraries Unlimited.

Futas, E. (ed.) (1995) *Collection Development Policies and Procedures*, 3rd edn, Oryx Press.

IFLA (2001) *Guidelines for a Collection Development Policy Using the Conspectus Model*, http://ifla.queenslibrary.org/VII/s14/nd1/gcdp-e.pdf.

Johnson, P. (2009) *Fundamentals of Collection Development and Management*, 2nd edn, American Libraries Association.

Smyth, E. B. (1999) A Practical Approach to Writing a Collection Development Policy, *RBM: A Journal of Rare Books, Manuscripts and Cultural Heritage*, **14** (1), 27–31.

Straw, J. (2003) Collection Management Statements on the World Wide Web. In Mack, D.C. (ed.), *Collection Development Policies: new directions for changing collections*, Haworth Information.

Notes

1 www.nla.gov.au/libraries/resource/acliscdp.html.
2 www.bbk.ac.uk/lib/about/strategy/colldev.pdf.
3 http://cityofpasadena.net/library/about_the_library/collection_development_policy/.
4 www.law.harvard.edu/library/about/collections/collection_development_policy.pdf.
5 http://gdl.cdlr.strath.ac.uk/documents/gdlcollectionpolicy.htm.
6 www.canterbury.ac.uk/library/library-policies/stock-collection-and-management-policy.doc.
7 www.lib.cam.ac.uk/CDP2008_9.pdf.
8 www.ucl.ac.uk/library/cmp.shtml.
9 http://library.nyu.edu/collections/policies/index.html.
10 www.vam.ac.uk/nal/policy/index.html.
11 www.cc-pl.org/index.php/About-Us/library-policies.html.
12 www.abcr.ac.uk/en/is/collections/policy.
13 http://library.montclair.edu/staff/Coll_Dev_Policy_2009.pdf.
14 http://library.columbia.edu/services/collection_policies/general/materials_selector_responsibilities.html.
15 www.brookes.ac.uk/library/policy/cmp/cmpselect.html.
16 www.monterey.org/Portals/2/PDFs/Policies/Policy%20401%20Collection%20Development.pdf.
17 www.bradford.ac.uk/library/documents/library_collection_development_policy.pdf.
18 www3.uakron.edu/ul/policies/cdp-ebooks.html.
19 http://ifla.queenslibrary.org/VII/s14/nd1/gcdp-e.pdf.
20 www.sussex.ac.uk/library/assets/documents/policies/collectionmanagementpolicy.pdf.
21 www.oclc.org/collectionanalysis/.
22 http://library.columbia.edu/services/collection_policies/general/collection_depth_indicators.html.

23 www.hsl.virginia.edu/admin/policy/collection-evaluation.cfm.

24 www.omahapubliclibrary.org/index.php?option=com_content&view=article&id=194.

25 www.library.fau.edu/policies/cd_fau.html.

26 www.ala.org/ala/issuesadvocacy/intfreedom/librarybill/index.cfm.

27 http://ww2.cityofpasadena.net/library/collection.asp#Purpose.

28 www.cc-pl.org/index.php/About-Us/library-policies.html.

13

Information literacy for the academic librarian in the digital information age: Supporting users to make effective use of the collection

Tracy Mitrano and Karrie Peterson

Introduction

Information has never been more abundant. Technology can store, transmit, mine and recombine information at volumes and rates exponentially greater than any other time in history. Internet searches identify thousands of potentially relevant sources. What is the role of the collections librarian in this inherently disruptive environment? Academic librarians once enjoyed recognition as information gatekeepers. They also acted as the stewards of content. With budgets constraining library selection and preservation roles, and as concerns about space have resulted in more licensing and less ownership, authority now lies in the facilitation of user-meaningful access. Information literacy (IL) plays a central role in this complex landscape.

IL is not only the academic librarian's job, it is the responsibility of everyone participating in the academic community: librarian, scholar, teacher and student. It proffers a constantly evolving vocabulary, from 'site' to 'search,' that a user must master in order to begin informed searching. Critical inquiry lies at the core of its functionalities: discernment of sources, curiosity about authenticity, intelligent assessment of different points of view and disciplinary perspectives. It requires attention to new and ever-changing concerns such as technical security, cyberspace privacy, legal concepts such as intellectual property, and ultimately, internet ethics. IL is the passport not only to research but also to both personal and professional identity in the 21st century.

This shift in the role of the collections librarian from judgement to process will be examined by considering issues raised by

- the traditional research environment
- the new era
- new challenges for scholars
- IL instruction in the digital world
- user abilities and expectations in respect of skills, behaviours, experience and preferences
- the synergies between collection management and IL.

A traditional research environment

First, some definitions.

IL is variously defined, as information fluency, digital age skills, media or information literacy, and 21st-century skills. Identified by governments and cultural organizations as essential for citizens, IL touches educators at all levels of institutional study and across disciplines. While all libraries address IL, this chapter will focus on academic libraries.

IL skills can be described as specific competencies for being able to articulate information needs, and then to find, evaluate, manage and use information (ACRL, 2000). A general heuristic definition is that IL skills enable a person to function effectively in an information environment to access resources, assess their relevance and quality, parse, dissect, compile and recompile data into coherent form which may then be synthesized to create new knowledge. It can also be seen as a cycle in which information abilities are applied to problem solving, beginning with knowing that information is needed, and advancing through many steps that include understanding how to find and evaluate information, create new knowledge and ethically handle information in the course of life activities (Horton, 2008). IL also integrates relevant legal issues such as copyright with policy concerns, academic integrity (or plagiarism), technical security, computer updates and patches, online privacy, appropriate use of social media and internet identity, and the use of defined programs for specific activities, such as LinkedIn for professional networking.

Traditionally, collections librarians built the collections and provided the appropriate finding tools to use them, while IL, or user education librarians trained students and others to use the finding tools to access the materials effectively. As services matured and library networks developed, local collections remained of great importance, but librarians increasingly helped users with tools for accessing relevant materials not all of which would be owned by the institution's library. Today, as discussed below, librarians have merged those services.

Through searching indexes leading to journal articles, monographs, government information, data sets, conference proceedings and other published formats, scholars could gain a comprehensive overview of any topic. Scholars relied on the library to find everything that mattered because most knowledge was funnelled through scholarly publishing channels – authored and peer reviewed by fellow academics and disseminated by publishers that actively marketed to libraries.

Libraries were also a gateway for scholars seeking primary resources – letters, manuscripts, photographs, maps or other archived materials – by providing the catalogues and indexes to unique materials that often required travelling to the owning institution for access.

Scholars also need to be broadly aware of their field, and to know about current developments. Many libraries established services to meet this need by circulating current journals to faculty before shelving them, or by distributing tables of contents as an alerting mechanism, or by presenting the current journal literature for easy physical browsing. As journals moved to electronic formats, libraries discovered additional ways

– working with the vendors – to provide current awareness alerts for scholars.

In a more general way, researchers and academics also counted on libraries to preserve the record of scholarly knowledge – every journal or monograph, no matter how obscure, would find a home in some library. Libraries were the ultimate backstop for scholars following citation trails. Students and faculty could count on a vast network of library collections for verifying the claims of others by checking sources themselves.

Information literate scholars, skilled in using the catalogues and indexes, were able to evaluate the status of publication types, and developed strong intuitions about where relevant information would be produced and published. They were also able to manage their research materials, keeping track of and appropriately citing sources consulted.

In this more traditional environment, IL librarians worked together with collections librarians to ensure that scholars knew how to take advantage of efficient library services. Promoting hidden collections, such as microfiche or microfilm sets, by featuring specialized indexes was a common shared effort. Another collaboration between instruction librarians and collections librarians involved providing feedback for vendors of electronic indexes to journal literature, with requests to make their products more user friendly, more robust in terms of user-desired functionality, or more inclusive.

Students, beginning university studies with less understanding of the process, required concentrated instruction and were often guided towards IL skills in conjunction with assignments.

An undergraduate might have the research strategy bounded by their lecturer, for example, being told to use a dozen scholarly sources. Master's or Doctoral degree candidates would be expected to perform a comprehensive review of all the literature revolving around their research topic which, at that level, could include visits to other libraries, interlibrary loan (ILL), and combing through microfilm collections.

Instruction librarians, consequently, taught the use of indexes, bibliographies, catalogues, union catalogues, finding aids, locally developed tools and citation manuals as part of the research process.

In the context of doing academic research, an information literate student was able to use the library and its tools, consult with librarians as needed, manage the information collected through the research process and present their own information product in appropriate form. In short, IL consisted of many of the same elements as it does today, but in a more static world.

A new era

The end of the previous era is not measured by a particular date so much as by the increasing tendency of users to disregard the library as the sole gateway to all relevant information. So what has changed?

The information scarcity of yesteryear has become the information tsunami of today, bringing the global world of research to everyone's fingertips, in coffee houses or at home in slippers. Search engines have grown more sophisticated. The world wide web allows users to be consumers and publishers of information and new types of information that are not part of a traditional scholarly commercial publishing stream, and therefore are not indexed or collected by libraries, now matter to users (blogs, web-based projects, etc). There are many implications of the networked, digital information environment, among them:

- It is now possible to know of more resources on a topic than anyone could read in a lifetime.
- Metadata schemes range from controlled vocabulary to social tagging, but information about and knowledge of how to use those schemes is neither uniform nor obvious.
- Research has become data driven due to the ability of computers to manage and process data, but there is no mature system in many disciplines for handling data to foster discovery, long-term access and interoperability.
- Developments such as open educational resources or the requirements of research funding agencies increasingly mean that information can be made available outside traditional publishing streams and purely academic avenues of discourse.
- In a media rich world, text is no longer the only medium that counts – scholars are keen to access images, video, sound and data compiled in increasingly complicated and rich ways often described contemporarily as 'social media'.
- Digitization and digital imaging by museums, archives and other institutions holding cultural materials have made it possible to present surrogates for unique materials and artefacts on the web, making these items widely 'available'.
- New technologies have disrupted old business models – including scholarly publishing and legal paradigms – sometimes placing libraries in the cross-hairs of copyright infringement litigation.
- New social norms have challenged traditional academic policies such as those concerning the citing of sources and plagiarism, and ethical conduct in civic discourse about ideas, politics and personal identity.

Scholars still have their traditional tasks, but also some new ones. They need to do comprehensive research to maintain current awareness, and rely on scholarship for tracking citations and sources. But they also need to filter out information; approach new resources with the ability to figure out their technical functionality; puzzle out the social, political and economic context of information; appreciate distinctions between what is technically available and legally appropriate; struggle, when necessary, with the tensions and gaps that exist among all the factors that affect use of the internet, such as market pressures, technical code standards and antiquated laws to maximize use of the myriad resources not only to exploit resources to their advantage but also to participate in that same spirit in the dynamic, semiotic internet environment.

New challenges for scholars

As publishing, research and sharing of collections evolve with the development of the world wide web, scholars face new challenges:

- Both novices and experts must decide when research has been up to the required standard for the task at hand – when is enough, enough? Finding aids in any library leads to copious resources. If the limit for what is proper to identify and consult is no longer the institution's own library, then how far does it extend?
- Advanced scholars may worry that their own library has become an insufficient gateway to a comprehensive search. Collection budget cuts aside, they may wonder if Google is perhaps more complete, or that their own library's website is missing tools essential for comprehensive research.
- It can be harder for scholars to feel they 'know' online tools and indexes when content and interfaces change continuously. New business models confuse users. For example, the index to journal articles from a single publisher can be mistaken for a discipline-wide index; two different online resources in the field of chemistry might appear the same to an undiscerning user, but one may be continuously updated and a dynamically changing database while the other version is a static, one-time purchase of the database as published at a particular point in time (Garritano, 2010).
- Search tactics need to be changed according to the data that is being searched, and the search tool's functionality. For example, search terms in a full text database should be adjusted depending on whether the text is in modern or older language. Searching tactics also depend on metadata schemes, such as controlled vocabulary. But users frequently do not know how a searching mechanism works, and how to craft searches for best results.
- Scholars also cannot easily identify how intellectual property constraints may affect their research. For example some article aggregators must exclude certain articles due to intellectual property issues, and this is not easy for scholars to monitor.
- Users 'lose their place' in research because they don't understand the business, or conceptual models behind the categories of information that we have inelegantly connected for them using OpenURL protocols and link resolvers. Technology still fails on occasions when we try to connect one proprietary source, such as an index, to another, such as a journal subscription.
- New information types are often valuable *because* they are significantly different from traditional resources. For example, in the Web 2.0 world, a blog author whose posting is ambiguous can be questioned for clarification, or receive important comments that are worthy of quoting. How does this evolving type of information resource fit into a standard literature review?
- Users are faced with nuanced and complex evaluative tasks. Evaluation is not a litmus test of whether or not a resource is academically worthy, but requires placing the resource in a political, economic, historical and social context.
- Current awareness now requires new approaches. In the wide-open territory of the web, finding what might be important and filtering out what is not is daunting.

Many scholars, bypassing traditional library resources, have turned to news aggregators, RSS feeds, blogrolls, Twitter or other social networking tactics to stay connected with research in their field. Constructing effective networks has become an essential skill. Data is now frequently available online, rather than being tabulated into static presentations, which requires users to correctly manipulate the interface as well as draw appropriate conclusions.

* The web can appear 'flat' to undergraduates who lack understanding of how information is generally disseminated, causing them to entirely miss information from the proprietary' hidden web'.

Information literacy instruction in a digital, networked world

IL instruction at many institutions has evolved over time to become an integral part of the academic library's mission. Most academic libraries at least pay homage to the idea that students who graduate from the parent institution should leave with skills that will enable them to succeed in a world of digital, networked information. Some, such as Cornell University, have gone much further to develop and implement programs that train faculty to include primary, electronic research into their curriculum, even, if not especially, in large undergraduate core courses across disciplines. The Cornell Undergraduate Competency Initiative, based on a similar program at the University of California at Berkeley, is now in its fifth year.[1]

Instruction in IL faces a host of challenges: identifying the necessary skills; outreach to new partners such as information technology specialists, higher education legal ethics experts, and faculty; effective communication with users and the creation of new methods of instruction.

The scope of what must be learned has expanded exponentially, but without an accompanying curricular framework. Understanding the information landscape and developing good intuitions about the kind of information that may exist on a research question develops over time and with practice. While one-shot sessions may work for tool training, teaching for deeper understanding requires more sustained interaction with students.

Librarians have attempted to address these problems by further developing instruction programs, and in some cases have benefited from mandates issued by institutions or governments requiring IL instruction. Collaboration with partners is critical to success: staff from all areas of the library, higher education specialists in student services, information technology specialists, law and policy experts with an eye to relevant topics such as copyright, and most important, teaching faculty. Collaborators bring necessary expertise, and combined resources can sometimes be greater than parts, whether in the development of online information, digital literacy programs, or seminars or workshops that actively train faculty in how to bring IL instruction into the classroom.

User abilities, expectations and preferences

Contemporary teaching and learning strategies continue to probe information-seeking behaviours, although the situation is so much in flux that observation of these endeavours should remain highly and critically self-conscious and frequently 'ping' the efforts of other institutions as well as the broader culture, law and politics of the internet.

Two questions frame research considerations: how skilled are users, and what are their important preferences and behaviours in light of the overall environment?

Skills

In respect of skills, people have mixed levels of comfort and expertise with digital interfaces. An experienced humanities researcher is not necessarily more expert in using a search engine than an undergraduate computer science major. At the same time, the veteran researcher will have a deeper understanding of the ways in which knowledge is created and disseminated in their discipline. Consider another example: compare the different kinds of knowledge brought to the task of interpreting a newspaper image by a social historian and a young student adept at digital image editing. Both technological knowledge and contextual understanding are essential aspects of IL.

Observers of information science note that although the popular press makes much of the technologically savvy generation, 'the information literacy of young people has not improved with widening access to technology; in fact, their apparent facility with computers disguises some worrying problems' (CIBER, 2008, 12).

An annual US study finds that college students rate their IL skills highly:

Eight out of 10 (80%) said they are very confident in their ability to search the Internet effectively and efficiently. Almost half (45.1%) rated themselves as very skilled, and another third (34.9%) rated themselves as experts. Although students' assessments of their ability to evaluate the reliability and credibility of online sources of information and of their understanding the ethical and legal issues surrounding the access to and use of digital information were lower, overall ratings are still high. Students whose technology adoption responses categorize them as innovators and early adopters ranked their technology and information literacy skills higher than other students.   (Smith, Salaway and Caruso, 2009, 16)

Technical facility does not equate to knowledge. Disabusing users who believe that their technical skills are sufficient remains a central task of librarians, or, for that matter faculty and everyone involved in the enterprise of teaching and learning.

Behaviours, expectations and preferences

Research behaviour is closely related to issues involving technical skill management. A key report based on a survey of thousands of American college students describes students frequently using a single research strategy for different kinds of research tasks, struggling with context and the beginning of the research process in which the students need to frame the research inquiry. At the same time, they infrequently consulted with librarians for help – to a much lesser extent than in the survey taken the preceding year (Head and Eisenberg, 2010).

User expectations and preferences also count. As generations of digital natives reach college age, user expectations become a pre-eminent concern for libraries. Those expectations will undoubtedly continue to evolve given their non-school-related use of new technologies (Adamson et al., 2008). Libraries have spent the last several years moving towards perceived trends such as 24/7 services, online social networking, and dis-intermediated online documentation for users eschewing standard reference service. However, some faculty remain sceptical about adapting to the preferences and expectations that digital natives bring from their experiences. Given varied opinions among faculty, should libraries, then, adapt to emerging behavioural trends or strive to change the behaviour and understanding of users?

It is sometimes said that if libraries do not adapt, they will become irrelevant. It may not even be left to libraries to make that choice, given the market pressures upon them and the growing number of commercial ventures intent on seeking profit in higher education, including training in areas such as research skills. Nowhere is this pressure felt more than in the area of online learning, where disruptive technologies developed in the commercial sector are bearing down in ways bound to affect newer library services just being established. For-profit online learning, a growing part of the UK market share in higher education,[2] is also making significant in-roads in the US sector and poses a host of challenges to traditional, not-for-profit higher education. Worthy of treatment as a separate topic, the impact of outsourcing of any variety of services, work product and education to or via for-profit corporations – possible and facilitated by electronic communications – are the proverbial 'game-changers'. Technological in nature, these initiatives have profound effects on virtually all aspects of library collections, not least management of digital collections. Librarians alone cannot assuage this challenge but must be aware of it at every level of service.

The glass is not necessarily half empty, however, the crisis does indeed suggest opportunity. Libraries are in an excellent position to take up the global challenge to help citizens acquire much-needed IL skills in step with an understanding of emerging preferences, behaviours and abilities of our users. As expressed by Brindley (2009, 5):

> So what does it all mean for great libraries? In principle, it is simple. Libraries and information services must step up to the plate to provide services that meet the needs of this new generation, and ones that add value well beyond the search engine. Libraries must work to understand the needs and expectations of the virtual schoolchildren and virtual scholars, and swiftly move their emphasis to the digital reality and future.

In short, academic libraries still have an opportunity to teach not only the skills, but also the intellectual and moral development of the whole person. We can both provide the instrumental instructional skills for students to find future employment and impart the message that education is an inherent service to society. We should play to these strengths of our work and take full advantage of these opportunities.

Building synergies for collections work and information literacy

The discussion above suggests areas in which libraries might build synergies between collections work and IL efforts. We can group them thematically:

1 Bringing users from the open web to library collections and services.
2 Presenting library materials in an instructional environment.
3 Building digital collections with embedded tools for using the materials.
4 Continuing to develop the evidence base.

Bringing users to library collections

While library collections may no longer be the only place where scholars find useful information, they provide a central core of quality, filtered information anticipated to meet user needs. It is still important for users to learn what resources libraries offer and how to use them effectively.

Libraries are connecting their collections to Google Scholar and providing users with toolbar utilities to enable any web search or highlighted term to be quickly repeated in the library catalogue.

Research has demonstrated that college students do not necessarily turn to Google first, but often begin research with the course reading list (Head and Eisenberg, 2010). Librarians have put library resources in students' paths by linking to research guides or other resources from course websites. As these and learning management systems evolve, there will be new opportunities for connecting students in useful ways with relevant library materials.

Students also consult with networks of acquaintances in the course of searching for information, and libraries have begun to make their presence known in virtual spaces such as Facebook and Twitter.

Libraries are digitizing important collections and using search engine optimization (SEO) techniques to ensure that scholars discover, exploit and contribute to the growing body of digitized library resources.

A key reason to use libraries, invisible to many users, is the quality of metadata applied to resources in order to aid discoverability. Users have become accustomed to the flexibility of keyword searches in full text documents and have learned to cope with the lack of precise results. However, there is rich value in the controlled vocabulary that libraries have used to identify resources, and ways need to be found to help users identify metadata, and to take advantage of the controlled vocabulary without a steep learning curve (Pradt Lougee, 2002). The semantic web, social tagging, or other new metadata schema may pave the way for automated processes to achieve the level of precision in searching and retrieving resources that can be attained when the metadata is supplied by specially trained cataloguers.

Presenting library materials in an instructional environment

Libraries, with their relatively defined constituents, can do something commercial entities aren't likely to attempt: embed instructional help in the interfaces and content that students access in the process of learning.

This would mean a major shift towards thinking of IL instruction as embedded in the collections, for students to find *while* they are doing their work, as opposed to thinking of IL instruction as a service presented through workshops, class sessions or online tutorials to prepare students *for* their work. For example, a student who begins a search at the local library catalogue might be prompted to click on a link labelled 'What are the pros and cons of using this tool?' Embedding such cues within the research helps to frame IL as a process of serious critical thinking.

Embedded 'instruction' might help some challenges, such as reaching students with intelligent instructional support targeted to their knowledge level. For example, a student interacting with a research guide might be provided with context-specific help whenever certain terms were highlighted, and the research guide content itself might change as a result of how a student interacts with it by becoming more relevant to the research purpose (Ofcom, 2006).

Here are some specific ideas for presenting collections within an IL instructional framework:

1 Present collections and finding tools as part of the learning library landscape

Presenting the information landscape in a compelling, visual way becomes an essential approach to the enterprise. For example, shining a critical light on Google as a for-profit corporate entity in contrast to library tools helps students to appreciate how business models can affect search and that organizations can manipulate the ranking of results. It is all too easy to assume that the top position is due to some inherent quality in the information source, service or product, rather than an ability to pay for that position. Differentiating between tools and information types is challenging for students, and providing the means for them to compare bigger pieces of the information landscape in context can aid their critical thinking skills. Informative visual interfaces might effectively replace the standard search boxes. Those simple search boxes, as a rule without design and aesthetically unpleasing, obfuscate the treasure trove of information behind them.

2 Use transparency and reveal, rather than hide business models

Seamless access to full text is highly prized by users, hence the development of OpenURL linking between indexed citations and full text journal articles. However, students who do not understand the business models that underpin the availability of information on the internet at large may become confused or misled about that information. Transparency of the business models helps users evaluate sources, especially in a digital landscape where the profit motive has become intertwined with the availability of information.

3   Find ways to present collection items that help users evaluate information

Students need to learn how to put the information they are encountering into social, political and economic contexts. This is not a checklist kind of task, although there may be some basic elements, such as peer review. Studying how experts evaluate information might foster more complex evaluations. For example, an experienced scholar may review the context of a government report and characterize the purpose and content in more nuanced ways than a novice. What might the expert's evaluative process suggest in terms of scaffolding content to prompt users towards a good evaluative process?

4   Let users help make collections more discoverable

Social tagging can serve IL goals. Students not only need to find information 'at their level' or appropriate to their task, they need to learn to articulate better their information needs and characterize the kinds of information that will meet their needs. Some semi-structured opportunities to tag resources may help students learn to articulate their needs and characterize resources and can, for example, supplement vendor 'tagging' of clinical research or book reviews.

5   Leave better 'breadcrumb' trails

Clicking around the internet can be confusing, especially when the scholar does not understand the conceptual landscape – for example, when the user does not readily recognize that they are in a library catalogue vs a journal article index. An IL 'you are here' view could help users visualize the information landscape from the perspective of their current task.

6   Interact with users

Libraries can play a key role in helping users speak back to the purveyors of online information in the same way people use social technologies to shape every other business in their lives. Interfaces now should be sophisticated enough to teach the user – while they are searching – how to get better results, and if users were permitted to directly provide data to vendors and libraries about the problems they are having, both libraries and commercial providers would benefit. Electronic books, often accessed through clunky, awkward and confusing interfaces, might evolve more quickly with transparent user feedback streams.

Embedded instruction that gets students thinking about IL topics is most likely to succeed where it is engaging, imaginative and interactive and results in real, practical advantage for the user – it cannot simply be one-way announcements and point-of-need tips. Collections librarians interact with collections; their interactions with scholars bring content and users into a collective, dynamic orbit. Genuinely meaningful interactive instruction also brings into stark relief the role of the collections librarian in helping scholars process and become a part of the vast, digital information landscape.

Building digital collections with embedded tools

As scholarship evolves, and online research projects become more common, how will libraries collect and provide access to these resources? New resources have features very different to those collected today. They are likely to be works in progress, interactive, surrounded by rich conversations happening in real-time or asynchronously, and have evolving linkages to other online works. The best uses for these kinds of collections may not be immediately apparent to scholars. How libraries provide a frame for 'what you can do here' without pre-empting uses that scholars will uncover for themselves is a question that reveals the delicate balance that a librarian must always maintain between scholar and user. The global, interactive internet culture has blurred the lines between and among the roles of librarian, researcher and user. Collection librarians must maintain a tricky and precarious balance.

One aspect of developing and embedding tools within collections is highlighted in a well known example about historical research:

> If you wanted to do a biography of Alexander Hamilton's [one of the USA's revolutionaries and founding fathers] years in office, it would be pretty manageable. It's not unreasonable to think of a scholar over the course of a career, actually familiarizing him or herself with most, if not all, of the source documents, assuming they can get into the right archives to see them. The scale is a human scale.
>
> When you start thinking of somebody who wants to write a history of, let's say, Bob Rubin's [a highly placed official in President Clinton's administration] role in the Clinton administration – to take a parallel instance – the volume of evidence is unthinkable. No one person could possibly observe, much less absorb intellectually, the volume of information now available for research. We start thinking about having to have automated tools in order to simply deal with the flood of evidence. (Lynch, 2009, 233)

Tools to solve these new problems are already being created by scholars, but their immediate availability, along with the materials themselves are key issues for IL for students especially. While libraries have always presented tools such as citation managers, many other research devices will need to be presented and explained, such as data visualization, text analysis and mechanisms for comparing large numbers of resources along various vectors, such as key concepts addressed or numbers of times cited. Librarians will have to master these.

The desire of users to put the content they have collected into forms that enable them to use these great tools will also drive discussion with commercial content providers, since digital rights management (DRM) concerns can have the effect of locking down content and restricting some research practices.

Continuing to develop the evidence base

Identifying good data and practices to demonstrate effectiveness can help libraries in two ways:

- as evidence of the value of the library in the overall teaching and learning mission of the parent institution
- and to point towards ways that libraries, in a changing world, can appropriately adapt their services.

Recent trends in both higher education and academic library practice point towards increasing requirements for analytics to be woven into the decision-making process. The need for librarians to collaborate across library units, across campus and across institutions is widely noted, along with the sharpening call for accountability (ACRL, 2010).

This is good news for libraries that already contribute to student learning but which have lacked tools to demonstrate their value. Analytics, or the gathering and interpretation of data about the effectiveness of services and programs, can be time consuming and labour-intensive, and much more likely to be done if there is a wide degree of interest and support for making it happen. Often making the benefits of having carefully tweaked and tailored services clear to scholars goes a long way to garner the support needed to realize the efforts involved.

This trend complements the on-going work of collections librarians. Traditionally, they have made good use of data for selection purposes by benchmarking home collections against peer institutions, and measuring the use of various resources. Usage data also can indicate a certain 'return on investment' where very expensive resources that are heavily used can be more productively compared with little-used resources that are also very low cost. But how do collections contribute to student learning? And how can collections beyond the library's control be measured?

Collaboration between collection librarians and IL instruction efforts may result in new ways of measuring the contribution of collections to student learning. For example, tracking the usage of resources in conjunction with a course could indicate that students are consulting resources appropriately. Analysing how content is packaged and presented to users can reveal how the resources are used, what additional 'help' links are clicked on, or even how students answer 'self-test' questions as they are researching, thus bringing us closer to knowing how content and presentation contribute to student learning.

In turn, libraries can better present content with instructional scaffolding if we improve our ability to collect information about problems scholars encounter doing their research. As we have seen in the preceding discussion about user expectations and preferences, analytics can help shape services, if not also spark innovation. Collaborative approaches can be especially important in areas where there isn't a simple right answer about the way to proceed in shaping services for users. For example, libraries may feel the impetus for change coming from reports that describe emerging technology trends, such as the *Horizon Report* (Johnson et al., 2010) which recently highlighted the growing interest in mobile phone applications. How can innovation in this area be approached intelligently, when it is still too early for 'best practices' to solidify? Bringing together both instruction librarians and collections librarians to plan solutions helps ensure that all aspects of the user experience will be addressed. Instruction librarians bring significant tacit knowledge about users' skills and understanding, and long experience rolling out new services and interfaces for users. Collections librarians contribute their experience of presenting huge amounts of content and a wide variety of formats ranging from video to music scores to books, as well as their interest in designing services that can help them track usage. Combining these approaches can help a library respond appropriately to data about emerging technologies by merging their knowledge to ensure that new innovations are prioritized around users' actual needs and presented in a way most likely to result in user adoption.

Conclusion

As technologies, the market, social norms and laws change, so, too, do scholarly uses of library resources in research and learning. Adapting library collections and the attendant services requires an understanding of the new intellectual approaches and information technology skill sets required to meet these challenges. Historically, scholars relied on the library for services ranging from preserving the record of scholarship to providing efficient current awareness services. As the information landscape has shifted, users have turned to other settings when they no longer regard the library as the exclusive source of information or the best provider of resources. The information tsunami requires librarians to help develop in users a deep understanding of how to approach information, especially in the digital realm. For example, it is no longer adequate for a collections librarian to offer a static set of indexes and finding tools. In the digital age they must be able to present the latest information technologies – increasingly mobile in nature – to the user, as well as an informed and highly critical approach towards the appreciation and evaluation of new resources both in and outside the walls of the library.

The new world of networked information, in which our constituents can be both consumers and producers, means that IL incorporates understanding of legal, technological and ethical constraints. In short, the scope of what our users need to grasp to be both good scholars and digital citizens has grown exponentially. However, there is not a commensurate growth in the time people have to master all aspects of information fluency skills. Therefore, library services of the future must incorporate strategic relationships across campus and throughout the library to assist users towards informed facilitation of their research without requiring that faculty or students commit to time-consuming stand-alone activities such as workshops and tutorials. Embedded assistance adds the kind and quality of value that distinguishes using the library from a generic internet search. It adds trust to the relationship between librarians and users. In a virtuous circle, the more often our scholars use library services, the more we can continue to enhance their understanding and skills, and the better collection librarians can serve higher education's missions.

With this in mind, you might like to reflect on the following questions:

• As a professional working in the areas of collections, how might you structure ways

to stay up to date with the concerns and challenges of your user community?
- How might you present a concept, such as federated search, to users via a website? What different tactics might you try to embed your explanation of it in the context of user activities?
- What might be some ways to involve all stakeholders in improving the way that e-books are presented in the library collections?
- As a collections librarian seeking to make sure that resources are known to the right researchers, what measures can you envision using to monitor this?

References

ACRL (2000) *Information Literacy Competency Standards for Higher Education*, www.ala.org/ala/mgrps/divs/acrl/standards/informationliteracycompetency.cfm.

ACRL (2010) *Top Trends in Academic Libraries*, http://crln.acrl.org/content/71/6/286.full.

Adamson, V., Bacsich, P., Chad, K., Kay, D. and Plenderleith, J. (2008) *JISC & SCONUL Library Management Systems Study: an evaluation and horizon scan of the current library management systems landscape for UK higher education*, Sero Consulting Ltd with Glenaffric Ltd and Ken Chad Consulting Ltd March, www.jisc.ac.uk/media/documents/programmes/resourcediscovery/lmsstudy.pdf.

Brindley, L. J. (2009) Challenges for Great Libraries in the Age of the Digital Native, *Information Services & Use*, **29** (1), 3–12.

CIBER (2008) *Information Behaviour of the Researcher of the Future*. A CIBER Briefing Paper, 11 January 2008, www.ucl.ac.uk/infostudies/research/ciber/downloads/ggexecutive.pdf.

Garritano, J. R. (2010) Trends in Chemical Information Literacy and Collection Development, 2000–2009, *Science & Technology Libraries*, **29**, 235–57.

Head, A. J. and Eisenberg, M. B. (2010) *Truth Be Told: how college students evaluate and use information in the digital age*, Project Information Literacy Progress Report, http://projectinfolit.org/.

Horton, F. W. Jr. (2008) *Understanding Information Literacy: a primer*, UNESCO, unesdoc.unesco.org/images/0015/001570/157020e.pdf.

Johnson, L., Levine, A., Smith, R. and Stone, S. (2010) *The 2010 Horizon Report*, Austin, Texas: The New Media Consortium, www.educause.edu/ELI/2010HorizonReport/195400.

Lynch, C. (2009) Lecture: impact of digital scholarship on research libraries, *Journal of Library Administration*, **49**, 227–44.

Ofcom (2006) *The Consumer Experience*, London, UK: Office for Communications, http://stakeholders.ofcom.org.uk/binaries/research/consumer-experience/research1.pdf.

Pradt Lougee, W. (2002) *Diffuse Libraries: emergent roles for the research library in the digital age*, Council on Library and Information Resources (CLIR), www.clir.org/pubs/reports/pub108/contents.html.

Smith, S. D., Salaway, G., Caruso, J. B. (2009) *ECAR Study of Undergraduate Students and Information Technology. Volume 6*, EDUCAUSE Centre for Applied Research, www.educause.edu/Resources/TheECARStudyofUndergraduateStu/187215.

Notes

1 http://infocomp.library.cornell.edu/.
2 http://chronicle.com/article/For-Profit-Higher-Education/64748/.

14
Supporting users to make effective use of the collection

Ruth Stubbings

Introduction
As illustrated in the other chapters of this book, readers' expectations and the collection and development strategies of libraries are changing in this digital age. The move to a greater reliance on electronic information is influencing how society searches for and uses information and is impacting on how libraries and their collections are viewed and used.

In the public arena, the British Government is keen to provide more and more information on the internet. This ranges from local government to health information, and how individuals can get involved in the 'Big Society'. To this end, the British Government launched two initiatives. The first was the Information Matters strategy, which recognized that 'More information is being created and held today than ever before. It is the lifeblood of virtually every service we use as citizens, whether run by the public or private sector' (Knowledge Council 2008, 2). The Information Matters strategy aims to enhance and create standards on how government departments find, use, store and make information available. The strategy promotes the concept that government staff had responsibilities as 'creators, custodians and users of knowledge and information' (Knowledge Council, 2008, 3) and that they required skills and tools to meet these responsibilities. The second was the 'Digital Britain' initiative. The Digital Britain Interim Report highlighted the need for Britain to develop both the technological and skills infrastructure to succeed in the digital economy. The report argued that for the UK to 'maximise the digital opportunity, we will need to ensure a population that is confident and empowered to access, use and create digital media' (DCMS & DBERR, 2009, 66). The report of the Digital Britain Media Literacy Working Group (Ofcom, 2009, 9) divided the skills individuals need to operate in today's society as digital life skills and digital media literacy skills.

In academia, there has been a radical shift from print to electronic information in terms of electronic searching tools as well as the electronic full text of journals and textbooks. Many university libraries have moved to buying not only current journals electronically, but also archives of back issues and are seriously considering, if they have not already done so, discarding back copies of print journals so that space in the library building can be more innovatively used. University libraries are also heavily involved in the open access agenda and are helping academics to promote their research outputs by depositing their articles in institutional or subject repositories, as well as in peer reviewed journals. With the growth in student numbers, university libraries are keen to provide greater access to set texts, and e-books can help them to achieve this.

With this growth of e-information, what are the implications for how readers find and use information?

Searching for and using information

In the UK 71% of adults have access to broadband (both fixed and mobile) and 40% have a social networking profile[1]. The European Commission state that over 50% of Europeans use the internet daily, but highlights that 30% have never used it at all.[2] As governments see the internet as being important, they are investigating how to increase access to it. Ofcom regularly ascertains how people access and use the internet, but less work is being carried out on how to enhance individuals' information literacy skills. In a recent study, Ofcom (2010a, 4), reported that although more respondents than in 2007 are likely to say they are confident in searching for information on the internet, a large percentage are still not confident in judging the quality of a website. In addition, the respondents were more likely to learn how to make the most of the internet from family, friends and trial and error, and 61% of parents who responded to a survey on children's media literacy agreed that 'My child knows more about the Internet than I do' (Ofcom, 2010b, 4). This raises implications about how the public will be able to take part in the digital society.

The assumption that young people know how to find information quickly and easily has been challenged by the CIBER research group at University College London. CIBER investigated this through an analysis of the literature and argue that we may be making assumptions that are not necessarily true. CIBER (2008, 22) contend that there is no evidence to prove that young people's search skills have improved or declined with the growth of the internet and that more investigation is needed. However, the report highlights that although students may be confident in their searching skills, they often use natural language, perhaps illustrating a poor understanding of their information needs, and they are less confident in critically evaluating the information they find. They are often impatient, do not want to spend time searching for information, and many do not find library-provided resources intuitive.

The CIBER report (2008, 30) highlights that information protected by passwords runs the risk of being ignored by young people, especially those who have developed coping strategies for finding information based on using search engines. CIBER notes that young people associate closely to brands, such as Google and that they are 'promiscuous, diverse and volatile' (CIBER, 2008, 9) when searching for information. Libraries and the resources they provide are therefore competing against a strong market brand. CIBER argue that 'the problem is one of both raising awareness of this expensive & valuable content and making the interfaces much more standard and easier to use' (CIBER, 2008,

30). Good quality information literacy is one tool available in our armoury. Librarians in public and school libraries, as in other sectors, have a role to play to help individuals, especially young people, make the most of the internet, whilst also pointing them to alternative information sources that may suit their needs more.

With the growth of electronic information, research continues to indicate that in academia, as elsewhere, information searching and management behaviours have begun to evolve and change. The Joint Information Systems Committtee (JISC, 2010a, 4) indicates that there is a greater reliance not only on electronic search tools, but also on the ability to access the full text of an item, especially journal articles, in electronic format. So there is a strong movement away from visiting a library to find the full text of an article in print to expecting to be able to access it online. This reflects research in the USA. Schonfeld and Housewright (2010, 4) argue that researchers originally relied heavily on libraries to find books, journal articles and other research material and this is no longer the case. In their survey of faculty attitudes to information they found that they prefer electronic academic information and use subject specific search tools; search engines such as Google and Google Scholar; and following citations from bibliographies to find the information they require.

Inger and Gardner (2008) discovered that researchers have shifted from using library catalogues and web pages to find known references, to using databases and search engines. Schonfeld and Housewright (2010, 13) argue that with this increased use of electronic information there has been a shift in how faculty members view the library. Respondents to their survey see the library as being more important in terms of purchasing the material they require than as an information intermediary. They give a note of caution and suggest that 'the declining visibility and importance of traditional roles for the library and the librarian may lead to faculty primarily perceiving the library as a budget line, rather than as an active intellectual partner' (Schonfeld and Housewright, 2010, 13). This should concern libraries because as JISC (2010a, 39 & 50) highlights, readers' perceptions of libraries are slow to change. Currently many associate libraries with books rather than the electronic resources on offer and therefore they will not recognize the important part library staff play in both selecting and helping readers navigate to content.

Students in Higher Education (HE) institutions have greater access to electronic information than at any previous time. In the UK with the growth of student numbers and introduction of fees, students are less likely to buy textbooks and expect libraries to have a large range of multiple copies. To meet these expectations, libraries are turning to e-books, although not all subject areas are well catered for and therefore print copies are and will continue to be important in some subject areas. As the Horizon report preview (NMC, 2009, 4) points out, electronic books are now accessible on a greater variety of e-readers and the experience of online reading is becoming more comfortable. In fact it has entered the mainstream in the consumer world, especially of novels. Attwood (2009) notes that the JISC e-book observatory project reports that e-books were used for 'grazing' information rather than for continuous reading, meaning hard copies and e-books are complementary. JISC (2010b, 2) argue that students and researchers have become 'power browsers' and only use small extracts from e-books and e-journals.

In some subject areas, especially the social sciences and humanities, students are expected to use journal articles to support their studies. Although some students are quick to grasp the opportunities that electronic journals have opened up, for others it has created barriers and confusion (authentication and differing search interfaces) and they struggle to find good quality academic information quickly and easily.

Since libraries are spending significant amounts of money on good quality information, readers need to be encouraged to make the most of these resources and exploit them to the maximum. Librarians can and should play a key role in lobbying publishers for more intuitive interfaces, whilst teaching readers how to find, critically analyse and present information back to others in a range of formats. The challenge for information professionals is to ensure that readers can use the information, whether print or electronic, provided by libraries both easily and effectively.

What is information literacy?

With the vast growth of information being made available in a variety of media (audiovisual, electronic, face-to-face and print), there is a continuing recognition that the ability to find, manage and present information to others is important for both individuals and society as a whole. The ability to find and use information has been described in a variety of ways. These include: information skills, information literacy, information fluency, i-skills, digital skills, digital literacy, media literacy, transliteracy and many more. Below is a brief synopsis of just a few definitions and models.

The Chartered Institute of Library and Information Professionals (CILIP) defines information literacy as: 'knowing when and why you need information, where to find it, and how to evaluate, use and communicate it in an ethical manner.'[3]

CILIP break down information literacy into several components:

- A need for information
- The resources available
- How to find information
- The need to evaluate results
- How to work with or exploit results
- Ethics and responsibility of use
- How to communicate or share your findings
- How to manage your findings.

The CILIP definition is deliberately broad in nature, as it recognizes that individuals discover information from a variety of sources (people, the media, research and published information sources) and that they use information in many different ways. Although the components appear like steps, there is an understanding that individuals may have different starting points depending on the subject context, their own knowledge and what they are trying to achieve.

The Society of College, National and University Libraries (SCONUL, 2007) have developed the Seven Pillars of Information Literacy model (Figure 14.1). It is similar to that of CILIP, as it describes information literacy as having seven components including:

- Recognizing an information need
- Distinguishing ways of addressing the gap
- Constructing strategies for locating information
- Locating and accessing information
- Comparing and evaluating information
- Organizing, applying and communicating information
- Synthesizing and creating information.

The model particularly stresses that information literacy includes the use of information to 'further develop ideas building on that synthesis, and, ultimately, create new knowledge in a particular subject discipline' (SCONUL Advisory Committee on Information Literacy, 1999, 8).

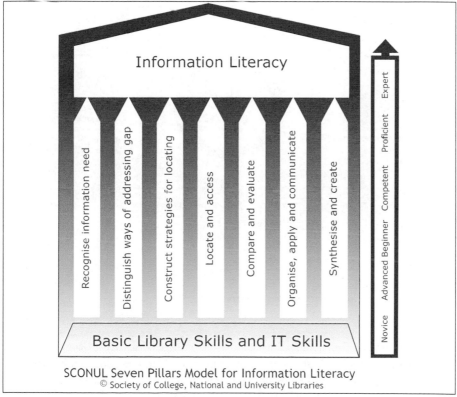

Figure 14.1 *SCONUL Seven Pillars Model for Information Literacy*
Image reproduced under the Creative Commons Licence

The model suggests that underpinning information literacy is an individual's ability to use libraries in general and IT. In addition, it recognizes that individuals may have different levels of proficiency in different aspects of searching and using information. The model has been criticized as being too step driven and linear, but I would argue that the authors never intended the model to be viewed in such a formal and rigid manner, and considered information searching to be iterative (SCONUL Advisory Committee on Information Literacy, 1999, 8), recognizing that individuals would find and use information differently, dependent on their starting point, subject knowledge and what they are trying to achieve.

JISC (2005, 3) have developed the concept of i-skills for staff in higher education. They define i-skills as the ability to: '. . . identify, assess, retrieve, evaluate, adapt, organize and communicate information within an iterative context of review and reflection.'

The i-skills model developed for JISC is reproduced in Figure 14.2. The important aspect of this model is the explicit link to the creation of new knowledge and self reflection.

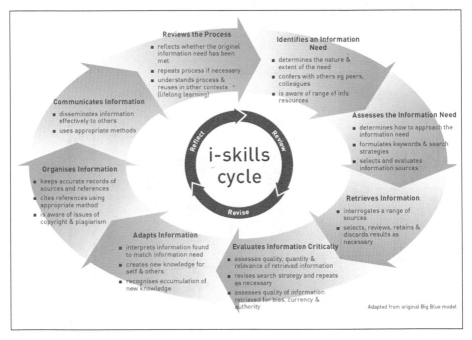

Figure 14.2 *The i-skills cycle*
Reproduced with permission from JISC

Since the growth of data being published in a wider range of formats, Beetham, McGill and Littlejohn (2009, 72) argue that the link to a wider range of publication and communication tools should be made. They state that 'information literacy needs to be broadened to include – or be supplemented with – communication and media literacies. It makes little sense to support information literacies in isolation from other communications and media practices'. I would argue that this is true, but would add that a definition that is too closely linked to one way of communicating information may be too restrictive and not truly reflect how people find and use information.

The report of the Digital Britain Media Literacy Working Group (Ofcom, 2009, 4) divided the skills individuals need to operate in today's society as digital life skills and digital media literacy skills. The report defined digital media literacy as 'the ability to use, understand and create digital media and communications'. This complements Ofcom's definition of media literacy which is 'the ability to access, understand and create communications in a variety of contexts'. Ofcom admits that their focus is on electronic media and state:

> Media literate people should be able to use the Internet to find information and accept that sometimes what they find may represent a particular view rather than a statement of objective fact. They will be able to control what they and their children see to avoid being offended. They may also be confident enough to be able to order and pay for goods and services online and to create their own website and contribute to a chatroom discussion.[4]

It does not matter which term or definition is used, as long as it is broad enough to encompass all formats of information, searching behaviours and ways of using information. For this chapter these capabilities shall be referred to as information literacy (IL).

Why is information literacy important?

In 2005 the Alexandria Proclamation (Garner, 2006, 3) made clear that 'Information Literacy lies at the core of lifelong learning. It empowers people in all walks of life to seek, evaluate, use and create information effectively to achieve their personal, social, occupational and educational goals. It is a basic human right in a digital world and promotes social inclusion of all nations.'

The importance of information and the skills to find and use it, is regularly discussed amongst librarians, but it is also recognized by governments, even if the exact term is not used. For example, in the UK, the then Prime Minister Gordon Brown (Brown, 2007) in his speech on liberty and planned constitutional changes at the University of Westminster stated 'This is the century of information. Our ability to compete in the global economy, to protect ourselves against crime and terrorist attack, depends not just on natural wealth or on walls or fences but on our ability to use information.' In addition, US President Barack Obama proclaimed October 2009 as a National Information Literacy Awareness Month in the USA (Obama 2009) and acknowledged that 'rather than merely possessing data, we must also learn the skills necessary to acquire, collate, and evaluate information for any situation. This new type of literacy also requires competency with communication technologies, including computers and mobile devices that can help in our day-to-day decision making'.[5] The development of readers' information literacy skills is not just important in academia, it is important in life in general. Readers are becoming more and more reliant on the internet and are relatively happy to 'get by'. Their ability to find and differentiate between information sources varies greatly and can impact heavily on how well they interact with library resources and therefore information in general. So that resources purchased by libraries are not under-used, librarians need to further enhance readers' information literacy competencies. As Inger and Gardner (2008, 19) point out 'No-one can police or predict where users will choose to start their research, their choices reflect a complex array of their perceptions of the starting point characteristics, brand awareness, budgetary considerations and which sites they trust.' Libraries can help raise their readers' understanding of the information landscape and library brand awareness, both through traditional marketing techniques, and also by developing their readers' information literacy competencies.

Developing readers' information literacy competencies in UK HE

Resources in the UK HE library sector have been put towards enhancing students' information literacy skills and teaching has become a core part of a librarian's role. Courses are being designed and delivered by library staff to students in various formats including face-to-face, online, blended learning, formal classroom time and informally on the enquiry desk. The content of IL courses has often concentrated on the mechanics of how databases work. Librarians should move away from this type of mechanistic training and aim to teach the subject specific information landscape and the more important higher-level thinking skills, such as problem solving, critical evaluation and communication that underpin the research process.

To help readers develop their IL skills, librarians need to have a good understanding of:

- the information landscape
- information literacy
- pedagogy
- the institution's aims and objectives.

The information landscape

Librarians should already have a good understanding of the information landscape in general, but they need to develop a comprehensive overview of the particular subject areas they support. This will include a basic knowledge of the subject, key authors, texts, journals and databases. This knowledge can be developed through: reviewing existing stock; perusing reading lists and dipping into some of the key texts; reading reviews of the books academics and researchers order; attending lectures; discussing the topic with librarians from other institutions; and talking to lecturers about where they publish (books, working papers, journals, conferences, etc.) and how they use information for their teaching and research. An understanding of a specific subject landscape will help the librarian purchase the correct stock that will meet the information needs of a diverse range of readers, for example, a first year undergraduate, taught post graduate or a professor. It will assist the librarian in selecting whether the print and/or electronic format of an item should be purchased; choosing the correct number of multiple copies; and allocating the correct loan status to an item. For example, a key text for undergraduates will often have large numbers of multiple copies purchased, with at least one copy being placed in a high demand collection, ensuring a wide circulation of the item, while if a text is mainly targeted at researchers, only one copy may be purchased and it will often be placed as a long-loan item, allowing the reader time to reflect and synthesize the majority of the content of the book.

Information literacy

An understanding of a specific subject information landscape will also help the librarian place information handling and management into context for specific readers and make information literacy relevant to their audience. For example, a first year undergraduate may need to further develop their problem-solving skills so that they can formulate a research question and a more complex search query. When a student reaches their final year, they may need stronger guidance to move away from relying on a general search engine and books, to using information databases to find current journal articles and conference papers. Without this guidance many undergraduate students may struggle, both to understand the importance of good quality academic information to their studies and the most effective practice in finding it. This lack of understanding could cause the resources to be under-used and this will impact on whether subscriptions are renewed or new editions purchased. In contrast, a mature researcher will most probably not need guidance on how to formulate a search strategy and the resources available. However, they may need updating on the quick-changing trends in publishing, for example, open access; different mechanisms for assessing the impact of their research output, for example, how to work out their h-index; as well as changes to the search interface of their favourite databases. An in-depth knowledge of the subject specific landscape will help a librarian design courses that meet the participant's needs at the right time, therefore making the courses more relevant to them.

Pedagogy

In the past, the more traditional elements of IL, such as formulating and carrying out a search strategy, have often been seen as the domain of the librarian, while the teaching of good practice in the creation of new knowledge, especially synthesis and writing skills, has been the preserve of academics. Librarians should recognize that with the growing importance of social networking and the open access agenda in publishing, their role has expanded and that they can play a key part in developing a reader's ability to evaluate, synthesise and present information to others. When teaching undergraduates and taught postgraduates, this could be by helping them to understand and avoid plagiarism; developing their referencing skills; as well as the basics of essay and report writing. If a librarian does not have the confidence to teach these skills on their own, they should consider co-teaching with academics and with staff from other support departments such as academic writing centres, research offices and graduate schools. Greater collaboration with others will not only further develop a librarian's skills and confidence, but will further raise the profile of the library and its resources, both with staff and students. Both will see librarians in a broader role and be more likely to seek advice on a wide range of issues relating to academic skills, including effective practice in finding and managing information.

For librarians to effectively teach IL, they need to develop an understanding of pedagogy. As mentioned earlier, researchers, especially young researchers, rely heavily on the internet and often feel they know how to find information that will suit their needs. These young researchers often wonder what IL classes can offer them. For IL courses to be successful, librarians need to understand pedagogy so that they can:

- design classes with appropriate content
- use a variety of teaching methods that suit a range of learning styles
- create stepping stones so that the learner can move from understanding to the application of knowledge and skills
- develop hooks and activities that motivate the student to actively partake in the learning experience
- evaluate the learning and teaching event, so that improvements can be made.

The development of undergraduate students' IL skills is best achieved by giving them opportunities to work together to problem solve and find good quality, relevant information for a real task. This can be effectively achieved utilizing both lectures and workshops in PC labs with the final result being linked to formal assessment. Sadly, librarians are often constrained by timetabling and may only be given one lecture slot to teach IL. A well designed learning event that includes student activities such as self-reflection, brainstorming and discussion is therefore essential. Consideration should also be given to utilizing blended learning, so that the face-to-face teaching is used to explore and discuss concepts, while the virtual learning environment (VLE) is used to instil basic facts and the mechanics of searching particular databases and information sources. A good quality learning experience will help a student recognize the importance of IL both to their everyday life, study and work. It should also introduce and encourage them to use a greater range of information sources provided by a library, rather than just relying on the internet.

For IL teaching to be effective it should have a subject focus and be embedded into the curriculum and research process. Librarians can find it hard to convince academics to set time aside both in their busy working day and in the curriculum for IL teaching for a number of reasons. These include:

- the fact that academics are generally able to find what they need to support their research themselves
- minimum class contact hours and the lecturer wishing to use the time to teach the subject

- lack of understanding of IL by the lecturer and how it can benefit them and their students
- a belief that IL and study skills are taught in other modules
- a belief that students already have these skills because they can use a computer and search the internet.

A library and library staff can begin to overcome these barriers by taking both a top down and a bottom up approach to embedding IL into the everyday life of an institution.

Librarians in collaboration with university enterprise and research offices should be playing an important role in developing academic and research staff's understanding of all the different ways they can promote their research outputs and raise their research profiles. Such activities highlight how librarians can add value to the research process and often encourage queries relating both to effective search practices and stock. They remind research members of the institution that the library is not just a custodian of books and study space for students, but contains and facilitates access to many valuable resources that will help the researcher.

Institutional aims and objectives

A clear understanding of the institution's aims and objectives, especially in relation to the curriculum and research agenda, can help librarians negotiate for IL to be embedded into the teaching and research of an institution. For example, where does your institution wish to sit within the teaching and research league tables? Does your institution aim to further develop the international learning experience; increase widening participation; develop more collaborative research; and encourage entrepreneurial behaviour of staff and students? All of these agenda items and more, can be used as hooks to encourage an institution to adopt a developmental approach to IL.

Consideration can be given to developing an IL strategy or framework similar to that of Loughborough University Library (2010) that highlights how IL benefits both staff and students. It may include a description of the types of attributes and skills researchers may need at different points in their studies or career. The framework will be more effective if presented to and ratified by a key university committee. However, such frameworks can still be used when negotiating with academics to embed IL into particular programmes and modules, even if not ratified, as it can be used as a discussion tool. Cardiff University Information Services (2009a) has created an excellent range of resources that highlights the importance of IL to both academic staff and students.[6] In addition they have developed the popular *Handbook for Information Literacy Teaching* designed to help librarians teach IL effectively (Cardiff University Information Services, 2009b). The Open University have also created the Information Literacy Toolkit (Open University, 2011) that is designed to help library staff develop both their own and their students' IL competencies. These tools help to raise the profile of IL and lay the ground for successful negotiations.

Librarians can speak to lecturers in their own language thus illustrating that they have an understanding of learning and teaching theory and the research process. In particular, librarians should seek to explore the learning outcomes of modules and use these to demonstrate clearly where IL sits naturally within the curriculum. Librarians can use examples of teaching they have delivered for other departments, as well as hooks, such as prevention of plagiarism or raising a person's research profile, to persuade both individual academics and departments to embed IL teaching into the curriculum. Librarians should also encourage champions within departments to promote information literacy to their colleagues. Word of mouth can be a very effective way of highlighting the positive benefits of IL teaching.

Conclusion

The ability to find and use information is defined and described in many different ways. No matter how we describe it, the important factor is that information can empower both individuals and society. If librarians do not proactively develop readers' IL skills, they will continually 'get by' with what they find on the internet and the library's importance to an institution will decline as will their budgets. Any budget reduction will prohibit the purchase of appropriate stock and lead a library to be further seen as irrelevant to an institution, thus creating a catch-22 situation. Librarians should be proactive, step forward and help readers to further develop their skills in this area, so that they understand the value of and can effectively utilize the resources purchased for them by their libraries.

Here are some questions for you to consider, which will help you decide how to take the IL agenda forward in your institution.

1 Has your library developed an IL framework?
2 Do you and/or your colleagues have a teaching qualification as well as a library qualification?
3 Do you share effective teaching practices with colleagues?
4 Do you understand the aims and objectives of your institution?
5 Who are the major stakeholders in learning and teaching and research in your institution? Do they have an understanding of IL?
6 What hooks can you use to encourage IL to be embedded into the curriculum?

References

Attwood, R. (2009) Librarians Desperate for E-books as Demand Outstrips Supply, JISC finds, *Times Higher Education*, 10 September 2009,
www.timeshighereducation.co.uk/story.asp?storycode=408039.

Beetham, H., McGill, L. and Littlejohn, A. (2009) *Thriving in the 21st Century: learning literacies for the digital age (LLiDA project)*, JISC,
www.jisc.ac.uk/media/documents/projects/llidareportjune2009.pdf.

Brown, G. (2007) *In Full: Brown speech on liberty* [delivered at the University of Westminster on 25th October 2007], BBC News, http://news.bbc.co.uk/go/pr/fr/-

/1/hi/uk_politics/7062237.stm Published: 2007/10/25 14:43:52 GMT.

Cardiff University Information Services (2009a) *Handbook for Information Literacy Teaching*, www.cardiff.ac.uk/insrv/educationandtraining/infolit/hilt.

Cardiff University Information Services (2009b) *What is Information Literacy?* www.cardiff.ac.uk/insrv/educationandtraining/infolit/whatisil.html.

CIBER (2008) *Information Behaviour of the Researcher of the Future: a CIBER briefing paper*, University College London.

DCMS (Department for Culture, Media & Sport) and DBERR (Department for Business, Enterprise & Regulatory Reform) (2009) *Digital Britain: the interim report*, Cm 7548, HMSO, www.official-documents.gov.uk/document/cm75/7548/7548.pdf.

Garner, S. D. (ed.) (2006) *High-Level Colloquium on Information Literacy and Lifelong Learning Bibliotheca Alexandrina*, Alexandria, Egypt, November 6–9, 2005. Report of a Meeting Sponsored by the United Nations Education, Scientific, and Cultural Organization (UNESCO), National Forum on Information Literacy (NFIL) and the International Federation of Library Associations and Institutions (IFLA), UNESCO & IFLA, http://archive.ifla.org/III/wsis/High-Level-Colloquium.pdf.

Inger, S. and Gardner, T. (2008) *How Readers Navigate to Scholarly Content: comparing the changing user behaviour between 2005 and 2008 and its impact on publisher website design and function*, Abingdon, Simon Inger Consulting, www.sic.ox14.com/howreadersnavigatetoscholarlycontent.pdf.

JISC (2005) *Investing in Staff i-Skills: a strategy for institutional development*, JISC, www.jisc.ac.uk/uploaded_documents/JISC-SISS-Investing-v1-09.pdf.

JISC (2010a) *The Digital Information Seekers: findings from selected OCLC, RIN and JISC user behaviour projects*, JISC, www.jisc.ac.uk/publications/reports/2010/digitalinformationseekers.aspx.

JISC (2010b) *Digital Information Seekers: how academic libraries can support the use of digital resources*, JISC, www.jisc.ac.uk/publications/briefingpapers/2010/bpdigitalinfoseekerv1.aspx.

Knowledge Council (2008) *Information Matters: building government's capability in managing knowledge and information*, HM Government, www.nationalarchives.gov.uk/services/publications/default.htm.

Loughborough University Library (2010) *Information Literacy: embedding IL into the curriculum*, www.lboro.ac.uk/library/skills/custrain.html. Last updated: 13 October 2010.

NMC (2009) *2010 Horizon report: preview*, Austen: The New Media Consortium, www.nmc.org/pdf/2010-Horizon-Report-Preview.pdf.

Obama, B. (2009) *National Information Literacy Awareness Month, 2009. By the President of the United States of America. A proclamation*, Washington: Office of the Press Secretary, The White House, www.whitehouse.gov/the_press_office/Presidential-Proclamation-National-Information-Literacy-Awareness-Month.

Ofcom (2009) *Report of the Digital Britain Media Literacy Working Group*, Ofcom, http://stakeholders.ofcom.org.uk/market-data-research/media-literacy/medlitpub/media_lit_digital_britain.

Ofcom (2010a) *UK Adults' Media Literacy: research document*, 17 May 2010, Ofcom, http://stakeholders.ofcom.org.uk/binaries/research/media-literacy/adults-media-literacy.pdf.

Ofcom (2010b) *UK Children's Media Literacy: research document*, 26 March 2010, Ofcom, http://stakeholders.ofcom.org.uk/binaries/research/media-literacy/ukchildrensml1.pdf.

Open University Library (2011) *Why Information Literacy: information literacy toolkit*, www.open.ac.uk/iltoolkit/index.php. Last updated: 13 January 2011.

Schonfeld, R. C. and Housewright, R. (2010) *Faculty Survey 2009: key strategic insights for libraries, publishers and societies*, New York: Ithaka, www.ithaka.org/ithaka-s-r/research/faculty-surveys-2000-009/Faculty%20Study%202009.pdf.

SCONUL Advisory Committee on Information Literacy (1999) *Briefing Paper: information skills in higher education*, SCONUL, www.sconul.ac.uk/groups/information_literacy/papers/Seven_pillars2.pdf.

SCONUL (2007) *The Seven Pillars of Information Literacy Model*, Last updated: 2007, www.sconul.ac.uk/groups/information_literacy/sp/model.html.

Notes

1   http://media.ofcom.org.uk/facts.
2   http://ec.europa.eu/information_society/newsroom/cf/pillar.cfm?pillar_id=48.
3   www.cilip.org.uk/get-involved/advocacy/learning/information-literacy/pages/definition.aspx.
4   http://stakeholders.ofcom.org.uk/market-data-research/media-literacy/about/whatis/.
5   www.whitehouse.gov/the_press_office/Presidential-Proclamation-National-Information-Literacy-Awareness-Month/.
6   www.cardiff.ac.uk/insrv/educationandtraining/infolit/whatisil.html.

15

Engaging with the user community to make your collection work effectively: a case study of a partnership-based, multi-campus UK medical school

Jil Fairclough

Introduction

This chapter will explore methods for engaging the user community and maximizing the use of library collections. It will use as a case study the Brighton and Sussex Medical School (BSMS), a partnership involving the University of Brighton, the University of Sussex and Brighton and Sussex University Hospitals NHS Trust in the UK. Practical examples will be used to highlight where strategies have resulted in increased usage of collections and increased engagement with the user community.

A library provides services for a community of users and develops its collections and services to match the needs of those users. It does this within a budget, supporting the strategic goals of the institution. In any library the collection is its main draw, but in a global digital world where information is offered from a wide range of sources, libraries have competition. It is essential, therefore, that librarians ensure that their collections work effectively and that they match their collections to their user community's needs. To do this effectively it must not simply respond to its regular users, but be proactive in pre-empting the changing needs of its whole community; it must operate through the mantra 'know thy user'. This is not new, of course. In his textbook on book selection published in 1930, Drury suggests '. . . the right book for the right reader at the right time' (Drury, 1930, 1). He also states that 'a qualified selector, acquainted with the demand from his community and knowing the book and money resources of his library, chooses the variety of books he believes will be used, applying his expert knowledge' (Drury, 1930, 2).

Scientific publishing: a short history

To understand collection management in the subject area of medicine, it is worth briefly reviewing scientific publishing post-Gutenberg. The first printed book *De Sermonum proprietate, sive Opus de universo* by Rabanus Maurus was printed in 1467 – over 540 years ago. The first scientific journal, *Philosophical Transactions of the Royal Society* (science being then known as natural philosophy) appeared in 1664, over 340 years ago. Scientific publishing remained the same more or less for the next 300 years. The print journal was the method of disseminating scientific information. Publishers published print journals;

research was published in those journals; those who needed to access the research bought a subscription to the journal. In 1992 this all changed, with the advent of the *Online Journal of Clinical Trials*, the first medical peer-reviewed electronic journal.

Since 1992 scientific publishing has seen massive change, particularly with the advent of the open access movement. Publishers of open access journals use alternative business models, where – using the 'gold' model – the author pays a fee on acceptance for publication. This is in contrast with the traditional business model where the library (or individual) pays a subscription fee. An example of an open access journal is Public Library of Science (PLoS) Medicine, which was launched in 2004. Whilst having achieved an impressive impact factor of *13.01*[1] in a relatively short period, the PLoS group proposes that, rather than the journal itself being assessed, individual articles are assessed on their own merits. Using a range of indicators and measures at article level, such as how many times an article is cited, downloaded, mentioned in blogs, added to social bookmarks and rated and assessed by the community, the information itself becomes the commodity rather than the journal. This usage data can produce maps of scientific activity. The MESUR project[2] has produced such maps, developing impact metrics based on online usage of articles and showing relationships that are created between articles thereby revealing how information is used by a community such as science. The notion that a library has a tangible collection owned by the institution has changed radically in the last 20 years, reflecting the ways in which scholarly communication is now produced, disseminated, accessed and consumed.

The establishment of BSMS

Brighton and Sussex Medical School (BSMS) opened in 2003, the result of a government initiative to create more UK doctors (Howe et al., 2004), and one of four new medical schools in the UK. BSMS consists of three partner institutions working together – the University of Brighton (UoB), the University of Sussex (UoS) and Brighton and Sussex University Hospitals NHS Trust (BSUH). Thus the partnership involves two higher education institutions working with the NHS.

Since 2003 BSMS has grown rapidly. With just 130 students and a small number of staff in its first year, the school is now at full capacity with 700 undergraduates and much increased levels of staffing. The first cohort of students graduated in 2008.

There is no one physical medical school library; staff and students use existing libraries at UoS, UoB and the NHS library at Royal Sussex County Hospital and other NHS site libraries. When establishing BSMS, the immediate need was to provide a digital and physical library environment to support the growth of the curriculum. A librarian was appointed to strategically co-ordinate the establishment and delivery of library services to the BSMS community across geographically dispersed locations across three partner institutions. It was essential to engage fully with the new user community to achieve this.

Marketing BSMS Library Services

There are numerous definitions of marketing, but the one which is most useful for not-for-profit organizations is . . . 'the organization's task is to determine the needs, wants, and interests of target markets and to deliver the desired satisfactions more effectively and efficiently than competitors, in a way that preserves or enhances the consumer's and the society's well-being' (Kotler, 1994, 29).

This places the emphasis on the well-being of the society, or – in library terms – the user community, in this case BSMS. The BSMS user community now includes undergraduate and postgraduate students, teaching staff (who are often practising clinicians as well), faculty academics, researchers and administrative support staff. Thus the task is to deliver the 'desired satisfactions' to the BSMS user community.

Marketing is necessary to help engage the user community and maximize use of resources. The traditional strategy of production and targeted distribution of printed materials such as posters, bookmarks, post-it notes and supplier 'freebies' is necessary. Current awareness strategies, which include distributing regular e-mail updates and using social networking sites are also necessary in promotion activities. However, these are only a part of the picture.

Many of the marketing strategies described in this chapter, are often referred to as 'outreach', which implies that the library has to extend outwards. This chapter argues that the reverse is true; that the library needs to be embedded into the daily work of the institution.

When asked which one method works best, the answer is 'all of it', altogether at the same time and continuously. This chapter will focus on three ways in which the library is embedded in BSMS:

- the librarian as a member of BSMS staff
- the librarian as teacher
- the librarian as expert in the product.

The librarian as member of staff

The librarian is a valuable resource to the institution and as such needs to be involved in all activities of the medical school in order to support the teaching, learning, research and day-to-day activities of the school.

To make the collection work effectively the librarian needs to know the users: on an individual level and on a collective level by their division, their speciality, their year group. In respect of the student population, this means having a detailed knowledge of the curriculum; knowing what modules are taught and where, who teaches them and to how many students. It is also important to know what the assessments for the modules are and their hand-in dates. In respect of teaching staff this means knowing them individually, the subjects they teach, their research, who they work with and what other roles they perform within the school. In respect of researchers, this means knowing what their area of research is, who it is funded by and who they are collaborating with. It means personal contact and what has been described as 'walking the halls' in order to build and strengthen relationships between user and library.

At BSMS the librarians are members of BSMS staff, with the Medical School Librarian involved in the strategic activities of the Medical School. This includes:

- Sitting on the curriculum planning committee, where curriculum process and management is managed.
- Sitting on the student affairs committee, to feed back to students on library services and to receive feedback from students.
- Sitting on the Academic Board, to participate in strategic decisions.
- Attending Module Review Boards to participate in the review of the whole module, including the use and impact of recommended resources.
- Sitting on interviewing panels for admissions alongside other members of faculty/teaching clinicians.
- Sitting on the Research Sub-Committee to participate in strategic decisions and process relating to the research agenda.

It is only by acquiring an in-depth working knowledge of the day-to-day activities of the medical school that informed decisions regarding library collection management can be made. Understanding how information resources are used by its user community and for what purpose they require the resource will inform decisions relating to:

- the quantity and location of collections
- how to best make those collections accessible
- how to understand functionality requirements
- how to achieve the right balance between print and electronic resources
- the currency of resources
- retention issues.

As well as informing collection management decisions, this information is also useful for budget purposes.

The librarian as teacher

The General Medical Council (GMC) is the UK accrediting and registering body for medicine and in *Tomorrow's Doctors* (General Medical Council, 2009) 'sets the knowledge, skills and behaviours that medical students should learn at medical schools.' The GMC also sets the standards for 'teaching, learning and assessment'. One of the key outcomes for undergraduates is laid out under 'the doctor as a scholar and scientist' which states requirements for undergraduates to be able to 'apply scientific method and approaches to medical research'. The requirements include:

- critical appraisal of the scientific literature
- the formulation of simple relevant research questions
- applying findings from the literature to answer questions raised from clinical problems.

The requirements also state that undergraduates must be able to 'use information effectively in a medical context'. It is in these areas that librarians can provide the expertise to teach this knowledge, thereby supporting the aims and objectives of the medical school in their requirements for the outcomes of the curriculum.

The Medical School Librarian, as the school's information specialist, teaches information skills to students on the core curriculum throughout the whole five years. BSMS provides a structured learning approach within a 'spiral' curriculum, which is an incremental approach to learning that builds on knowledge by revisiting topics and increasing the level of a student's understanding (Harden and Stamper, 1999). In line with this approach, the academic skills programme beginning in the first eight weeks of the first year, includes teaching by librarians covering referencing, writing skills, avoiding plagiarism, using bibliographic software, and finding, using and appraising information. Basic critical skills are introduced with the lecture 'Finding the Right Information'. Students are asked to help make an informed decision about buying a new car. Should they ask a guy in the pub who used to own one of these cars? Should they consult the car makers' website? Should they refer to a published large-scale survey of users of this car over a specified period of time? Using this analogy, students are introduced to the idea of critical skills, which is further explored through the example of Wikipedia. Using a straightforward show of hands, students are asked if they use Wikipedia, which generally results in approximately 80% raising their hands. Students are then asked to raise their hands if they would be happy if their doctor made a clinical decision relating to their healthcare using Wikipedia as the sole source of information. This usually results in between 2–10 students out of a cohort of 138 indicating they would be happy with this approach. The exercise lays the foundation for a more critical examination of information sources and students can then be introduced to the key sources used in the medical field such as systematic reviews and guidelines.

Basic search skills are introduced at this early point and built on in year two. In year three students are introduced to evidence-based resources, advanced search strategies to identify best available evidence and the critical appraisal of papers. This is delivered as part of the Clinical Foundation Module on the core curriculum which covers key skills required to support clinical practice. Teaching on the curriculum provides the opportunity to further 'know thy user', by giving first-hand access to students and for the library to reinforce itself as the natural source for advice and guidance in information management.

As well as teaching information skills on the curriculum, it is also essential to embed high-quality information resources into the curriculum. In an online environment where users expect to move from one piece of information to another seamlessly, librarians need to ensure that this happens within the learning environment. BSMS uses Blackboard as its virtual learning environment (VLE), and students access all their learning materials from Studentcentral, the University of Brighton's brand name for the VLE. To make those natural links to recommended resources, librarians ensure that reading lists in module handbooks indicate titles which are available online, creating direct links to these online texts, provide direct links from library catalogues to e-books, and embed links from module areas to appropriate e-resources. Working closely with academics as part of the delivery of the curriculum, librarians create tailored links to recommended resources for particular assignments or particular teaching events. For example, year five students attend three themed one-day conferences during their final year and online resources are made available to them to support their learning. Working closely with the learning technologists, who, at BSMS are part of the library services team, librarians provide tailored links to learning resources as part of the year five online module, Clinical and Professional Studies (Howlett et al., 2009).

This module is delivered completely online through Studentcentral, and consists of over 500 cases, each with up to ten questions for students to work through (see Figures 15.1 and 15.2). Over half the cases include multimedia of various types including ECGs, X-rays and video. Links to the most appropriate online resource, including library collections, are created as part of the feedback section for each case, to provide enhanced learning for that topic. Examples of resources include links to e-books subscribed to by the library, freely available guidelines from the National Institute for Clinical Excellence (NICE),[3] the BNF online,[4] articles from journals subscribed to by the library and clinical knowledge summaries.[5] Resources may be recommended by the writer of the case, or

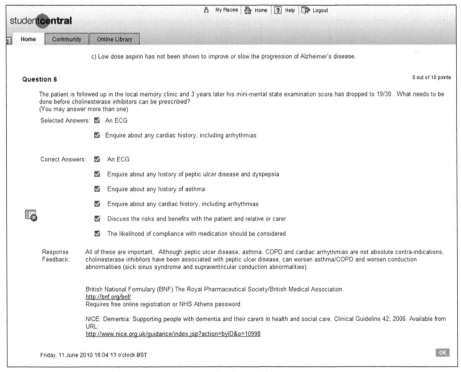

Figure 15.1 *Screenshot from Studentcentral, showing how links to learning resources, including those from the library collections are made*
© *University of Brighton, 2011*

more often left to the librarian to select the most appropriate and relevant available resource. Applying this in-depth knowledge of resources that the librarian has, and ensuring seamless linking from the teaching and learning area to resources embeds the librarian as a valued member of the curriculum team.

By embedding resources, including library collections, students are continually being directed to library collections for their information requirements, as well as reinforcing the library as the point of expertise in the provision of learning resources.

The librarian as product expert

'Build it and they will come' is not always the case with library collections, particularly in a multi-campus, partnership institution where navigating multiple online systems is currently necessary. It is not enough to provide a range of high-quality online resources and expect users to find them and use them, particularly for users who now operate in a global online information landscape.

It is essential that the librarian understands the way in which any resource is used and the purpose for which it is required. The library collections of the institutions that constitute BSMS differ as they serve different (but often overlapping) user communities. For example, the NHS library will require more clinically based journals than those required in a university library. Online resources which provide evidence-based summaries or digests, such as BMJ Best Practice,[6] Clinical Knowledge Summaries,[7] Map of Medicine[8] and the Cochrane Library[9] will be important working information tools for the clinician,

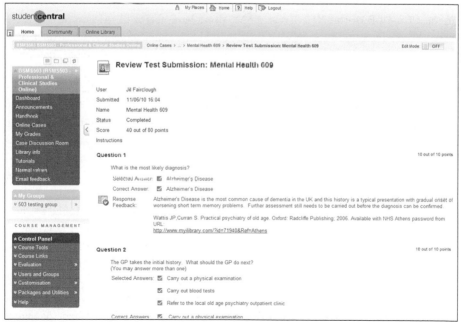

Figure 15.2 *Screenshots from Studentcentral, showing how links to learning resources, including those from the library collections are made*
© University of Brighton, 2011

whereas the peer reviewed high-impact journals will be the key information sources for academics within the medical school.

Enabling resources to follow students

The model established at BSMS ensures that the physical location of resources follows the students. Students can use any of the BSMS libraries but in the first two years students are based at the UoB/UoS sites and use the nearest libraries, which are the university libraries. Wherever a module is taught, the library on that location stocks the multiple copies of books on the reading list for that module. For example, anatomy in the first year is taught on the UoS site. Multiple copies of books supporting anatomy, funded by BSMS library services, are placed in the UoS library, whilst ensuring that one copy of each is available in each of the other two partner institutions libraries. In year three, students move to the BSUH hospital site where they are based for the remainder of their three years. The final year, although based at BSUH, includes three clinical placements at other regional hospitals. The location of physical resources, such as books, continues to follow the students, with the BSUH library being the home for physical resources supporting years three, four and five. In addition, the NHS hospitals across the counties of Sussex and Surrey, where students carry out clinical attachments, receive funding to resource their libraries to support students on placement.

Access

BSMS users consider themselves as belonging to the BSMS community, rather than those of the UoS, UoB or the NHS Trust. BSMS users have access to the libraries of these three partner institutions, each with their own library management system, their own library website providing the portal to subscriptions-based resources, their own authentication systems for online resources, their own processes for providing services such as interlibrary loans (ILL) and their own opening hours. It was therefore deemed important to develop systems which provide seamless as possible accessibility to library resources, whilst retaining the BSMS identity for users. An example of this was the development of the BSMS library membership card which provides physical access and borrowing capabilities for the user in all three libraries across the two universities and the NHS Trust. This provides the user community with the required BSMS identity whilst at the same time providing seamless access to physical collections.

Students also have access resources from mobile devices. MoMEd (Mobile Medical Education) is a BSMS initiative which provides personal digital assistants (PDAs) for all year three, four and five students. The PDAs are provided with a suite of selected resources on a memory card called *Dr Companion*, produced by MedHand International.[10] Resources have been selected based on known use of electronic and print resources and include the *Oxford Handbook of Clinical Medicine*[11] (along with other Oxford handbooks), the *British National Formulary* (BNF)[12] and *BMJ Clinical Evidence*.[13] When managing collections within budget, it is currently the case that resources are paid for, albeit in different formats, several times. In an ideal world, it would only be necessary to purchase in one format, but this is not possible at the present time. In the case of books, for example, some titles are bought in print format in multiple copies, as students still require and borrow them in this format, but they also use those same titles as e-books as well as in the format required for use on PDAs. At present, the next stage for MoMEd is to move to usage of resources via smart phones. The MoMEd steering group is made up of the Director of Undergraduate Studies, who also leads the Medical Education Unit, BSMS Clinical Fellow, BSMS IT Manager, BSMS Learning Technologist, Medical School Librarian, IT administrator and BSMS IT technician. This brings the librarian's skills in information resource selection, procurement and user utilization to the project.

Balance between print and electronic

Users, their needs and the purpose the resources are used for will influence whether resources are made available in print or electronically. For example, an NHS library could stock a collection of good surgery books, but the purpose of providing these texts needs to be understood. Who are the users of these surgery books? Medical students? Surgeons? Healthcare professionals? Patients? If surgeons and related healthcare professionals require these texts to support their everyday practice then one has to ask how useful this collection is in print. The library has to find ways of making the information that surgery staff need accessible at their point of need. This might mean purchasing surgery texts as electronic books, or it might be that an alternative online resource, such as an online multimedia package, is of more use to those users, or it might be that a clinical librarian is assigned to the surgery team. The clinical librarian works with a clinical team providing a rapid literature search service, so the resource becomes the librarian. If the purpose of those surgery books is to support surgeons in training studying for examinations, or for medical students undertaking a surgical rotation as part of undergraduate studies then print books are more likely to be required.

For the BSMS community the availability of electronic books (e-books) has been the norm as they have been purchased and provided by library services since the establishment of BSMS and users know no different. Users benefit from a range of selected titles including the Oxford Handbooks and Textbooks titles, which are well used. e-books are selected according to the purpose for which they are used and how the information within is used. The number of books borrowed from the BSMS libraries has not reduced with the availability of e-books. Medical students regard e-books as an additional resource to print books, using them as quick look-up tools. Students still borrow print books in the quantities they always have. This is not the same for journals where users have almost entirely converted to online resources. BSMS have not acquired journals in print format, buying online only (wherever possible) to fulfil users' needs.

Retention and currency

BSMS has developed a collection management policy in co-operation with its partner libraries to provide collections for the BSMS community and support their requirements. NHS and university libraries will have differing policies reflecting the needs of their user communities. For example, the NHS libraries for the counties of Kent, Surrey and Sussex (including the BSUH library) have developed a stock withdrawal policy which provides guidance on what to retain on the library shelves, which serves the NHS user community.[14] For example, anatomy is exempt and books on this subject will be kept until they are no longer usable. However, pharmacology books are only kept for five years and indeed formularies (such as the BNF) are only kept for two years. This is to ensure that only the most up-to-date information is being used by healthcare professionals. The university libraries have different policies on retention to that of the NHS library, with the emphasis being on education and research. BSMS students are taught to use, as part of their information skills teaching, up-to-date resources and therefore BSMS libraries want to stock only latest editions. This can be achieved easily when purchasing e-books, using the annual subscription model, where the provider replaces older editions by latest editions as a matter of course. This requires very little management by the librarian.

Functionality and cost

The Higher Education Funding Council (HEFCE) and the Service Increment for Teaching (SIFT) are the two main funding streams for BSMS libraries. Ideally, users require one online portal from which they can access all online resources. However, the two budgets are provided specifically to purchase resources to either NHS-based students or to HE-based students, making the one portal delivery a challenge. Therefore, the way in which budgets are allocated across the three partner institutions' site libraries does affect collection management and delivery. Managing a collection effectively ideally requires one budget, which can be deployed across the libraries to purchase physical and online resources to accommodate the requirements of the community irrespective of whether their environment is the NHS or HE.

The cost of online resources is inextricably linked to their functionality. Without adequate functionality the resource will not get used, however good the content. E-books are a good example and the selection process for e-books must include functionality criteria. The delivery of e-books is not as well developed as that for journals, and publishers continue to experiment with business models for purchasing and methods of delivery. At present, this has resulted in a variety of platforms for e-book delivery, including specific e-book providers such as MyiLibrary[15] and aggregators such as Wolters Kluwer Ovid,[16] who provide a search and discovery platform for e-books from various publishers. However, increasingly, individual publishers are developing their own platform for delivering their e-books which forces the user to navigate a myriad of different platforms. Users are unconcerned whether the information comes from Oxford University Press or Elsevier, for example. The advantage of using e-books to access information is to be able to search across the whole collection of e-books to obtain the information required. Users will, however, trust the library to offer high-quality, appropriate texts. This is where the knowledge and expertise of the librarian is essential. However good e-book content is, if the library cannot make it easy to find, access and search across it, then it should not be bought.

Conclusion

It is essential for librarians to understand the changing needs and 'desired satisfactions' and demands of their user community; or simply to 'know thy user'. To do this they must market their collections, but they must also market themselves – their roles in adding and offering expertise. These roles include the librarian as a member of staff, the librarian as a teacher and the librarian as an expert in resources. The librarian as the developer of the collection has to understand the users, their needs in terms of the product itself as well as the ease of accessing that product. In a growing and ever-changing global information landscape, the library and its collections need to embed themselves firmly in the institution's day-to-day activities, with the librarian providing the expertise required to navigate, access and utilize information.

Glossary

BMJ	British Medical Journal
BNF	British National Formulary
BSMS	Brighton and Sussex Medical School
BSUH	Brighton and Sussex University Hospitals NHS Trust
GMC	General Medical Council
HEFCE	Higher Education Funding Council
MoMEd	Mobile Medical Education
NHS	National Health Service
NICE	National Institute for Health and Clinical Excellence
PDA	Personal Digital Assistant
RSCH	Royal Sussex County Hospital
SIFT	Service Increment for Teaching
UoB	University of Brighton
UoS	University of Sussex
VLE	Virtual Learning Environment

References

Drury, F. K. W. (1930) *Book selection*, American Library Association.

General Medical Council (2009) *Tomorrow's Doctors: outcomes and standards for undergraduate medical education*, General Medical Council, www.gmc-uk.org/static/documents/content/TomorrowsDoctors_2009.pdf.

Harden, R. M. and Stamper, N. (1999) What is a Spiral Curriculum? *Medical Teacher*, **21**, 141–3.

Howe, A., Campion, P., Searle, J. and Smith, H. (2004) New Perspectives – approaches to medical education at four new UK medical schools, *BMJ*, **329** (7461), 327–31 (p. 236).

Howlett, D., Vincent, T., Gainsborough, N., Fairclough, J., Taylor, N. and Vincent, R. (2009) Integration of a Case-based Online Module Into an Undergraduate Curriculum: what is involved and is it effective?, *E-Learning*, **6** (4), 372–84.

Kotler, P. (1994) *Marketing Management: analysis, planning, implementation and control*, 8th edn, Prentice Hall.

Notes

1 Thomson Reuters, Journal Citation Reports ® (JCR®), 2009. 'The impact factor is a measure of the frequency with which the average article in a journal has been cited in a particular year or period'. Thomson Reuters,
www.thomsonreuters.com/products_services/science/academic/impact_factor/.

2 MESUR, Measures from scholarly usage of resources, www.mesur.org.

3 www.nice.org.uk.

4 www.bnf.org.

5 www.cks.nhs.uk.

6 www.bestpractice.bmj.com.

7 www.cks.nhs.uk/home.

8 www.mapofmedicine.com.

9 www.thecochranelibrary.com.

10 www.drcompanion.com.

11 Longmore, M. et al. (2010) *Oxford Handbook of Clinical Medicine*, 8th edn, Oxford University Press.

12 www.bnf.org.

13 www.clinicalevidence.bmj.com.

14 www.ksslibraries.nhs.uk/groups/cag.

15 www.myilibrary.com.

16 www.ovid.com.

Index